THE
CONSULTING
BIBLE

THE
CONSULTING
BIBLE

EVERYTHING

YOU NEED TO KNOW
TO CREATE AND EXPAND A
SEVEN-FIGURE CONSULTING PRACTICE

ALAN WEISS, PhD

WILEY

JOHN WILEY & SONS, INC.

Published by John Wiley & Sons, Inc., Hoboken, New Jersey.
Published simultaneously in Canada.

For general information on our other products and services or for technical support, please contact our Customer Care Department within the United States at (800) 762-2974, outside the United States at (317) 572-3993 or fax (317) 572-4002.

Designations used by companies to distinguish their products are often claimed by trademarks. In all instances where the author or publisher is aware of a claim, the product names appear in Initial Capital letters. Readers, however, should contact the appropriate companies for more complete information regarding trademarks and registration.

Wiley also publishes its books in a variety of electronic formats. Some content that appears in print may not be available in electronic books. For more information about Wiley products, visit our web site at www.wiley.com.

ISBN 978-0-470-92808-0 (pbk); ISBN 978-1-118-02359-4 (ebk); ISBN 978-1-118-02360-0 (ebk); ISBN 978-1-118-02361-7 (ebk)

Printed in the United States of America

10 9 8 7 6 5 4 3 2 1

This book is dedicated to all those who have ever entered this profession, improving the condition of their clients, and thus improving the lives of those around them.

Ergo, this book is dedicated to YOU, and to your success.

Contents

Introduction   **xiii**

Section I   Genesis: Consulting as a Profession   **1**

Chapter 1

Origins and Evolution: From Whence We Came   **3**

The Role of a Consultant   3
The Ongoing Need   6
Various Forms   9
Examples of Success   12
The Future   15
   Trend 1: Reestablishment of Corporate Loyalty   *15*
   Trend 2: HR Becomes the Incredible Shrinking Function   *16*
   Trend 3: Insourcing   *16*
   Trend 4: Volunteerism   *17*
   Trend 5: Right-on-Time Learning   *17*

Chapter 2

**Creation: How to Establish and Improve
Your Firm's Presence**   **19**

Legal   19
   Incorporation   *19*
   Protection   *21*
Financial   22
   Insurance   *22*
   Retirement   *23*
   Normal Conditions   *23*
Administrative Support and Resources   24
Emotional Support and Resources   27
   Inordinate Fear of Risk   *27*

Time Demands and Loss of Attention 28
Dueling Careers 28
Two Available Structures 30
The True Solo Practitioner 31
The Firm Principal 32

Chapter 3

Philosophy: What You Believe Will Inform How You Act **37**

Value Trumps Fee 37
Reducing Labor Intensity 40
Identifying True Buyers 43
Conceptual Agreement 46
Objectives 46
Measures of Success 47
Value 48
Leveraging 49
Principles of Leverage 50

Section II   Exodus: Consulting as a Business   53

Chapter 4

The Journey: How to Market Your Value
Rapidly and Profitably **55**

Creating Gravity and Attraction 55
Reaching Out Effectively 59
Viral and Social Media Implementation 62
Creating an Accelerant Curve 64
Shameless Promotion 67
Technology Strategies 70

Chapter 5

Presence: How to Be an Authority and Expert **75**

Creating and Nurturing a Brand 75
Expanding Products and Services 78
Considering Alliances 81
Referral Business 84
Client Referrals 84

Nonclient Referrals 85
Indirect Referrals 86
Retainer Business 87
Global Work 90

Chapter 6

Celebrity: How to be *the* Authority and Expert 95

Thought Leadership 95
Authorship 98
Value-Based Fees 101
Subcontracting, Franchising, Licensing 104
Subcontracting 105
Franchising 106
Licensing 106
The Talent Prevails 107
Reinvention 107
Creating Communities 110

Section III   Deuteronomy: Consulting Methodology 115

Chapter 7

The Perfect Proposal: How to Write a Proposal That's Accepted Every Time 117

Assuring Success 117
Find the Economic Buyer 118
Establish a Trusting Relationship with the Economic Buyer 118
Demonstrate That You Are a Peer of the Buyer, Not Lower-Level People 119
Always Create a Definitive Net Time and Date 119
Conceptual Agreement 120
Objectives 121
Measures of Success, or Metrics 121
Value 122
The Nine Components 123
1. Situation Appraisal 123
2. Objectives 124
3. Measures of Success 124
4. Value 124
5. Methodology and Options 125
6. Timing 125

7. *Joint Accountabilities* 125
8. *Terms and Conditions* 126
9. *Acceptance* 127
How to Submit 127
Never Suggest Phases 127
FedEx the Proposal 128
Create a Time and Date Certain to Review 128
Don't Add Bling 129
Before Submitting, Ask One Key Question 129
Be Prepared for Success 129
How to Close and Launch 130
The Buyer Wants to Meet 130
The Buyer Says That Some More People Will Look at the Proposal 130
The Buyer Loves Option 3 but Only Has Budget for Option 2 131
The Buyer Attempts to Negotiate Price 131

Chapter 8

Implementation: Magic Formula: Rapid Results with Low Labor Intensity **133**
The Role of the Buyer and Champion 133
The Buyer Must Exemplify the Desired Behavior 134
The Buyer Must Enforce Subordinate Accountability 134
Buyers Must Use Their Clout Where Needed 135
The Buyer Is Your Partner and Must Act like One 135
The Key Stakeholders and Influence Points 136
Avoiding Scope Seep 139
Midcourse Corrections 141

Chapter 9

Disengaging: It's Been Nice, but I Really Must Be Going **145**
Demonstrating Success 145
Obtaining Referrals 148
Obtaining Repeat Business 151
Expansion 152
Addition 152
Transference 153
Exploration 153
Creating Testimonials and References 154
Prepare the Buyer 154
Always Provide Options 154
Seek People Other Than Your Buyer 155

Use Multimedia 155
Provide Examples of What You Need 155
Guarantee Nonabuse 155
If Requested, Write It Yourself with Options 156
With References, Stipulate What's Expected 156
Long-Term Leverage 156

Section IV   Acts of the Apostles: Implementing Consulting Methodologies 161

Chapter 10

Interpersonal Methodologies: People First 163

Coaching 163
Facilitating 166
Conflict Resolution 169
Objectives 169
Alternatives 169
Conflict over Objectives 170
Conflict over Alternatives 171
Negotiating 172
Musts 172
Wants 173
Skills Development 175

Chapter 11

Teams and Groups: No One Is an Island 179

Leadership 179
Succession Planning 182
Career Development 184
Teams versus Committees 187
Communications and Feedback 190

Chapter 12

Organization Development: All the King's Horses, and All the King's Men ... 195

Strategy 195
Change Management 198

Cultural Change   201
Crisis Management   203
Innovation   206

Section V   Proverbs: Consulting Success   211

Chapter 13

Ethics of the Business: What's Legal Isn't Always Ethical   213

When Bad Things Happen to Good Consultants   213
  Case Studies   *213*
Financial Follies   216
Protection and Plagiarism   219
When to Refuse Business or Fire Clients   221
Doing Well by Doing Right   224

Chapter 14

Exit Strategies: Nothing Is Forever   229

Building Equity   229
Licensing Intellectual Property   232
Achieving Life Balance   234
Finding Successors and Buyers   237
Transitioning   240

Chapter 15

Payback and Reinvestment: We Build Our
Houses and Then They Build Us   245

Mentoring Others   245
Advancing the State of the Art   248
Participation in the Evolution   252
The Future   254

Physical Appendix   259

Virtual Appendix   265

About the Author   267

Index   269

Introduction

This is a book conceived and created for the independent consultant and boutique consulting firm principal. Having established that, let me point out in the second sentence of the Introduction that the strategies, concepts, methodologies, and experiences described herein are equally valid for the partner and practitioner in a larger firm. My seminal work on consulting practices, *Million Dollar Consulting*, has been read by over half a million people since the first edition was published in 1992.

So a logical question is: "How will this book be different?"

This is my most comprehensive book on consulting; that is, it tackles the profession from establishing a practice through seven-figure success, from acolyte to star. It will be updated and revised as needed, but there will also be continuing and organic additions through the online Virtual Appendix, available to you immediately at http://summitconsulting.com. Simply go to the site's bookstore, select this book, and click on "Appendix." There is no charge to access this at any time.

My latest thinking is incorporated here, including such recent intellectual property as the Million Dollar Consultant® Accelerant Curve; the role and creation of thought leadership positions; an expanded Market Gravity™ Wheel; the Market Value Bell Curve; and how to become an object of interest (OOI). Naturally, these are all incorporated into the context of societal, technological, and economic conditions and likely trends. And I'll be demonstrating how to establish a success equilibrium in ongoing periods of volatility, *and how to create your own volatility*.

Finally, one of the critiques of my earlier works I'm happiest about (and laugh at) is that I don't explain how to evolve into a large firm with employees, assets, and infrastructure. Those critics don't get it.

I'm a solo practitioner, I have no staff, and my margins are 90 percent—I keep what I make. This is a bible to lead you to that land, where you are totally independent, are reliant for victory or defeat on yourself alone, and can invest in your own future, your profession, and your legacy, because you are creating the greatest wealth of all, discretionary time. You'll find advice herein on how to build a firm as one of two viable business models. But keep in mind that you don't want to spend 40 years wandering to try to find the perfect model. You deserve to be successful along the way.

I've given this book a noble name because ours is a noble calling. Whether you are a newcomer or highly experienced, I will show you how to become superb at attracting and helping clients, so that you can enrich your life and the lives of those around you.

But first, you have to believe.

— Alan Weiss
East Greenwich, RI
March 2011

Genesis

Consulting as a Profession

The origins, evolution, and basic requirements of successful consulting. Some realities are self-evident and eternal.

Origins and Evolution
From Whence We Came

The Role of a Consultant

One day, somewhere in the mid-Pleistocene Epoch, after the last glacial period, a man was trying to create a stronger point on his stone spearhead so that he could better hunt and slay the peccaries that fed his clan and protect himself from dire wolves that fed *on* his clan. He did this in the only way he knew how, which he learned watching his father—he laboriously abraded the sides of the point on a larger rock.

On this day, however, a stranger happened by who might have been seeking more interesting surroundings, or was exiled from his clan, or, one could readily assume, simply was lost. Observing the work on the spearhead, the stranger demonstrated that the point had to be ground on a harder rock, not a softer one, and indicated how to choose them. Not just any rock would do. And, indeed, his method worked and the hunter fashioned a sharper spearhead more quickly. The stranger was offered thanks, provided with food, and bestowed with a lion's tooth. He then went on his way once again, well fed, and with a talisman.

Consulting had been born.

The Gospel
The role of a consultant is to improve the client's condition.

It may or may not have happened that way, but you can't prove it didn't. Consulting—advice, counsel, suggestions—has been around since people began living together. Claims of "the oldest profession" have been misapplied to another career, though some would claim that consulting can also be somewhat meretricious if performed with poor motives or lack of skills.

Our job is to improve the client's condition. Doctors are consultants, and one of the first things they learn in medical school is *primum non nocere* (first to do no harm). When we walk away from a client, the client's condition should be better than it was before we arrived, or we've failed. (That "we" may mean both the client and we have failed, but we share in the failure in any case.)

It's that simple.

However, we are engaged in *management* consulting as solo practitioners and small firm principals (or consultants and partners in large firms). And that pursuit did not begin when sloths as large as a tree waddled about the earth. It began and then flourished within some of our lifetimes.

The first management consulting firm was A.D. Little, founded in 1886 by a professor from MIT. It was mainly a technical research firm at the outset. Booz Allen Hamilton was founded by Edwin G. Booz of the Kellogg School at Northwestern University in 1914 and was the first to serve both industrial and governmental clients. (It wasn't until after the Great Depression's onset that these independent consultancies expanded to embrace more professionals and offices.)

Many, perhaps most, chroniclers of management consulting trace the origins to Frederick Winslow Taylor, the famed guru of time-and-motion studies in the early 1900s who purportedly spawned the industrial engineers and consultants who measured efficiency. There are two things wrong with this simplistic Genesis. First, it was governmental regulation combined with the exigencies of World War II that established consulting as we know it. And second, Taylorism was based on a great lie—Taylor fudged his numbers. In measuring efficiency (say, of a man shoveling coal), Taylor would calculate the size of the shovel, the distance to be traversed, lifts possible per minute, and so on. *But he never did calculate the fatigue factor inherent in virtually all physical labor.* People tend to get less efficient the more they work. When this became apparent, Taylor simply made up numbers out of thin air to accommodate this inconvenient reality. His work was discredited during his lifetime.[1]

From those beginnings[2] management consulting grew dramatically, primarily in the United States. The egalitarian nature of U.S. democracy was conducive to the belief that even senior people could use help (as opposed to, say, the European belief that high office was to be held by family ties, school connections, nobility, or bestowal by absolute authority), and that it was a sign of strength and insight and not weakness or incompetence to ask for help.[3] Only after the global transformation as a result of

World War II was management consulting transported overseas from the United States.

Prior to the war, however, governmental regulation actually promoted independent consulting. As opposed to the shop mentality of Taylor, management consulting was more focused on dealing with organizational structure—bureaucracy, if you will. The outside experts (see Figure 1.1) were accountants, engineers, lawyers, and similar professionals who worked for merchant banks.

In the mid-1930s, New Deal legislation such as the Glass-Steagall Act prohibited banks from engaging in nonbanking activities, so they could no longer employ and bill out the experts. Yet the banks continued to urge their clients to utilize experts to protect their loans and investments and ensure effective management.

Hence, independent management consulting was boosted by Depression-era government regulation.[4] James McKinsey, for example, assiduously pursued banking relationships to secure the consulting business that the banks themselves had once provided for their clients.

The war also represented seismic shifts in demographics and learning, most relevant for our purposes because of the large movement from an agrarian to an urban culture, and the introduction of mass training for people who had never been developed in such a manner before, nor so quickly, including women in manufacturing jobs. After the war, management consulting clearly had two components, shifting from merely specific, content-related expertise to also embrace *processes* that consultants mastered that were applicable in a variety of public and private enterprises.[5]

You can view the relationship in Figure 1.1. A consultant who is strictly a content expert (brake pads, air traffic control, medical malpractice) and has no processes to apply or transfer to the client may be thought of as an expert witness at a trial. His or her expertise is sought in a specific area for a finite duration. If there were no brake pads or air traffic control, the consultant would be irrelevant.

On the horizontal axis is the ability to apply processes and to transfer them to the client. If that is purely what's done, and there is no content expertise at all, then we have the equivalent of a facilitator, who can run group meetings and prevent mayhem but who brings no intellectual capital or property to the table.

I submit to you that the diagonal represents the power in consulting: the consultant who can apply and transfer skills and who also has an impressive ability to tackle content areas. That person becomes a collaborator with and partner to the client, and is far more valuable (can demand higher fees) than either colleague at the maximums of the other axes.

Recent phenomena have included the move of traditional audit and accounting firms into more generalized management consulting. The trust

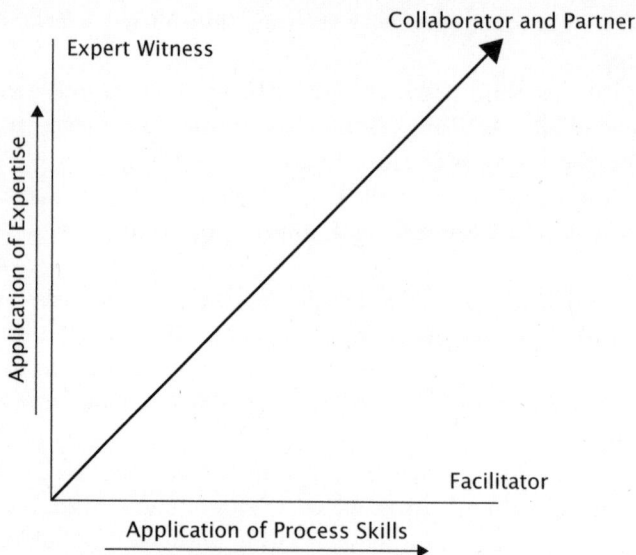

FIGURE 1.1   Relationship of Skills and Content

placed in them in dealing with company finances was simply transferred to other areas of the operation, albeit with mixed results—the audit mentality has resulted in time-based billing, which I'll discuss at length later as unwise, unethical, and unforgivable.

Finally, bear in mind that IBM derives the greatest percentage of its profit not from hardware and not from software, but from its consulting operation. That should tell you a great deal about the future. No one really knows how much revenue is derived by the total management consulting profession, but I'm guessing globally it's over $400 billion.

The Ongoing Need

We've established that our role is to improve the client's condition. That client is the person who is authorizing our payment out of his or her budget. I call that person the *economic buyer*. The buyer is our client, not the organization. A client is a human being, not an inanimate entity.

I know you prefer to list General Electric or Boeing as your client, and we all do such things. But very few buyers have the authority to hire you on behalf of the entire organization, and even those that do—CEOs, board chairs—are almost always hiring us for a limited scope of action. Your allegiance is to the economic buyer, the person whose condition is to be improved. (Only if you find that the buyer in ethical or legal conflict with the organization should you abrogate that allegiance.)

"Need" for the buyer comes in three flavors:

1. *Preexisting needs.*

   These are age-old, traditional, and valid needs now and tomorrow, and may include such areas as customer relations, market expansion, strategy, conflict resolution, innovation, and so on. Even the pharaohs had team-building needs, but they chose to take care of them with whip methodology.

2. *Needs you create.*

   All clients know what they want, but few know what they need. No one knew they needed a belt-mounted device connected to headphones to play music, but Akio Morita at Sony created the need with the Walkman (despite internal advice not to pursue it because no one wanted it). That was the grandfather of the iPhone, which is one of the most popular consumer products in history. When you see a request for proposal (RFP), which is really a predetermined alternative ("We seek a three-day leader training workshop to include case studies . . ."), that's an arbitrary alternative created by people who know what they want but probably not what they need. (Is the leadership problem a result of poor attitude and not poor skills?)

3. *Needs you anticipate.*

   Globalization, increased volatility, changing societal mores, technological advances, and other waves of change should enable any consultant to predict future needs for the client, such as the need to manage remote teams that never see each other, to outsource some services while insourcing others, and to create new levels of internal computer security.

The Gospel

All clients know what they want. Few know what they need. That difference is your value-added.

You can see in Figure 1.2 that your value distance is the difference between what the client states is wanted and what you demonstrate is really needed. That's often accomplished merely by asking this complex question: "Why?"

> "We want a leadership training program. Can you design one?"
>
> "Yes, but why do you want such a program?"
>
> "Once people get to district manager, our attrition rate goes way up. They are obviously not prepared for the job."
>
> "That's one possibility. But the increased travel, management pressure, and dealing with administrative requirements might also be causing tremendous stress and unhappiness, right?"
>
> "Well, yes."
>
> "Then shouldn't we investigate, ascertain the real reasons, and formulate appropriate responses? Training might not accomplish enough."

One of the primary flaws of unsuccessful consultants is that *they accept client wants as the real need.* The need is almost always beyond and above the stated want. If you simply satisfy the client want (no value distance) or advance it slightly (small value distance) your value is not very great.

However, if you demonstrate to your client that the real underpinnings of the issue need to be addressed, you can broaden the project, best delight the client, and, not surprisingly, charge the highest fee.

This concept of need is critical to consulting success. No one, but no one, cares about your mission, or vision, or values, all of which are now monotonously pontificated on countless consultant web sites:

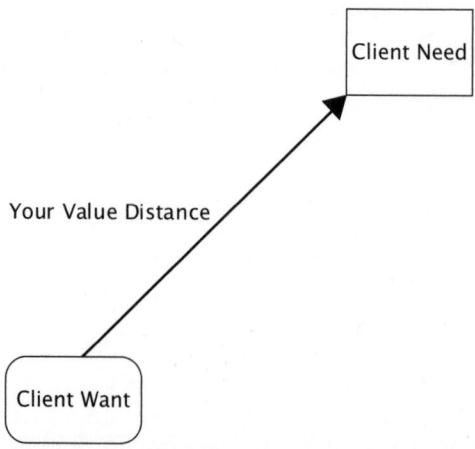

FIGURE 1.2   Value Distance

"We believe in the highest level of integrity and ethics."

Oh, too bad, I was looking for an unethical consultant.

Your own beliefs and value and firm history are irrelevant and hugely boring to buyers. What fascinates them are their *own* history, values, and beliefs. The more you cater to what's in it for them, the more successful you'll be in holding their attention. And always bear in mind that buyers have two sets of needs: professional and personal.

Thus:

- Never settle for what a buyer claims is wanted (even if the word "need" is employed). Probe to find out what conditions prompted the initiative to scratch that particular itch.
- Always seek professional needs (e.g., self-directed teams that create seamless client interfaces without duplication or confusion) and personal needs (e.g., I want to stop acting as a referee between teams and between team and client).

No matter what type of consulting you're undertaking, these facts are immutable. However, the various forms do have some distinctions.

Various Forms

Everyone today is a consultant. There is no barrier to entry, which is the blessing and the curse. When I wrote *Million Dollar Consulting* in 1991, I found that a palm reader on the boardwalk of Atlantic City has to pass more tests and conform to more regulations than any independent consultant. I would bet that's still true today, though no one claims to be a palm reader in an attempt to cover up that they're in fact between jobs, as the actors like to say.

Let me create a fundamental schism right here:

- A consultant is someone who improves the client's condition by providing skills, behaviors, content, advice, experiences, and other factors unique to that individual over a designated time. The consultant is a peer of the buyer and creates assignment parameters in consultation and agreement with the buyer. The consultant provides intellectual capital, often in the form of intellectual property. Outstanding consultants charge fees based on value.

- A contractor or subcontractor is someone who performs work for the buyer at the buyer's direction and discretion, acting as a temporary employee, helping to implement work assigned by the client. A contractor is, in fact, a temporary employee, and is almost always paid by the time unit, usually hourly. They are peers of other, internal implementers. They bring no unique intellectual capital in most cases, nor is that what the buyer is paying for.

Many of you are having a case of the vapors or have gone to have a shot of Scotch, and I hope it's the aged stuff. But that's my story and I'm sticking to it.

As some of you are thinking, many people calling themselves consultants simply are not. My educated guess over the past 25 years of good economies and bad ones is that there are only half as many true consultants as are claimed.[6] If we eliminate those between jobs just claiming to be consultants to save face and those who are really subcontractors who are not sharing consulting DNA, we may have about 200,000 consultants in the United States, and perhaps twice that number globally.

And I believe only about 50 percent are sustaining decent lifestyles without additional support (their spouse's income, the oil well in the back yard, Aunt Tillie's bequest), and perhaps 20 percent are making high six-figure and seven-figure incomes. But that's a story for later in the book.

You may also have noticed, to your horror, that perhaps 90 percent of people calling themselves information technology (IT) consultants are, in reality, just paid help without the benefits.

The Gospel

If you are a pair of hands and not a brain, then you're not a consultant. You're probably a very inexpensive employee.

I've personally mentored IT consultants all over the world, and have helped them to become true consultants, peers of their buyers, and charging for their value. But this is a tough sell. Most IT resources are simply doing—writing code, fixing bugs, testing new relationships. They are not bringing their own intellectual capital or serving as partners and advisors to the chief information officer or chief technology officer (who should be their buyers).

Thus, the actual world supply of consultants is smaller than believed and the need is constantly growing, meaning that your potential to be in that top

20 percent is pretty high if you approach the profession with at least the diligence of a palm reader.

How hard can that be?

I've reproduced an earlier graph with more detail in Figure 1.3.

I advocated the diagonal approach earlier, and you can see that it's based on three factors, not just two:

1. The degree to which you bring useful content to the client.
2. The degree to which you bring useful processes to the client.
3. The degree to which you create trust with the buyer.

Content: The client is already immersed in content, which is often the problem—they are breathing their own exhaust. (I once had to remind officers at Mercedes-Benz that they had auto experts falling out of the rafters, but that wasn't solving their customer service problems.) However, your ability to apply best practices from content you've been involved with elsewhere (and it doesn't have to be identical content, just analogous content) is highly valuable. The degree to which you move up the vertical axis depends on your interaction with the client, from sitting in a room by yourself to casual contact to public representation.

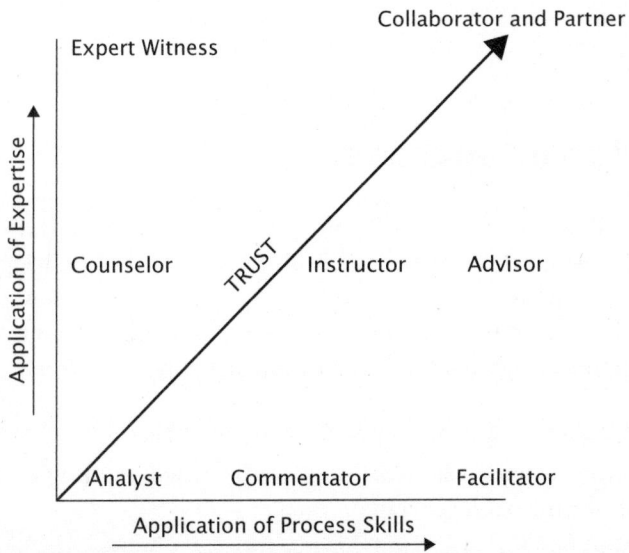

FIGURE 1.3 Content, Processes, and Trust

Process: You can superimpose processes that are universally applicable and that the client may be missing or simply not very good at. Most content-heavy clients are not adept at the processes of conflict resolution, or priority setting, or strategy, simply because their time is overwhelmingly devoted to content matters. As you move along the horizontal axis, you once again move from "back stage" to "front stage."

Trust: This is the key factor to propel you to the top right and become a true partner with your buyer. You can swiftly and efficiently build trust by:

- Being introduced by a peer of the buyer.
- Having a commercially published book.
- Creating proprietary intellectual property and models.
- Behaving and dressing like a successful businessperson.
- Offering value early and frequently.

Let me define trust: *It is the honest-to-God belief that you're acting in the other person's best interest.* That means that I'll accept even criticism well, because I know it's meant constructively. But if I don't trust you, I'll be wary even of compliments, worried about some hidden agenda on your part.

Consulting can take many forms, and it has in popular jargon. But I'm rejecting those who simply use the title because they are looking for full-time work and those who are merely implementing as part-time employees. That may sound elitist, but consulting is a noble profession, and we need to set some standards, since no one else seems to be doing so.

Let's see what success looks like.

Examples of Success

It's easy to talk about "new levels" and "great success" and "turbo-charge your career," but what do those metaphors really mean? Do they mean more clients, more money, more time?

First, let's describe what constitutes a successful consultant, generically. He or she can be recognized by the following attributes:

- A track record of helping improve clients' conditions over several years.
- Buyer testimonials in writing and on video attesting to the specific results the work generated.
- Working for firms and people beyond a narrow niche (and ultimately, as broadly as possible).

- Working nationally and internationally.
- Delivering value by remote and alternate means beyond physical presence.
- Sufficient income to sustain one's desired lifestyle, including appropriate savings and planning.
- A brand and presence in the market creating widespread knowledge of who the consultant is in that market and immediate credibility with prospects.
- Peer respect and a place in the profession where the consultant is recognized and cited.
- Intellectual property encompassing print, audio, video, and electronic distribution channels.
- A personal life in sync with one's professional life and the discretionary time to pursue one's interests continually.

One of the consultants I began mentoring about eight years ago was making about a half million dollars at the time and working almost constantly, the stereotypical one-man band. Today, his business is about $2.5 million; he uses five subcontractors on a regular basis, turns down business that doesn't interest him, has a pipeline extending out two years, *and takes 12 weeks of vacation each year.* Some of his typical vacations include swimming from one Caribbean island to another, and taking a month-long private air tour of a dozen world sites.

You may not need a million dollars of income[7] or three months of vacation, but you get the idea. You should be able to attain what you reasonably desire in life, and even beyond that. If I had ever had a business plan and created even stretch aspirations 30 years ago, I *never* would have imagined or predicted I'd be where I am today. Never.

The Gospel

A market plan will move you forward. A business plan will kill you, because you'll hit it.

Success means having an evolving marketing plan that you tend to daily. Since many aspects of it are passive, you can take long vacations and still have it work for you. But success doesn't ever mean having a business plan, since these are notoriously inaccurate and become dismal, self-fulfilling prophesies.

If you plan to increase your revenues by 20 percent, or bring on four new clients, or expand your web site, you may just do that—at the expense of having done much more! You don't want to increase revenue by 20 percent; you want to maximize revenue, maximize new client acquisition, and expand your web presence (what about a blog?).

> When I was being interviewed by the then-CEO of State Street Bank for a $350,000 assignment, he said to me, "We've increased net new revenues by 22 percent compounded annually over my watch, the last five years. Why do we need you?" In the next three seconds I was going to make or not make a third of a million dollars.
>
> I said to him, "How do you know it shouldn't have been 34 percent?"
>
> He thought for just a moment, smiled, and said, "You're hired."

Let's return to a familiar refrain: Real wealth is discretionary time. Money is merely fuel for that wealth. Ironically, many consultants chasing after success are like dogs chasing cars. They probably aren't going to catch the car and, if they do, what are they going to do with it? Ironically, too many people are busy earning so much money that they are actually eroding their wealth.

Now couple that premise with another tenet—TIAABB: there is always a bigger boat.

The point isn't to have the most; it's to have what you need for your purposes, assuming those purposes will grow as you do. Families, interests, philanthropies, friends, and other involvements usually demand more and elevated support as one matures. That's natural and expectable.

When we vacationed in St. Barth a few years ago, every major slip in the inner harbor was occupied: six yachts that had to be worth $25 million each tied up bumper to bumper like Hondas in a supermarket parking lot. Out in the bay were a dozen more that couldn't fit in the inner harbor.

There is always a bigger boat. The point is to be able to acquire the right boat for you at any given time and move on to new ones when appropriate for your needs, not someone else's needs or ego challenges to you.

I raise these attributes and philosophies of success early so that you can assimilate them as you learn the strategic and tactical approaches that follow in the chapters ahead. These are the generic parameters of success that I've observed and enjoyed over decades in this profession. The specific ones will depend on your lifestyle, your interests, and your intentions.

Finally, the best way to achieve success by any measure in the consulting profession is to be a generalist, not a specialist. The hackneyed refrain "Specialize or die" sounds like New Hampshire's license plate motto ("Live free or die").

My refrain is "Generalize and thrive." It's a simple equation: The more prospective buyers you have, the more opportunity you have to close business. The more appealing you are to the more people, the more you will be sought.

Once you start adding adjectives to your value propositions, you continue to narrow your field until it will fit on the head of a pin. Which of these two value propositions is more appealing to more people?

1. We accelerate sales closing time while decreasing costs of acquisition.
2. We accelerate sales closing time while decreasing costs of acquisition in the New England, middle-market, mortgage-lending space.

The first will still interest the mortgage bankers. The second will interest *only* them.

The Future

Usually, future trends and projections are saved for the final chapter in a book. I'm changing that here, because if you're going to, in essence, prepare for the future in the chapters ahead, perhaps it would be a good idea to agree in advance on what the future might hold! As Socrates pointed out, "If one does not know to what port one is sailing, no wind is favorable."

So how do we tell the good winds and stay away from the doldrums?

Anyone who makes projections in a snapshot such as a book can be in serious trouble, since events can change so quickly. However, I'm going to mitigate that problem in two ways.

First, I am providing an appendix that is electronic on my site (http://summitconsulting.com), which means I can update it regularly and you will have ongoing access to it. Second, I'm going to focus not on the price of gold or the future of alternative energy, but rather on *processes and systems* that will influence our clients and, hence, us, in very broad areas.

Trend 1: Reestablishment of Corporate Loyalty

The pendulum will swing back toward more organizational/employee loyalty. There will be a small (historically) but key group of nonexecutives who will be critical for residual talent needs. They will be pursued and nurtured with bonus systems and outstanding benefit packages. They, in turn, will act as you see Google or Apple employees act today—entirely supportive of their compa-nies, providing innovation and ideas, and helping—through their presence—to recruit more of the same.

What it means for consultants: There will be needs including retention, people management skills, matrix management, compensation and incentive policies, and related requirements to ensure positive working environments. This is hardly unprecedented. At various points in the past Merck, Hewlett-Packard, Levi Strauss, and FedEx exhibited this profile.

Trend 2: HR Becomes the Incredible Shrinking Function

Human resources (HR) departments will continue to attenuate. Their transac-tional functions (benefits administration, relocation, and so forth) have largely been outsourced successfully over the past two decades. That leaves the trans-formational functions (change management, organizational redesign, succes-sion planning, and so on), which, by and large, HR has been excruciatingly awful at fulfilling, following every loony fad and buzzword written by every academic and training company guru. If you don't believe that, then consider the market in front of you and around you. It's not being satisfied within the organizations that need you. And at this writing, I can't think of one HR exec-utive promoted to CEO in a Fortune 500 company over the past decade. It has become a dead end.

What it means for consultants: We are cost-effective responses to trans-formational needs. We come, we improve, and we depart, with no benefits package, no vested political interests, and no intent on a corner office or retirement fund. Change management and organizational development skills will be in great demand, often best delivered by solo practitioners, rather than by outside firms descending with 50 people and creating a pseudo-HR department!

Trend 3: Insourcing

Customers will become increasingly weary of dealing with company represent-atives half a globe away whose management thinks that by wearing American baseball caps and speaking from scripts they can efficiently respond to U.S. patrons. ("My name is Alan Weiss and I live in Rhode Island." "Thank you, Mr. Alan, and what part of New York is Rhode Island in?") The savings gained from overseas help is being lost on two key leaks in the boat: The first failure is work having to be done at home to compensate for inadequate service; the second is customer flight from long waits and inadequate conversations. Delta Airlines is the first major carrier, for example, to officially bring home these functions.

What it means for consultants: Companies are not going to condone expensive service operations just because they're local. Technology will have to be maximized, wait times drastically reduced, and service personnel adept at quickly determining how to handle the request or complaint.[8] The merging of technology and human response will be a paramount cost savings requirement.

> ### The Gospel
>
> You don't grow in the consulting profession by getting better at what you've already done yesterday. You grow by anticipating tomorrow.

Trend 4: Volunteerism

We're going to see major increases in volunteering because of retired people with time on their hands, the American ethic about helping others (much stronger here than in Europe, where government is expected to provide such help), and companies lending executives to nonprofits, community organizers, and other social movements. However, as I've said on every board on which I've ever served in the arts and charity, "Nonprofit doesn't mean nonprofessional." The excuse "I'm just a volunteer" doesn't compensate for sloppy management, wasted money, and a disappointed constituency.

What it means for consultants: The nonprofit world, bereft of government funds and corporate donations for years compared to historical giving, has managed to survive to the extent it has through volunteers and intelligent management of resources. But tens of thousands of these organizations have disappeared. There will be a growing need to educate board members, staff, and management on how to acquire, train, evaluate, and retain volunteers. A poor volunteer is worse than no volunteer. And the money will be there, through donors, sponsors, patrons, and fund-raisers.

Trend 5: Right-on-Time Learning

I didn't say "just-in-time," which invokes a frenzied dash to me. I'm talking about individual professionals and corporate employees having access to a variety of platforms that can generate information immediately, from where a certain movie is playing to the best insurance rates for a newly married 28-year-old airline pilot. These will be accessible to both the buyer and the seller. But there can be too much access, so how do you narrow down what you need without winding up on Facebook for 20 hours in a row?

What it means for consultants: The concept of communities will flourish, where people are attracted by the value of (1) the organizer, (2) the other participants, and (3) the environment.

There will be simultaneous need for you to create your own communities as well as advise clients on how to create theirs. A complaint, don't forget, is a sign of interest. It's better to be expressed in the community, as are ideas and suggestions for other communities, which create buying trends.

Let's turn now to setting up your business and getting ready for action. If you already have a business, use these guidelines to validate that you're organized in an optimal manner for your own success.

Notes

1. See *The One Best Way* by Robert Kanigel (Viking, 1997) for a fascinating biography of Taylor and his work.

2. These were one-person shops at the outset, solo practitioners, even the legendary James McKinsey.

3. As evidence of this, the first management consulting conference was organized in 1888 by the German Post Office. According to records, nobody came.

4. Christopher D. McKenna of Johns Hopkins University and Oxford University has written extensively on these governmental factors that promoted independent consulting.

5. Edgar Schein is probably the preeminent authority and originator of the term *process consulting*. See his book *Process Consultation Revisited* (Prentice-Hall, 1998) and my book *Process Consulting* (Jossey-Bass/Pfeiffer, 2002).

6. That number is often claimed as about 400,000 by research organizations such as Kennedy Information in Peterborough, New Hampshire.

7. Five of my books have titles using "Million Dollar" because (trust me) a hundred thousand dollars is not what it used to be.

8. A single e-mail to a customer service address at Kent County Water Authority in Rhode Island generated a truck and work crew to pave a broken stretch of asphalt on my property the next day! Then I received a follow-up e-mail to make sure I was happy.

Chapter 2

Creation

How to Establish and Improve Your Firm's Presence

Legal

Incorporation

There are three basic options for incorporation or creating a legal business entity. You will occasionally hear from people who will tell you that you don't have to incorporate. Shun them—they are fools. You will, rarely, hear from a lawyer who will tell you that it's not necessary to incorporate.

Call the ethics committee of the bar association!

You incorporate to create a legal entity that can protect your personal assets, form a firewall to protect you, independently borrow money, create certain tax advantages, *and enable you to do business with major clients.*[1]

Always use an attorney and tax advisor who are profoundly well versed in small, professional services firms. Do *not* use someone who has helped close on your house, done your will, and is related to you in any way closer than seventh cousin, twice removed. (If it's illegal to marry them in your state, you shouldn't use them as advisors.)

Three types of entity:

1. *Chapter C.* This is the standard corporation in the United States, like Microsoft or United Airlines. I once favored it because there were benefits and tax advantages, but recent laws have removed them. Since you have to empty a Chapter C corporation of all cash before year-end or risk being taxed twice on the same revenue (once in the corporation and once when you take it as salary or bonus), it's no longer the best alternative for solo practitioners or small firms.

2. *Subchapter S.* In this form, all company revenues flow through your personal tax return. It is neat, simple, and efficient. There is no need to empty accounts, though you should maintain separate business and personal accounts and keep careful records of paper trails. One of my clients was a $1.5 billion, privately held construction company that was a Subchapter S corporation.

3. *LLC.* Limited liability companies (LLCs) are best for partnerships within a corporate structure, but in some cases a one-person LLC may be allowed. Owners here are members of the LLC and take shares, which do not have to be equal. It is a very popular and effective form, and is often used when one entity rents or leases to another (e.g., office space).

Your attorney and tax advisor can tell you what your options are for your state, personal objectives, amount of business, and benefits. Make sure that you maximize in your company's bylaws the kinds of deductions that are permitted because you want to pay for everything you legally can with *pretax, not after-tax* dollars. If you take the risks of entrepreneurialism, you ought to reap the rewards. Making $250,000 as a solo practitioner can be the equivalent of making $350,000 on someone else's payroll and tax structure.

Possible deduction examples:

- Noninsured medical expenses
- Certain club memberships
- Home office
- Business equipment
- Communications devices
- Professional development
- Travel accessories
- Remote technology

- Specialized clothing
- Certifications and licenses

The Gospel

This is a litigious society. That may be unfortunate, but it's true. Failure to protect your intellectual assets is the same as leaving your house unlocked and the newspapers piling up at the door, inviting a robber into an empty home.

Protection

Anything original that you write is automatically covered by copyright protection laws. You should, however, indicate that protection with either (but not both) of the following forms:

© Alan Weiss 2011. All rights reserved.

Copyright Alan Weiss 2011. All rights reserved.

You do not have to register copyrights with the federal government.[2] The reason to do so is strictly for lawsuits. Without such government notice, you can sue to remove plagiarism and violation of your copyright, but cannot collect punitive damages or damages for any business lost. If you have filed with the government, then you can sue to collect such monies. In 30 years and with tens of millions of words written, I've never filed with the government for further copyright protection. I have successfully shut down a half-dozen plagiarists.

For certain phrases, models, and materials (extensions of your intellectual property) you can apply for trademark (^{TM}) and service mark (^{SM}) protection. If they stand up to investigation and challenges (for prior use) you will be granted registration ($^{®}$), which is the highest form of protection.[3]

Trademarks and service marks are differentiated by products versus services as a rule. Don't attempt to gain this protection online, even though it appears inexpensive to do so online. Use a good trademark attorney. The cost will be between $600 and $1,000, depending on where you live and the nature of the protection, but the search will be exhaustive and all the paperwork and responses will be correctly handled. From application to registration granted can take nearly a year in some cases, but you can use the trademark and service mark indicators as soon as you apply.

As a rule, you cannot protect common phrases, but you can protect use as adjectives. I can't protect Million Dollar Consulting, but I can protect Million Dollar Consulting® College. Also, classes vary. My partner and I (in our LLC) have protected our offering, The Odd Couple® Workshop (for professional speakers), because it is in a different class from the theatrical productions (which surprised even me).

That's why you need a good, specialized attorney.

Financial

Insurance

You need the following insurance. Once again, if someone tells you otherwise, put your hands over your ears, shut your eyes, and scream as loud as you can. (Do not attempt this if driving.)

- *Errors and omissions (aka E&O or malpractice).* This protects you if a client claims the advice you provided caused loss and harm, or that you stole intellectual property and used it with one of the client's competitors. The amount of E&O insurance is usually based on the volume of your business, and a million dollars in coverage, at this writing, would cost about $2,500 for a firm with revenues in the low six figures.

- *Liability.* Coverage here is in case someone trips over the power cord on the projector you're using and breaks a nail, resulting in them suing you, the projector manufacturer, the power cord supplier, the facility you're in, and the inventor of shoes. This is very inexpensive, costing a few hundred dollars for six figures in coverage.

- *Disability.* You're more likely to become disabled than to die while in the consulting profession. You can sometimes obtain group disability coverage through trade associations, but individual polices are available, though pricey. The earlier you do this, the better, since premiums rise according to the age you are when you take out the policy. Considerations:
  - *Waiting period.* This is the period after the disability occurs during which no benefits are paid before the insurance kicks in. The longer the waiting period, the cheaper the premium.
  - *Amount of coverage.* Normally, these policies will not pay more than 80 percent of normal income, and for a consultant that can be hard to prove or average.

- *Return to your normal work.* Some policies pay only until you can obtain *any kind* of work.
- *Pay premiums out of your personal account.* If your company pays the premiums, they are considered a benefit and the proceeds are subject to tax if they are ever needed.

Obviously, you need to obtain the type of life, health, and property coverage you need for your lifestyle. Long-term care policies are also increasingly sought, and are also cheaper at younger ages. Your company can usually pay certain premiums for you, though these are often taxable benefits. Check with your tax advisors.

Retirement

Use whatever benefit plans make sense for you, but be sure to maximize your ability to put money away in a simplified employee pension individual retirement account (SEP IRA), 401(k) plan, and similar plans, which are deductible expenses for the company and have caps. Regular IRAs and Roth IRAs are also very worthwhile at younger ages. In many cases, company matching is allowed, though your contributions are from after-tax funds.

Be aware that if you have regular employees, benefit plans must extend equally to them, which is one of many good reasons to use only part-time and subcontracting help.[4]

Contribute consistently and maximally to your retirement programs. While there is some catch-up offered, you will usually lose the ability to make these contributions after early in the following year, denying yourself both a deduction and a contribution to your future. Even if you're just starting out, try to contribute at least partially to your allowed retirement funds.

Normal Conditions

Keep your business checking account separate from your personal accounts. You can create a savings account or money market sweep account to accommodate funds that aren't immediately needed. Be aware that almost everyone has some combination of these needs:

- Regular expenses: food, clothing, mortgage/rent, recreation.
- Special events: marriages, college, extended trips, and so on.
- Unexpected events: family help, illnesses, uninsured losses.
- Impulses: spontaneous purchases, ego needs.
- Lifestyle changes: new cars, house remodeling.

- Debt reduction: zero-out credit cards, one-time purchases.
- Nonretirement investments: stocks, bonds, certificates of deposit (CDs).
- Philanthropy: contributions and memberships.

Don't simply spend what you make, and don't spend it on whatever happens to be in front of you. Think about priorities, because you also have these business needs:

- Professional development
- New hardware, software, and technology
- Office support
- Nonreimbursed travel
- Marketing
- Communications

These can be sobering when viewed in this manner, but they are better viewed in daylight than hidden in dark corners. That's why lean and mean is best. I've never had a staff or part-time employees, and my office has always been in my home.

Don't mix personal and business funds, even in a Subchapter S corporation, until the year is nearly ended and you can be advised on distributions and bonuses. Try to establish a separate, business line of credit with your bank. If you have both personal and business accounts, you'll have more clout and probably obtain more credit.

The purpose of credit is to even out the unequal flows of revenue and expenses. Credit should be paid off as soon as possible. That is responsible and appropriate in business. People who tell me they "never use credit cards" and pay only by check are amateurs, and remind me of people who put the rent money in one envelope and the milk money in another. If you're not willing to confidently use credit, then you simply don't trust your own abilities.

Administrative Support and Resources

Here's an area that can cost you a bundle if you're not careful, and here's why.

When I was fired as president of a consulting firm in 1985 (the owner and I shared a mutual antipathy), I told my wife I was going to go out on my own and no moron would ever be in a position to fire me again. She said fine, what was I planning to do first?

"Get an office," I responded.

"Why?" she asked.

"I'll be out on my own."

"Why do you need an office?"

"I won't have any support staff otherwise."

"Are people going to come to see you, or are you going to go visit them?"

"Uhhhhhh . . ."

"If it turns out you need an office, then get one. But for now, why not forestall that expense?"

I still don't have an office, or a staff, or an assistant, real, virtual, or imagined (well, there is that picture of Michelle Pfeiffer). My two children went to private school from preschool through their undergraduate degrees at major universities. The total of those tuition payments was $450,000 (don't smirk—it's even worse now). I calculated that, over 21 years, a modest office with utilities, insurance, rent, repairs, and part-time help would have cost me . . . $450,000.

Are you getting the picture?

The Gospel

A staff is not important unless you need it to help you walk up a long and winding road seeking enlightenment. And that's true only if you have a bad hip.

Most virtual assistants require supervision, and many of them don't represent you well, since they're representing another dozen or so people, as well. I warned one woman, in Toronto, who answered the phone for one of my mentor program members, that I would personally try to have her fired if she wasn't more polite when I called.

Also remember that full- and even part-time employees often must be covered in the same benefit formulas and retirement plans that you implement for yourself and your family. And then there's illness, theft, personal problems, errors—do you really need these headaches? Most of us are refugees from larger organizations and the people management issues that thrive there, like mold in a damp cellar.

Here are six suggestions and resolutions:

1. *Tuck your ego away.* Having a staff doesn't elevate you in the eyes of the buyer. Telling someone your "people" will look into it will generate only levity.

2. *Learn to do simple tasks efficiently.* You should have invoice templates, sample proposals, automated expense statements, and so on. Use technology. Send clients or prospects letters from your laptop. Make sure all of your enclosures are in electronic form. (There are sample forms in my electronic appendix.)

3. *Learn to type, and I don't mean with your thumbs.* I can type 60 words a minute, and so can you. If you can learn to use a keyboard, then you can learn to type on it. (I love the airline counter clerks who have been using keyboards for 20 years and never bothered to learn to touch type. It's not rocket science. These days, even rocket science isn't rocket science.)

4. *Delegate and outsource.* I use the following regularly:
   - Automated answering service
   - Graphics designer
   - Printer
   - Audio studio
   - Videographer
   - Internet experts
   - International limo company
   - American Express travel services
   - Postage and packaging supplies
   - FedEx and UPS accounts

   You get the idea. These people and companies are available when you need them for fixed fees and rates (don't give them this book). I also make it a habit to pay local vendors such as my printer and designer first, because they are small businesses and always need the cash, and when I need a priority job they always put me at the top of their lists.

5. *Shift work to the client.* Your value is in results, not physical presence. Educate the buyer about how the client provides scheduling, administrative support for the project, security passes, parking, prompt reimbursement of expenses, internal follow-up, and so forth. Make your work *less* labor intensive; don't design it to provide work for a staff of your own. (We discuss this in detail in the next chapter.)

6. *Hire people by the hour situationally.* If you absolutely must, hire college students or community acquaintances (not friends!), or even part-time employees from agencies for a few hours or a day to get volume work done. But that should be a last resort.

Early in your career, practice lean and mean. Later in your career, check for the bloat that often accretes to a growing, successful practice. I've counseled and coached consultants making $350,000 annually who have two full-time and two part-time employees! I run a business in excess of $2.5 million with *no* employees.

One of the interesting and common reasons for staffs to be hired is that the consultant has very strong affiliation needs that were once met by a larger, corporate (or intimate, small-office) environment, but are now missing. The resolution for that is to find affiliation in other ways: civic responsibilities, socializing, professional associations, family gatherings, volunteerism, and pursuing hobbies with others.

In the worst case, if you don't have affiliation, get a dog. But don't get a staff. I love dogs and would do anything for them, but they've never cost me $450,000.

This last need leads me to a much more intangible but far more vital support requirement.

Emotional Support and Resources

Emotional support cannot be virtual, and it's the most important support in any consulting practice, whether nascent or mature.

Ideally, it comes from family, then friends, then acquaintances, then professional colleagues, then the helping professions (counselors). I've mentored too many solo practitioners and small firm owners who are laboring mightily for their families and whose families do not support them emotionally.

Here are some of the reasons and what you can do about them.

Inordinate Fear of Risk

Not everyone has the same risk tolerance. Moreover, if you don't have all the information *you tend to overestimate risk.*

In the chart shown in Figure 2.1, which I use with corporate clients, you can introduce to others the idea of your current position (status quo) and the relative risk and reward of your venture, idea, or initiative. The problem of risk is that there is usually no counterbalance. Certainly a risk of −5 accompanied by a possible reward of +2 is not worth taking, unless the risk can be mitigated. But a +4 benefit with a −2 risk is well worth it.

This kind of visualization will help you with family and conservative others (attorneys, bankers, accountants) to understand the difference between prudent risk and gambling. It also provides the ability to exploit the benefit (move from +3 to +4) and mitigate risk (move from −3 to −2) with some intelligent planning. Investing in a $50,000 conference center may make no sense emotionally, until you realize that last year you made $300,000 in conference revenues but had to spend $150,000 on retail conference space.

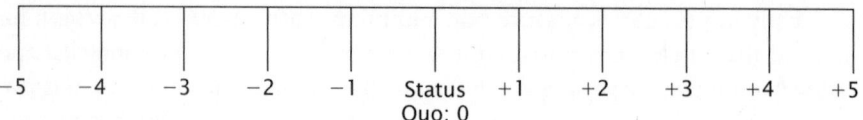

Question: What is the best and worst that might result?

+5= Paradigm-breaking improvement, industry leader.
+4= Dramatic improvement, major publicity.
+3= Strong benefits, organization-wide.
+2= Minor benefits, localized.
+1= Very minor improvement, barely noticed.
−1= Very minor setback, barely noticed.
−2= Minor setback, controlled locally.
−3= Public setback, requires damage control.
−4= Major defeat, financial damages, recovery time needed.
−5= Devastating losses.

FIGURE 2.1 Risk/Reward Ratio

Time Demands and Loss of Attention

You have to offset those occasions when you miss dinner, or miss a dance recital, or even miss an anniversary with those when you can be at an afternoon soccer game, take a long weekend vacation on impulse, or provide an extraordinary anniversary gift.

When I first began traveling (without benefit of modern technology and remote flexibility), I was on the road 80 percent of the time. I had two personal goals in that regard: First, I wanted to keep reducing it,[5] and second, I wanted to compensate for it. My kids, when I missed grammar school events, became accustomed to telling their friends I was in California or Florida or London, but also were quite proud to point me out on the sidelines during an afternoon soccer game or morning field trip. I wasn't there all the time when other parents were, but I was often there when other parents weren't.

It's never good to miss special days and special events. But these days on the calendar are meant to represent something far greater than a period of time passing, and it's that personal and loving experience that needs to be celebrated, no matter when that is.

Dueling Careers

Consulting demands time, especially to grow a thriving practice. If your significant other also has a career, then the two of you need to make common adaptations. You need to outsource! Hire help to mind the pets, watch the kids, clean the house, pick up the cleaning, mow the lawn, and so forth. If a dual income isn't sufficient to hire the resources that working couples require, then there is something wrong with the dual income.

Dual careers shouldn't become dueling careers. Look for ways to substitute for the mundane (cleaning the yard, painting the house) while safeguarding the sacrosanct (taking vacations, quality time with the kids, walks on the beach). This can't be a zero-sum game, where one benefits only if the other sacrifices. Both have to invest to reap the dividends.

Part of emotional support is eschewing the martyr's approach. The humorist George Ade observed once, "Don't pity the martyrs; they love the work."

Not everyone is in a relationship, of course, which makes it even more important to have an emotional support structure and proper resources. While other consultants can provide this, beware of too much commiseration ("Don't worry about losing that business; we're all losing business right now"). You want people around you who can tell you when it wasn't your fault *and when it was.* You want people who can help relieve the strain and pressure, but who can also demand accountability and responsiveness.

In short, you need trust. Remember: Trust is the honest-to-God belief that the other person has your best interests in mind.

Find those people who can be empathetic (they understand your position) but not sympathetic (they share your feelings and position, and therefore tend to be lost in the content). These resources may change as your business grows and/or as you mature. You will certainly outgrow some of them. This can be a very lonely endeavor if you aren't able to share the pressures, ask intimate questions, and filter unbiased advice. Try to find people who don't have a personal agenda, and include a cross section.

Don't accept all feedback as accurate or valid, but look for consistent patterns and feedback that is supported by evidence and behavior. Most important, never accept *unsolicited feedback,* which is almost always provided for the sender, not the recipient. If you listen to random suggestions, you'll be the ball in the pinball machine, being tossed and bounced by every arbitrary object in its path.

That just winds up being painful.

The Gospel

The myth about feedback is that it's always valid and worth considering. Listen only to those you respect and whom you ask. That discipline will save you years of grief.

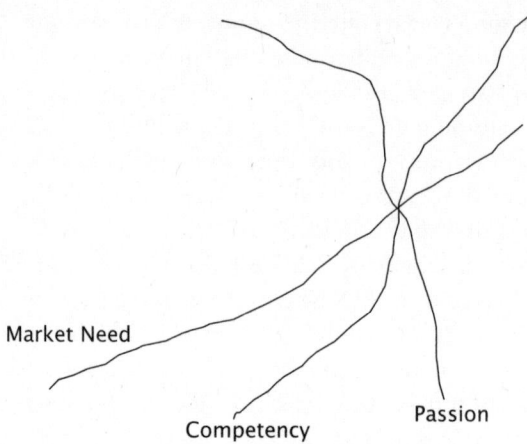

FIGURE 2.2 Where Do These Paths Intersect?

Here's why I've been so focused on your support system.

Your success is at the confluence of the three paths shown in Figure 2.2:

1. Market need, which you identify, create, or anticipate.
2. Competency to deliver quality work and results.
3. Passion to accept rejection and move through obstacles.

If you find market need and have passion but don't have the competency, you'll lose to the competition. If you have competency and passion but can't identify need, you have a story no one wants to hear.

If you have market need and competency but no passion, you have a nine-to-five job. And that's an environment most of us have fled from.

Your support system is the engine room for the passion. You need those fires stoked on a continuing basis. Some of us are better than others at providing the passion independently, but at some time or other we all need the support, the structure, the empathy.

Without passion you will be worse than lonely, and poorer than unsuccessful.

You'll be unfulfilled.

Two Available Structures

I'm going to make this simple: There are two available structures for a consulting practice. Both are viable. But to be betwixt and between is bizarre.

The True Solo Practitioner

When you are a true solo practitioner (aka independent consultant) according to the criteria we've discussed thus far (brains not hands, improving the
client's condition, and so forth), you work on your own, most often from your
home or a shared facility where you rent common space. If it's at all possible,
work from home, because it's far more comfortable and much less costly. If the
distractions are overwhelming, then find inexpensive shared space. Remember,
you go to clients; clients don't come to you.[6]

Every year, you maximize short-term and long-term income. In the short
term, you pay for all you can out of pretax income. You then maximize your
after-tax income in varying ways (depending on your legal status as Chapter C
corporation, Subchapter S corporation, or LLC). In the long term, you maximize your contributions to both pretax and after-tax retirement plans: SEP
IRA, traditional IRA, Roth IRA, 401(k), and so forth. You do not reinvest in
the corporate entity, other than acquiring the normal equipment and technology you need to stay current and effective. You probably operate on a cash
basis, recording income as it's received and deducting expenses as they are paid
(as opposed to an accrual basis).

The distinctions of the true solo consultant include:

- No staff, full-time or part-time.
- Home-based office.
- Outsourced routine needs, such as printing, graphics, web site design,
  and so on.
- Personal responsibility for key tasks, such as invoicing, correspond-
  ence, depositing money, processing credit cards, and so on.
- Personal credit funds the company until such time as receivables and
  critical mass of clients create corporate credit.
- No purchases of major assets, such as office space.
- Branding may be varied, but ultimate brand is one's name (e.g., "Get
  me Joyce Wilson").
- No plan to sell the business or leave it to family.
- Extensions of income include licensing intellectual property and royalties.
- Retirement and benefit programs created solely for the benefit of the
  consultant and family.

Some people who start out as solo consultants choose to move into the
creation of a firm later in their careers. That's fine, as long as key transitions
are clear. (And some firm principals choose to dissolve their firms and become

solo practitioners—more common than you might think, often caused by financial duress.)

The Firm Principal

Many consultants either begin or move into running a firm. That means that every year the principal must reinvest in the firm, with the intent of expanding business, personnel, goodwill, infrastructure, brands, and other accoutrements of what the accountants like to call a "growing concern." That's because the ultimate aim is to sell the business at some point as a multiple of revenues or earnings.

This requires more than merely consulting skills. The firm principal must exercise people management skills, delegation, recruitment, legal discretion, compensation, defections, and so on. Many consultants are refugees from large companies and managing people (including me). To return to this as the owner of the firm doesn't make the obligations any less daunting, frequent, or critical.

In firms, the benefit programs must be inclusive, so that employees derive identical or proportional advantages to the owner. This vastly increases expenses. Salaries and benefits also must be set and adjusted frequently and with care about equity across the board.

> ### The Gospel
>
> Never confuse a solo practice with a boutique firm, or attempt a hybrid. You'll be burdened with the disadvantages of both and few of the benefits of either.

The distinctions of the true boutique firm owner include:

- A growing staff, full-time and part-time.
- Serving as the primary rainmaker, with most people in support.
- Separate office space, either rented or owned.
- Outsourced specialty needs, but most skills onboard.
- Shared responsibility and delegation, especially of clerical functions, scheduling, finances, technology, and so forth.
- Discrete banking relationship independent of personal credit based on assets, property, goodwill, and so on.
- Branding that promotes the company, not the owner, so that an eventual sale will not demand the owner's continuing involvement.

- An exit strategy to sell the company at some finite point and to leave even if it requires a contractual relationship for some time; this sale may be to employees structured as a buyout over time from profits.
- Retention of licensing and royalty rights to increase the firm's value.
- The owner's salary would be considered as profit in the business at time of sale.

The danger occurs when a consultant has one foot planted on each side of the gorge, and the chasm begins to widen under the consultant's feet. By this I mean that the so-called firm is, in reality, a solo consultant supporting an unneeded staff and physical property. *Unless highly paid people bring in new business, they are not worth the money. Delivery people are a dime a dozen.*

I know that's anathema to many of you, but it's a harsh reality. There are tens of thousands of delivery people who solely implement, teach, and execute *because they can't market, and can't be rainmakers.* However much they will importune, their work is replaceable and not the reason for the firm's growth. The acquisition of new business is the reason for the firm's growth, and if just the owner is doing that, then he or she is acting as a solo consultant while carrying a very heavy backpack.

I call these murderous hybrids "consulting welfare states."

The Story of Phil

I mentored Phil for about 18 months some years ago. He was 47 at the time, about 30 pounds overweight, and failing at breaking his smoking habit. He had a staff of eight, all of whom were delivery people. Phil generated, through his rainmaking, about $450,000 a year. That's not bad for an independent consultant, but very poor for a firm of this size (which should be doing at least $2.25 million with that complement of professionals).

Phil and I spoke about once or twice a month, and it wasn't unusual not to hear from him some months when he was heavily booked with appointments. He traveled about 80 percent of the time, which was tough on his wife and two children.

After a two-month hiatus, I called his office. His wife answered and told me that Phil had passed away two weeks earlier, alone, in a hotel room in Boston. She hadn't been able to contact everyone yet to tell them. Some clients didn't even know.

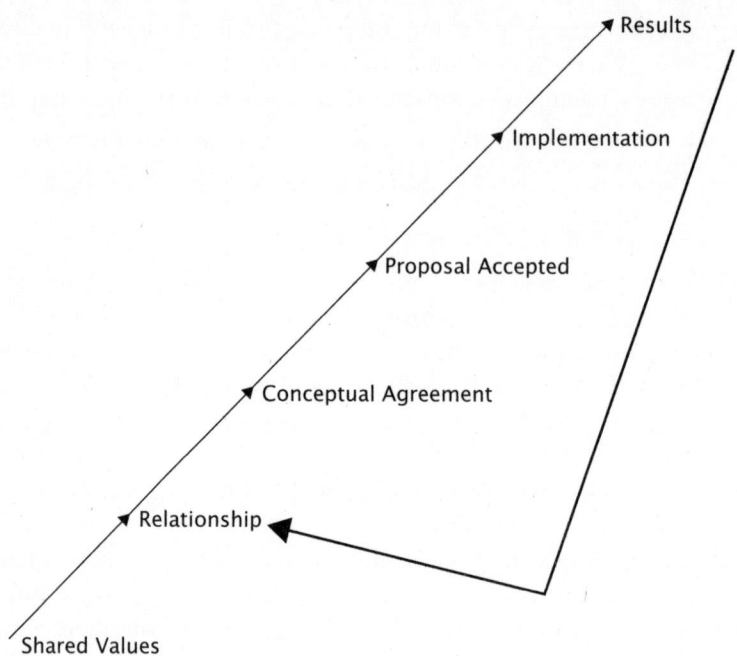

FIGURE 2.3 Consulting Model

I have never advocated starting out as a solo consultant and building a firm as a natural extension. I routinely make well over $2 million working out of my home with no staff at all. When I began, I made $67,000 my first year. The revenue has changed, but the structure of my business hasn't. Could I be making $4 million or building a $40 million firm? Perhaps. Maybe it's even probable. But I have no interest in doing so. Remember that wealth is discretionary time.

I can always make another dollar, but I can't make another minute.

I would urge you to consider the advantages of a solo practice and the vast disadvantages of building a firm. If you need affiliation, find it in other ways and by other means. Building a company is a very expensive and awkward way to create colleagues.

A very basic model for successful consulting appears in Figure 2.3. There's no reason in the world you can't do it yourself.

Notes

1. There are more reasons to list, but I don't want to use too much of my time or yours. One example: To reclaim value-added tax (VAT) from the United Kingdom when there on business, you have to have an IRS document that proves you are a corporation currently doing business in the United States.

2. U.S. Copyright Office: www.copyright.gov/.

3. U.S. Patent and Trademark Office: www.uspto.gov/about/offices/trademarks/index.jsp.

4. For you and for subcontractors, the IRS has rules about when a subcontractor becomes an employee, including that 80 percent or more of the person's income is derived from that single source. Check with the IRS web site or your financial advisor.

5. It went to 65 percent, then got reduced to 40 percent, hovered at 25 percent, and in the past few years has been less than 15 percent when I'm away and my wife is not traveling with me.

6. With rare exceptions, and when they do you can welcome them into your home or rent a private conference room in a hotel or club.

Chapter 3

Philosophy
What You Believe Will Inform How You Act

Value Trumps Fee

If you're discussing price and not value, you've lost control of the discussion. Every buyer would love to reduce price, but very few want to reduce value.

The Gospel
You will never be successful in this business charging by a time unit. And that is because it is unfair to the client and inequitable for you.

Fees are based on value. That value can be objective and tangible or subjective and intangible. We'll talk about conceptual agreement with buyers and creating tremendous return on investment (ROI) later in this chapter. But for now, let's focus on what may seem like a very simple relationship but is actually misunderstood by most consultants.

Our job is to improve the client's condition. We deserve to be paid for our contribution to such improvement. But our fees *must be consistent with the best interests of the client, not solely ourselves.*

The client's condition is improved objectively (e.g., profit, margin, market share) and subjectively (e.g., stress reduction, higher repute, seamless client interfaces); it is improved professionally (teams are more productive) and personally (they won't ask the buyer to constantly referee their conflicts).

Thus, we have the two traditional measures of improvement:

1. Objective and subjective business improvement.

2. Buyer professional and personal improvement.

Now add a third:

3. Speed of improvement.

The quicker you can improve a condition, the more valuable you are, since the client has that added time to reap the benefits of the improvements. If a project is estimated for completion in six months but you successfully complete it in three, the client is going to be extremely happy. The accrued benefits of speed:

- More time to benefit from improvements.
- Lower attendant expenses.
- Less organizational disruption.
- Ability to focus on new endeavors.
- Higher image and repute within the organization.

You get the idea. Speed is of the essence.

So then why charge for lethargy?

Any time you are charging by the time unit, you are in an ethical conflict with the client. The client is best served, as we've just established, by quick resolutions. But the consultant, in this structure, is best served (makes the most money) by taking the most time. That is more than impractical or an unwise business approach.

It's unethical to the client and unfair to you.

Hence, charge only based on value. We provide a variety of ways to do this under the "Conceptual Agreement" heading later in this chapter, but for now, consider this equation:

$$\frac{\text{Tangible benefits} \times \text{Annualized benefits} + \text{Intangible benefits} \times \text{Emotional impact} + \text{Peripheral benefits}}{\text{Fee}} = \text{Value}$$

Tangible benefits are usually capable of being annualized—the increase this year will be duplicated on a larger base next year. The intangible benefits have varying emotional impacts that are crucial ("I don't have that stressed feeling whenever I evaluate a subordinate"). And peripheral benefits include such things as being able to retain and attract top talent because of the project's success. (It wasn't a prime objective, but it's nonetheless a business benefit.)

The higher the numerators, the higher the denominator (your fee) can be and still generate tremendous value, which is the return on the investment. I urge that you provide at least a 10:1 return, which clients are not obtaining in any other endeavor or investment. (When I consulted with a manufacturing consulting firm in New York, it was providing its clients a 3:1 return, and the clients were delighted.)

The most ludicrous, bizarre, and dumb approaches to pricing are those that tell you to estimate your yearly financial needs (there's an easy one, right?), divide by your available hours (which means discretionary time is *not* your wealth because you're surrendering it), and divide to reach an hourly rate! I can assure you there are no seven-figure (or even mid-six-figure) consultants doing that who are leading a rational life.

Another idiotic source claims that you raise fees only when demand exceeds supply. Well, your supply is about 300 days a year—do you really want to work that hard? (One problem is that too many consultants leave harsh bosses in organizations to go out on their own and wind up working for a more demanding, more tyrannical boss.)

You base your fees on your contribution to the improved client condition, which is value. You may have to educate the client, but that's easy, even when they've been accustomed to consultants who don't know how to assess fees. Simply point out the reasoning for your fees:

Why Value-Based Fees Are Best for the Client

- No investment decision is needed every time the client may require your help.
- There is a clear cap on costs.
- Speed is rewarded, with its commensurate client benefits.
- The return on investment is clear and predictable.
- The client is better equipped to defend and justify the investment.
- There is unlimited access to you (which is never abused in reality).
- There is no confusion about motive (if the consultant recommends something, it's because it's needed, not an excuse to bill more hours).

The legal profession is S…L…O…W…L…Y learning to stop billing by 60-minute increments, but the vast majority of lawyers still bill by an hourly rate.

You don't want to be as dumb a businessperson as a lawyer.

Reducing Labor Intensity

Since wealth is discretionary time, reducing labor intensity is *as important* as raising fees. Years ago, my financial advisor told me that paying down debt was the equivalent of saving. I'm not a financial expert, but I am a consulting expert, and I can unequivocally tell you that reducing labor intensity is as critical as raising fees.

Too many people work like crazy to increase revenues while concurrently eroding their wealth. If you don't believe that, take a look at your friends, colleagues, and clients who choose to start working at 8 o'clock each morning and knock off at 8 o'clock in the evening. It doesn't make sense to own two boats if you don't have time to sail either one.

It's vital to understand this right at the outset, or to continue to remind yourself periodically during your journey. Here are the secrets to building a business while reducing your time investment.

1. *Do not deal with nonbuyers in your marketing.*

There are people who can't say "yes" but can say "no." So what answer would you most likely expect? Use nonbuyers only to help arrange introductions to the buyer (or at least identify the buyer). In general, you won't find a living, breathing buyer (someone who can write a check for your value) in human resources (HR), training, internal consulting, event planning, or meeting planning. If you attempt to wade through this morass of equivocation, you will find yourself mired in the La Brea tar pits observing mastodon bones. If this seems harsh (just because you can cite an exception or two), so be it. We're talking about your wealth here. More about this in subsequent chapters.

2. *Streamline your delivery model.*

The problem with a "six-step strategy model" or a "five-part sales improvement process" is that you feel honor-bound to deliver all those steps, irrespective of whether the client really needs them. (One client asked a colleague of mine if he could start with step 3. "No," said my colleague, "it's all or nothing.") The danger isn't merely in losing the engagement; it's in obtaining it and overdelivering just because you're in love with your own methodology. Can you do a five-day workshop in three days? Can you run six focus groups instead of a dozen? Can you visit four offices and not 10? You're the expert in consulting.

Never accept a consulting alternative from the client ("We're seeking a three-day leadership workshop for 20 managers"). They are usually both arbitrary and unduly labor intensive. Other than that, they're great. Every request for proposal (RFP) is really an arbitrary alternative seeking deliverables.

3. *Use the client's resources.*

Shift work to the client. This is neither a federal crime nor a cardinal sin. Use the client to schedule and to provide administrative support, office space, guides, past documentation, summaries, and anything else you can think of. Remember that when you transfer skills to the client you're increasing the client's benefit and your value (see Chapter 1). Make these divisions of labor clear in your proposal under "Client Accountabilities."

> I learned to run strategy formulation programs by plastering the room with easel sheets, often 60 or more. They had to be placed in order, edited, transcribed, and circulated after the session, which was more work and harder work than the actual interactions.
>
> Finally, it occurred to me to require that a trusted client administrative person be present, take notes, retrieve the easel sheets, transcribe, and submit to me for final approval before dissemination. That saves me a week of work over the course of a 90-day relationship. And it makes far more sense for client personnel to do this than someone you would hire.

4. *Outsource and delegate.*

If your significant other is going for the mail and household supplies, the trip can include business mail and office supplies. For example, you need access to people who can provide:

- Printing
- Graphics design
- Web work[1]
- Bookkeeping
- Tax work
- Travel planning
- Office design
- Proofing
- Research

Never outsource your marketing, because this is a relationship business, and as a buyer, I'd be offended if you had a third party or subordinate contact me instead of trying to do so yourself. Outsource back-room work, not front-stage work.

Always pay local vendors first. They are small businesses or solo practitioners like yourself, and cash is king. The faster you pay, the more you'll be a priority on those occasions when you need something done in a rush.

The Gospel

If you don't believe that wealth is discretionary time, the next time you make another sale try to concurrently make another hour.

---

5. *Subcontract.*

There are a great many people who can't market but can deliver quite well, and they would be happy to work for you. Don't hire them as employees, but as situational subcontractors (metaphorically, a pair of hands). Consultants tend to overpay delivery people because they believe that methodology is king, but results are the ace that trumps the king. Your relationship and generation of results are the key to long-term client projects and referrals.

The methodology and implementation are merely the engine room. You need stokers, not engineers.[2]

Here are ideal reasons to use subcontractors for a day or a month:

- There is legitimate high volume—focus groups, interviews, classroom sessions, customer visits, and so forth.
- You need specialized expertise. Part of the project involves financial, or technical, or mystical powers that you don't possess.
- You are bored. You can do it, but you may fall asleep during the interviews.
- You have other priorities. It makes more sense for you to be marketing in a manner only you can do than to be delivering in a manner almost anyone can do. (Key: Just because you can do something faster or better doesn't mean that someone else can't do it just fine for the circumstances. You don't use a howitzer to swat a fly. At least I don't.)
- You anticipate needing subcontracting in the future, and this is a good opportunity to acclimate and train your potential help.

Finally, as you build Market Gravity™ (which we'll discuss later), you'll be doing "reach out" and benefit from more attraction. The more buyers are drawn to you because of your brand and reputation, the less time you need to invest in finding them and educating them about your value.

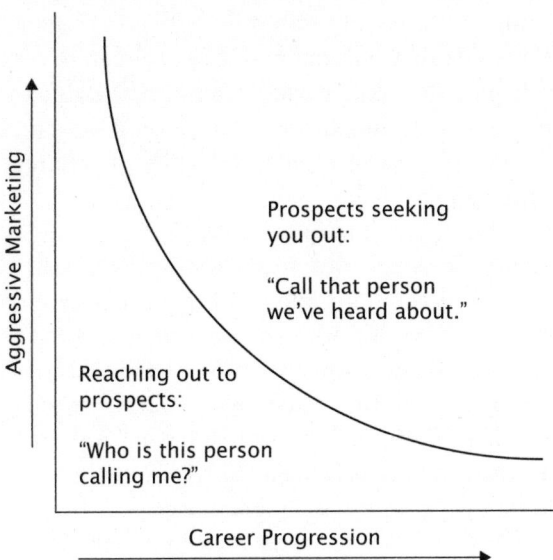

FIGURE 3.1 Reach-Out versus Gravity

You can see from the graphic shown in Figure 3.1 that as your career progresses, you should require less and less time to find clients, because they are finding you. If you veterans who are reading this aren't experiencing that great benefit, then read on.

Identifying True Buyers

The true buyer is that individual whom I've named the economic buyer. I've chosen this to differentiate this person from feasibility buyers who may evaluate an approach in terms of culture, or methodology, or need, *but who cannot make the decision to buy.*

And then there are the nonbuyers. We mentioned the ability to say "no" and the inability to say "yes."

What this amounts to is your steadfastness to reject acceptance and accept rejection. That is, you must reject the acceptance of those who cannot help you (either by signing a check or introducing you to someone who can sign a check) and accept the occasional rejection that is inevitable in this business as you deal with powerful, true buyers. Don't forget the illustration in Figure 3.1, which eases this dynamic by demonstrating that as you become more successful, buyers will come to you, making credibility and fees virtually moot, and reducing rejection substantially.

You can't afford to develop relationships with and be associated with low-level nonbuyers, because that collegiality will be as tough to remove as gum on Texas asphalt in August. You can descend from buyer heights to work with virtually anyone in the organization, but you can't ascend to work with significant buyers if you're seen as a peer of human resources, or training, or lower-level management in general.

An economic buyer can, metaphorically, sign a check. That is, he or she can cause the computer to spit out a check. You don't deal with purchasing or accounts payable, and you don't adhere to their rather arbitrary and unilateral payment practices. *They* deal with the terms that you and your buyer have agreed upon. (Buyers can also require manual checks when there has been an error or undue delay. Remember, when anyone says that payment takes, say, 30 days, it means that for 29 days the request sits on someone's desk, because computers can produce checks anytime at all.)

So how do you tell who the economic buyers are? I say "buyers" because in larger organizations there are scores or even hundreds. I dealt with a dozen different buyers in Merck alone over 12 years. You can't always tell them by title. One of my most significant buyers—he spent $250,000 per year for several years—had the title "International Director of Management Development." Conversely, some vice presidents can't buy a toothbrush in some organizations (find someone in a bank who is *not* a vice president).

In smaller organizations, the owner, or CEO, or president will be the buyer. In nonprofits, usually the executive director or managing director is the buyer. However, in most cases, most of the time, you can find the true buyer by asking these 10 questions of the person with whom you're dealing at the moment:

Questions to Determine the Economic Buyer

1. Whose budget will support this initiative?
2. Who can immediately approve this project?
3. To whom will people look for support, approval, and credibility?
4. Who controls the resources required to make this happen?
5. Who has initiated this request?
6. Who will claim responsibility for the results?
7. Who will be seen as the main sponsor and/or champion?
8. Do you have to seek anyone else's approval?
9. Who will accept or reject proposals?
10. If you and I were to shake hands, could I begin tomorrow?

There are often, among the nonbuyers, key recommenders who can speed your efforts to find the economic buyer. It's worth developing brief relationships with such people in order to have someone lower the drawbridge over the moat.

> ### The Gospel
>
> It's easy to develop long-term relationships with nonthreatening nonbuyers, but this results in nonpayment of your mortgage.

It's worth revisiting our consulting model chart (see Figure 3.2).

We begin with shared values—not spiritual or religious values, but business values. For example, I won't participate in downsizing work, because I believe it's unethical and the result of errors (and sometimes stupidity) in the executive suite. That's me; others may disagree. But I turn that work down based on differing values.

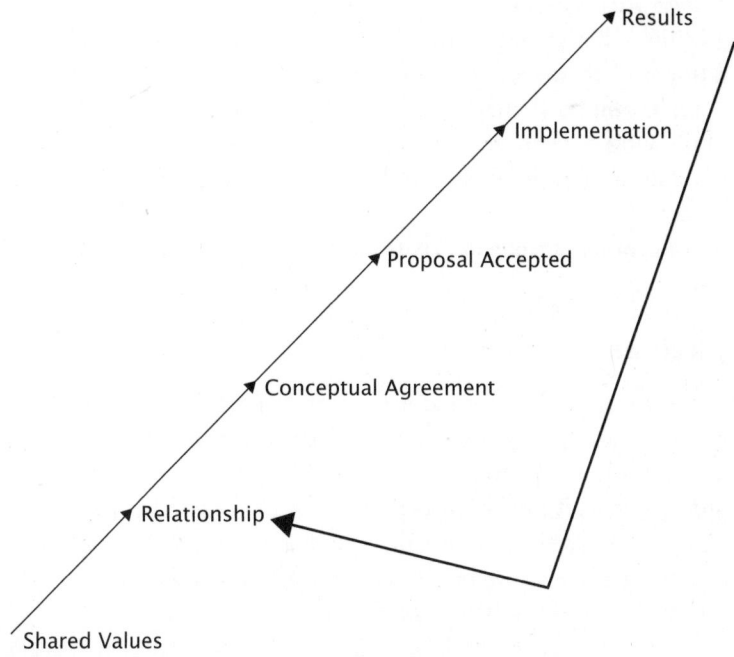

FIGURE 3.2 Consulting Model

If values are simpatico, then we forge a relationship with the economic buyer. And that requires finding the economic buyer, which is why we've taken the time to examine that process here.

The next step is developing conceptual agreement, which is the very heart of my consulting model, but can be accomplished *solely with an economic buyer*. Only buyers can sign proposals (the following step in the model), and only they can provide the details that will make the proposal of high value and justify your fees.

Most consultants stumble in trying to find the economic buyer and settle for lower levels because of self-esteem issues, feelings that they don't deserve or don't merit the attention of a key executive.

Get over it.

Conceptual Agreement

Once you've developed a trusting relationship with the economic buyer, you're positioned to establish conceptual agreement. We're in the middle of the chart, the sweet spot, and ironically, *the longer you take to develop a relationship and create conceptual agreement, the quicker you'll obtain projects.*

I know that sounds counterintuitive, but I simply mean this: The steps are rational in their sequence: No one is going to trust you with their objectives, for example, if they don't trust *you*, and you can't submit a proposal (the following step to conceptual agreement) without a congruence in the buyer's and your expectations and perceived value. (Nor can you arrive at a cogent fee.)

Conceptual agreement has three aspects: objectives, measures of success, and value.

Objectives

There are *always* business outcomes, never deliverables or inputs. They describe a component of *an improved client condition*. Hence, these cannot be inputs, because a training program or a focus group does not improve the client's condition, per se; it merely costs money! (You'll find that most gatekeepers and HR people talk solely in terms of inputs, and almost all RFPs are predefined inputs, e.g., a four-day strategy retreat and a safety audit.)

Examples of objectives might include:

- Reduce closing time for the average sale.
- Improve client reorder size and frequency.
- Reduce stress levels and resultant absenteeism.

Note that objectives can be both professional and personal, and can be tangible or nontangible. You derive objectives from the buyer by asking intelligent questions, and not stopping until you have plumbed all available responses. Here are 10 examples of questions:

1. What is the ideal outcome you'd like to experience?
2. What results are you trying to accomplish?
3. What better product/service/customer condition are you seeking?
4. Why are you seeking to do this work/project/engagement?
5. How would the operation be different as a result of this work?
6. What would be the return on investment (sales, assets, equity, etc.)?
7. How would image/reputation/credibility be improved?
8. What harm (stress, dysfunction, turf wars, etc.) would be alleviated?
9. How much would you gain on the competition as a result?
10. How would your value proposition be improved?

Hint: If a buyer does give you an arbitrary input or deliverable, simply ask why it's important and what it's supposed to produce.

Measures of Success

The second aspect of conceptual agreement is metrics, that is, the indicators or measures of progress and/or completion. This is important so that both you and the buyer can judge relative success at any given time, *and the success that occurs is attributable to your contributions in the project.* This is vital to demonstrate ROI and justify fees.

Examples of metrics might include:

- Time sheets showing rapidity of sales closing after first contact.
- Quarterly sales reports of client reorders and rapidity.
- Anecdotal reporting of stress levels at meetings and absentee reports submitted weekly.

Note that these can be both objective (based on empirical evidence) and subjective (based on perceptions and observed behavior). That's fine, as long as you and the buyer both agree on who will do the anecdotal reporting.

Questions to develop metrics may include the following 10 inquiries:

1. How will you know we've accomplished your intent?
2. How, specifically, will the operation be different when we're done?

3. How will you measure this?

4. What indicators will you use to assess our progress?

5. Who or what will report on our results (against the objectives)?

6. Do you already have measures in place you intend to apply?

7. What is the rate of return (on sales, investment, etc.) that you seek?

8. How will we know that the public, employees, and/or customers perceive it?

9. Each time we talk, what standard will tell us we're progressing?

10. How would you know it if you tripped over it? (Per Bob Mager)

Hint: If the buyer isn't sure of a measure, ask, "How do you know the quality or performance is not present now, and how would you know when it does occur?"

It's vital to establish effective measures with your objectives. Too many buyers claim they want to go "from good to great" based on a popular book, or to reach "world-class standards" based on someone's inflated mission statement. These mean nothing if you can't identify them. The legendary training expert, Bob Mager, has written in several of his books, "How would you know it if you tripped over it?"

Not bad advice.

The Gospel

Never skip or give short shrift to conceptual agreement. If you're so eager or anxious that you neglect it, you'll either miss the sale, obtain a smaller sale than you should have, or engage in an implementation likely to produce zero pragmatic results (and an unhappy buyer).

Value

This is the most overlooked aspect of conceptual agreement, but a crucial nuance, because here the buyer is actually stipulating the worth of the project, so you can demonstrate a dramatic ROI with your fee. For this reason, you must question about value relentlessly, until you've arrived at both business and personal impact of a successful project.

Examples of value might be:

- Improved margins for the average new sale.
- Improved profit per client annually.

- More focus on strategy and less on tactics and failure work by senior management.

Value can sometimes be the same as objectives; for example, profit is both an objective and of high value. But profit has significant and varied impact: more investment in research and development (R&D), larger investor dividends, more favorable repute with Wall Street, building a reserve fund, and so forth.

Never accept the surface or obvious, but help the buyer to articulate the full range of value possible.

Questions for this include the following 10 inquiries:

1. What will these results mean for your organization?
2. How would you assess the actual return (on investment, assets, sales, equity, etc.)?
3. What would be the extent of the improvement (or correction)?
4. How will these results impact the bottom line?
5. What are the *annualized* savings (first year might be deceptive)?
6. What is the intangible impact (on repute, safety, comfort, etc.)?
7. How would you, personally, be better off or better supported?
8. What is the scope of the impact (on customers, employees, vendors)?
9. How important is this compared to your overall responsibilities?
10. What if this fails?

Hint: If the buyer asks why this is important, simply reply that the impact of the project will help determine joint priorities, scope, resources committed, and so on. There shouldn't be any suspicion that you're asking this to increase fees, *because you've already established a trusting relationship*. You can see the reason for the sequence, and why it's so vital to maintain it.

Conceptual agreement—objectives, measures, and value—are as simple as these past few pages suggest, but are as vital to your success in consulting as anything you'll learn in any book. You'll see later, when we discuss proposals, how they will enable you to briefly but powerfully create a win-win proposition for your buyer.

And they create the basis for tremendous leverage.

Leveraging

Before leaving the philosophy of the business and pursuing specific marketing tactics, there is one more important strategic principle to explore: leveraging.

By "leveraging," I mean the ability to exponentially improve your odds, your success rate, your number of successful outcomes, and so on, *without any extra work, without relying on the alignment of the stars, and without bribing a public official.* I've found that we can all do quite simple things to stack the deck in our favor.

The Gospel

When you play with someone else's equipment, on their turf, using their rules, and allowing them to hire the officials, you are going to lose that game.

The earlier and better you learn to leverage, the more dramatically your business will grow, and the more it will become second nature to you. Archimedes said, "Give me a lever, and I can move the world."

All I'm asking is that you move a few clients.

Principles of Leverage

1. *Always provide a choice of "yeses."*

Never give someone a "take it or leave it" choice if you can possibly avoid doing so. In a proposal, always provide options. But even in a next meeting, you enhance your chances by saying: "We seem to need more time to establish objectives for the project. I can meet you tomorrow, same place, same time; or if you'd prefer to get off site, breakfast or lunch is possible Thursday or Friday; or, if you prefer to do this by phone, then I can do that any afternoon this week if I can have an uninterrupted hour of your time. What's best for you?"[3]

If you're dealing with a gatekeeper or intermediary: "You can introduce me to the vice president and set up a meeting for the three of us; or you can set up the meeting for me alone; or I can contact the vice president using your name. Which do you prefer?"

My estimate is that you improve the chances of a favorable response by at least 50 percent by providing a choice of "yeses." This is, as you can imagine, particularly crucial in proposals, and we'll delve into the technique more deeply once we arrive at that stage of the process.

2. *Never bundle; always unbundle.*

A colleague of mine, Paul, provided telesales training and improvement, which included:

- Discussions with management team
- Custom tailoring of program
- Personal delivery
- CDs and text materials
- Follow-up with buyer
- Spouse program
- E-mail and phone response for 30 days
- Two and a half days of onsite training
- Recording allowed for remote locations
- Inclusion in newsletter subscription
- Access to new intellectual property (IP) as produced

Paul charged $7,500 for this. I would have charged $75,000.

Paul threw everything but the kitchen sink into his offer. I would have broken these into options and menu items.

Paul focused on the deliverables. I would have focused on the results and value produced as a consequence of these deliverables.

Most consultants tend to bundle their products and services because they basically are insecure about their worth and want to provide as much stuff as they can to justify fees. That's why my system *begins* with conceptual agreement on outcomes and value.

Don't bundle. When you call a plumber, the plumber doesn't say, "And while I'm there fixing the drain, I can also caulk the tub and regrout the tile."

3. *Ensure that your full array of capabilities is manifest and understood.*

I actually still hear from consultants, "But if I claim to do all these things, won't I be seen as a jack-of-all-trades?" Isn't it ridiculous how empty rubrics, this one from the early seventeenth century, affect so many people supposedly living in a modern world? "Jack-of-all-trades, master of none." This isn't a zero-sum game, and we're not talking about laying bricks and tending cows.

A very good client of mine, the CEO of an insurance company for whom I had been working for two years, said to me, "Can you recommend a keynote speaker for the American Council of Life Insurance annual meeting of CEOs? I'm the program chair." It took me a day to convince him that I wasn't trying to create a gig for myself but that I was and am a highly sought keynoter.

He had never known. Why should he? I had never told him!

Here's how to do this gracefully:

- Provide all your capabilities in your electronic *and* written materials.
- Gather testimonials about *all* that you do, regardless of frequency.
- Cross-pollinate; for example, mention your consulting in your speeches, refer to a speech you made while talking to a consulting buyer, and so forth, whether it's coaching, facilitating, publishing, training—whatever.
- Never narrow yourself unduly. Maintain a broad value proposition. Don't focus on a niche. And ban the phrase "specialize or die" to the same trash bin as "jack-of-all-trades."

4. *Gain referrals ruthlessly.*

Learn this phrase: "Referrals are the coinage of my realm."

Repeat it to yourself whenever you can, then say it glibly to your clients, as in: "Referrals are the coinage of my realm, and I'm wondering who you know who could also benefit from the kind of value I've provided here." (Keeping with the choice of "yeses": "You may introduce us, or I can merely use your name, or I'll keep your name out of the conversation—which do you prefer?")

You should be asking all of your contacts for referrals at least once a quarter. Virtually no consultants do this well. They feel as if they are asking for a favor instead of setting up a win-win-win scenario: good for the ultimate referral, good for the person making the referral, good for you.

We all provide references to our doctors, lawyers, dentists, accountants, auto mechanics and so forth as a common courtesy. What's different here? Nothing. But those people don't often refer others to you because they usually have more knowledge about the dark side of the moon than your value. Make sure they know how you help people, so that they can serve as win/win/win sources themselves.

Never talk esoterically: "I'm in the team interactive performance space where we create self-direction in multidimensional harmony." Instead: "I help all organizations, large and small, maximize teamwork to create better performance and profit."

That, even a lawyer can understand.

Notes

1. One of the absolute *worst* time wasters is trying to maintain and administer your own web site or blog. Be the content expert, not the technical expert.
2. On the count of three, all together: "Wow, he's harsh!"
3. Note that you can agree to meet again by phone only because you've already established a trusting relationship in person.

Exodus
Consulting as a Business

The routes, techniques, and means to overcome obstacles and avoid wandering. It is legitimate and important to want to help people.

Chapter

4

The Journey
How to Market Your Value Rapidly and Profitably

Creating Gravity and Attraction

The Market Gravity™ Wheel is a representation of your options to attract people to you. The longer you're in business, the more you should be:

- Attracting people because of your repute and expertise.
- Gaining business through referral business from clients.
- Gaining business through repeat business from clients.

That combination should amount to about 85 percent of your annual business. If you accompany that with my belief that you need to jettison the bottom 15 percent of your business every couple of years, then you can see that you'll need to generate a modest amount of new business, but not that much.

Too many consultants are struggling *well into their careers* because they fail to implement this philosophy and strategy. They become immersed in the delivery of their work, don't market, and then face the feast-or-famine syndrome: Either they have work that they're being paid to deliver or they are desperately seeking such work.

They are neither ant nor grasshopper. They are road kill. Beware of the crows.

You should jettison the lower end of your client list because:

- The client is no longer profitable.
- You are bored with the work.
- The client is troublesome.
- The work is unpleasant.

Ironically, you're doing the client a favor as well as yourself. Many clients you keep solely through inertia or a false sense of loyalty. But your passion and interests are not present, so you cheat the client of your real value and efforts. Simply apply this language:

"My practice has moved on to a place where I can't provide the focus and attention that your issues deserve, and I'm going to recommend some people who will bring new energy and relevant skills to you. I'm thankful for your past business and support, but don't want to take advantage of that relationship and can't provide in the future what you're going to require."

Then move on.

In addition, you want to create new business for the following additional reasons:

- Improve or change your markets.
- Learn new skills and gain new experiences.
- Gain credibility with your client list and diversity.
- Improve your visibility.
- Create more interest and fun.

However, the vast majority of your annual revenues should come from existing clients and their referrals. Consequently, you can't afford to market solely when you're not delivering. You must be marketing at all times, meaning that a portion of your marketing effort is passive, in that it's in place and always working for you, while some is active and you're engaged even if you're also delivering.

Figure 4.1 depicts the classic Market Gravity Wheel I developed over a decade ago and have continued to evolve as technology and society have evolved, with the help of my technical expert and partner, Chad Barr, of the Chad Barr Group.

We discuss some of the major elements briefly here, and you'll see in the remainder of the book how they blend into your marketing plans.

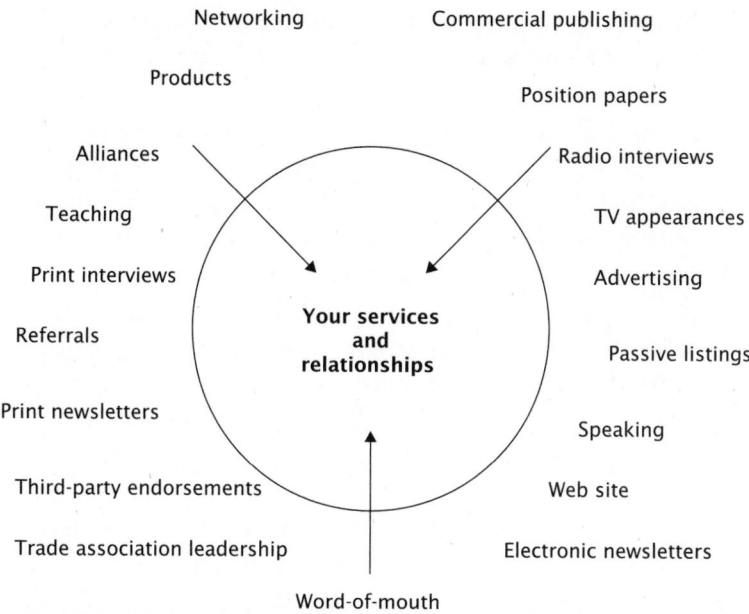

Creating Marketing Gravity

Pro bono work

Networking   Commercial publishing

Products

Position papers

Alliances   Radio interviews

Teaching   TV appearances

Print interviews   Advertising

Referrals   **Your services and relationships**   Passive listings

Print newsletters   Speaking

Third-party endorsements   Web site

Trade association leadership   Electronic newsletters

Word-of-mouth

FIGURE 4.1 Market Gravity Wheel

The Gospel

None of us in consulting was trained or educated to be a marketer. But this is the marketing business. So we had better get good at it.

- *Referrals.* We've already discussed the importance of asking for referrals at least quarterly, not only from clients, but from professional acquaintances, social contacts, civic involvement contacts, and others.

- *Commercially published books.* If referrals are the platinum standard, to be the author of a published book is the gold standard. More books are being published than ever before (at this writing only about 3 percent electronically, but that will obviously grow each year). *You do not need a best seller; you need a book that will cause buyers to say, "We need to talk to this person."*

- *Blogs.* Blogs are ideal sources to create and manifest expertise. You must have intellectual property, offer provocative ideas, post text/audio/video several times a week, and welcome commentary.

- *Networking.* Networking is best done with strangers who don't have preconceptions, and not to collect business cards, but rather to find one or two key buyers or recommenders.

- *Pro bono work.* If you can select a cause you believe in that can use your assistance on a board or committee, or where you can provide your skills (strategy, leadership, team building, and so on), you'll find yourself an instant peer of the executives and community leaders who are serving in similar capacities.

- *Position papers (white papers).* You can demonstrate your expertise and become an object of interest by creating brief (two- to five-page) papers on various aspects of your value proposition (e.g., "The Five Myths of Sales Compensation" or "Why Planning Is Killing Strategy").

- *Speaking.* Even if you are not a professional speaker (viz., also generating revenues through keynotes and training), you can still market by presenting in front of rooms filled with buyers and recommenders. This is best done through trade associations.[1]

- *Web site.* Your web site *is not* a sales vehicle. True buyers—which is why I've been so careful to specify who they are—*do not* troll the Web to find resources (though low-level people do). Your web site is a credibility site. Use it to highlight your thought leadership, intellectual property, and overall stature.

- *Testimonials.* As with referrals, ask for testimonials from every client, *during* and not after the project or relationship. Use the choice of "yeses." Ask if they'd rather provide a letter, be in a 60-second video, serve as a reference, or provide another alternative. Videos of happy clients on your web site are very powerful.

We'll delve into these further as we proceed, and you can see the highly varied additions and variations around the wheel. You don't have to do everything, but you should be engaged in at least a dozen options, and adding a few every single year.

Some elements may not be comfortable for you or in your comfort zone. But I can tell you this: The subtitle of this part of the book is "Consulting as a Business."

If none of the elements in the Market Gravity Wheel is in your comfort zone, then you're in the wrong business.

Reaching Out Effectively

Everyone, at some point in their careers, must reach out. This is commonly termed cold calling, and people will tell you that it's perfectly legitimate and the best way to market and sell. I don't believe that.

Put yourself in the buyer's shoes. Would you be responsive to someone you don't know calling or writing to convince you that he or she is the answer to a problem or the resolution of an issue you didn't know you had? Or one that isn't a priority? Or one that is something you'd rely on only with trusted advisors?

Do you, yourself, respond to those people who call with investment opportunities, or e-mail with a chance to help someone in a third-world country export their $45 million inheritance? Are you accepting or suspicious when someone *whom you've never heard of* offers you a deal too good to be true?

Cold calling works best for commodities, where low price can carry the day, quality is fairly standardized, and there is ongoing need. Purchasing agents are paid to find the lowest price on a certain type of computer, and people have become adept at walking into car dealerships with the manufacturer's invoice printed off the Internet and offering $100 above the dealer's actual costs.

But that's not going to be successful with Bentley, Bulgari, or Brioni. That's because those are commonly accepted high-quality brands that don't need to quibble or dicker, and in fact would damage their brands by doing so.

Thus, when you must reach out, don't cold-call; make the effort at least lukewarm. And the essential element in that effort is to create some level of trust, which is the antipodal position to being a stranger.

In Figure 4.2, the trust pyramid, you see how this can be done so that you're never pitching or relying on the dreaded and impossibly ineffective elevator speech.[2]

At the base is trust inherent in a referral. We've talked about that earlier. If you're successful, that will happen even without your stimulation.

But then we have trust based on manifest expertise. That means that your intellectual property is in circulation. (If you're worried about others stealing your ideas, then by all means lock them away in a vault, but also go into another business, because you won't succeed in this one with that level of paranoia.) You have materials, metaphors, and messages that abound, particularly on the Internet, which is the fastest way to achieve mass recognition.

Higher still is trust based on affiliation needs. That means that when you're networking (which is essentially a reaching out as well as gravity mechanism), you charm people; when you're at various events, people are attracted to you; you take leadership and volunteer positions. (One buyer said to me, "I don't know what project we can use you for, but I do know we need smart

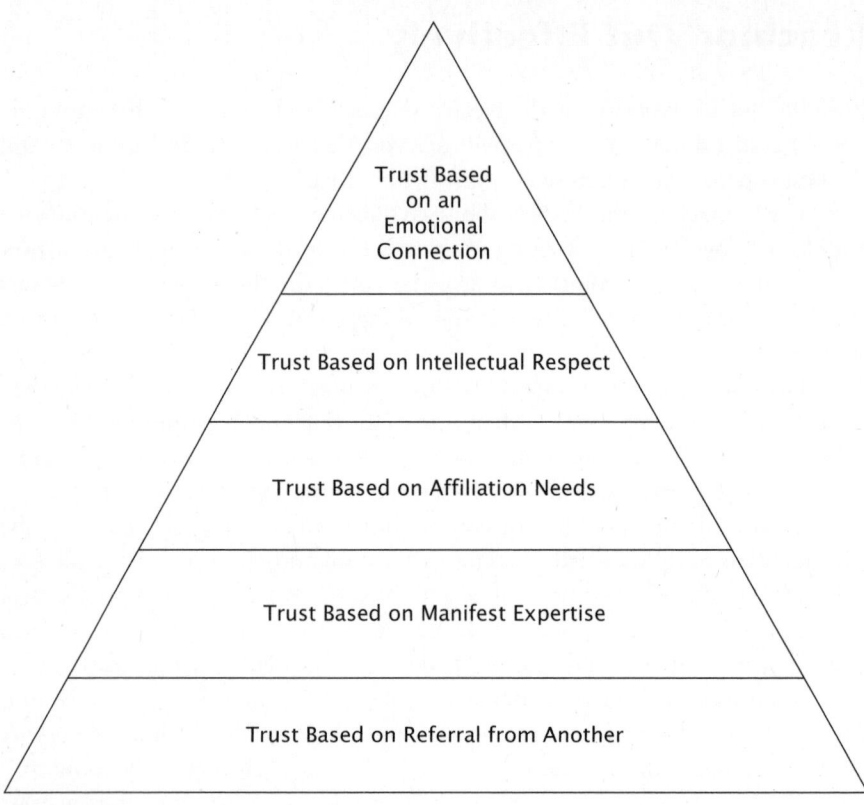

FIGURE 4.2   Trust Pyramid

people around, so plan to start next week and we'll collaboratively figure out something for you to do and what to pay you.")

Trust based on intellectual respect is especially important with powerful people, who are drawn to those who have written books, have spoken out provocatively, and aren't timid about manifesting their intellectual firepower and prowess. Expertise is outstanding ability in given areas. Intellect is the ability to be outstanding in *any* area.

The Gospel
Buyers choose commodities based on price. They choose business partners based on trust.

Finally, trust based on an emotional connection is the highest level to achieve. Keep in mind that this pyramid is not sequential; you are not toiling from the bottom up, but rather can enter at any level. How do you create this when you're reaching out and have no prior relationship? You find what's in your buyers' self-interests. Do they publicly support a certain charity? Are they fans of a particular sports team? Are they family oriented? Do they travel for pleasure? Do some homework, and evolve your approach through such emotional triggers.

The worst aspect of cold calling, by the way, is being successful. That's what I said! Because since your odds are about 10,000 to 1 that if you gain an early success you're going to be prone to keep at it, pounding the pavement, working the phones, sending direct mail—until you fail 9,999 times.

To summarize, Figure 4.3 provides another view of my consulting marketing model.

We'll continue to deal with these in detail. Let's turn now to a point I made earlier: How to use the Internet to accelerate your repute, brand, expertise, and word-of-mouth promotion—at virtually (no pun intended) zero expense and travel.

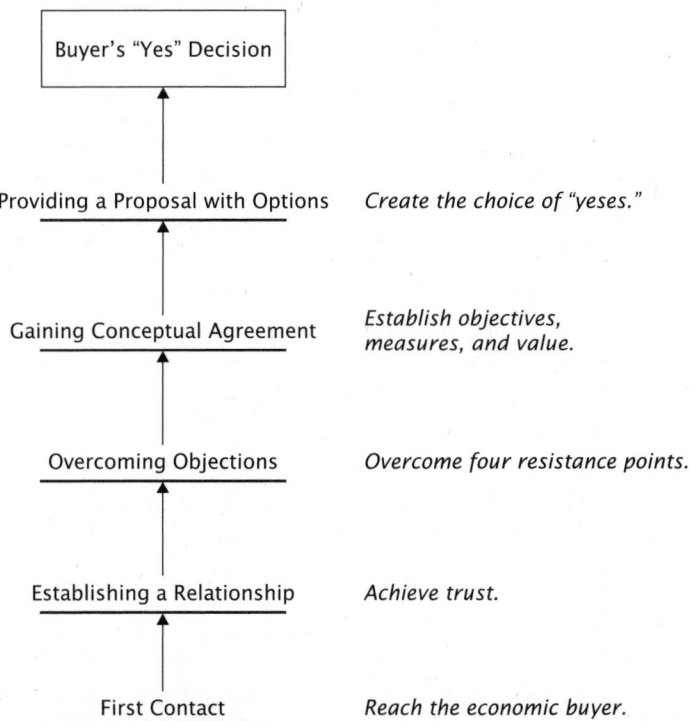

FIGURE 4.3 Consulting Marketing Model

Viral and Social Media Implementation

I know of few things—pet rocks, midi skirts, quadraphonic sound, absinthe—with more promotional noise and less practical application than so-called social media platforms. They have their utility if utilized correctly, but they can be huge time dumps if they are mistaken for daily marketing marvels.

Let's look at the cons and dispense with some myths, and then we can focus on the few valid pros:

1. *Social media amplify your message.*

   The trouble is that they amplify *all* messages, and create a cacophony amidst which it is hard to be heard at all. Picture yourself in a Boston bar on St. Patrick's Day. Everyone is screaming and enjoying themselves, most people are making no sense, and those who are can't be heard above the din. At least they have the compensation of drinking.

2. *You can reach customers for free and personally.*

   Not really. You might if you're in the real estate or diet business. But corporate buyers do not use social media to find and select consultants. Don't be swayed by research showing that X percent of corporate managers use the Internet daily to find information. They may well be using Google, or Wikipedia, or Amazon. But they are not searching for consultants! Would *you* choose a personal advisor from an Internet contact? If you would, please step away from any sharp objects.

3. *Even with a low percentage of interest, you'll be successful because of the huge number of potential contacts.*

   At this writing, LinkedIn tells me I have 6,142,687 people linked to me in one form or another. My offer to you is this: Tell me how to get 50 cents from each one and I'll split the money with you. If you have a mailing list of a million people, and not one is interested or could be interested in your services, you have a worthless list. You're better off with one solid buyer contact from a networking event than accumulating a thousand people a week on Facebook.

4. *People are successfully launching and building businesses on social media platforms.*

   Most of the people scratching out an existence are those who are selling services such as how to market on social media platforms! They are not marketing a tangible and haven't been successful selling a product or service on social media, but they are somehow experts, so they can sell social media marketing techniques. I will readily grant you that there are exceptions. But you don't build a practice on a detour or tough path; you build it on a paved road that already exists and on which you can build some speed.

Having established those negatives, here is how you can truly leverage social media intelligently and with a minimum of time invested, because these devices will proliferate, combine, and grow—and may already be more practical by the time you're reading this.

1. *Create a repository of intellectual property.*

I post on Twitter every morning. It takes two minutes, and I try to keep the post well under the Twitter maximum of 140 characters so that it can be retweeted. That's what helps to create viral reputations. I don't post platitudes, or others' quotes, or inane commentary about what food I'm eating. I post value: a business technique, a management insight, a sales innovation, and so on. At one point I numbered these, reaching 100 over 100 days.[3]

2. *Create uniqueness.*

I follow no one on Twitter, despite the fact that I have thousands of followers. While this infuriates some people (who are not buyers in any case) it helps to maintain my reputation as a contrarian and someone apart from the mainstream.

3. *Use multimedia.*

You can incorporate text, audio, and video on social platforms and blogs. Exploit this potential, so that you become an object of interest and others cite you. Show photos or videos of your work with clients, or speaking before a group, or client testimonials.

4. *Make major announcements.*

All sites have the provision to create splashes about important events. Let others know of your awards, accolades, workshops, publications, speeches, appointments, and so forth. You can post these in seconds, so that the chance of making that 1 in 10,000 contact is reasonable based on the time investment.

5. *Create groups.*

Become the thought leader of groups that focus on your value proposition, work, expertise, and methodology. Provide intellectual property and thought leadership. As the groups grow, seek out realistic references, connections, collaborations, and so on.

Overall, your investment in strictly social media platforms for work should be less than 30 minutes a day. (What you do for recreation and affiliation, which is far more logical on these sites, is up to you. But don't confuse the two. If you go onto a site to post a minute's notice and are still there two hours later, it's the equivalent of leaving your office and playing in the park.)

Your investment in blogging, which is somewhat different, should be higher. I'd advise you to post a minimum of three times a week. Keys:

- Use podcasts, videos, photos, cartoons, graphics, and text. Keep the blog varied, fresh, and interesting.
- Invite commentary and reply to it. Moderate the site to remove anything obscene, obviously promotional, or plain dumb.
- Keep most items brief, maybe a third to half a screen; some major articles might take up a full screen, but try not to go beyond that.
- Keep the site informational and valuable, with only soft promotion (e.g., in standing items in the margins or brief announcements). People will not return to what amounts to an advertising billboard.
- Don't be afraid to share your value. Post your ideas, intellectual property, and techniques. Be original and bold.

Blogging is very powerful when you already have a brand, but it can also create brands if you are interesting and aggressive. You can do this at any point in your career, and good blogs go viral very rapidly. Make sure you offer RSS feeds, so that people can be apprised of each new posting. Consider guest articles as well, which show that you are the center of expertise for your topics, to the extent that others publish there.

Creating an Accelerant Curve

We've discussed the benefits of drawing buyers to you and the necessity of reaching out to them on occasion. In professional marketing, the trick is to accelerate their scope, degree, and size of business with you.

Hence, we can consider an Accelerant Curve that views business as long-term and clients as lifelong.

On the left axis of Figure 4.4 is ease of doing business with you. In the upper left we would find free downloads, inexpensive booklets, modest teleconferences, pro bono work publicity, and so forth.

On the bottom axis is increasing intimacy and fees (and, counterintuitively, decreasing labor intensity, as we'll soon see). Thus, the left-hand side

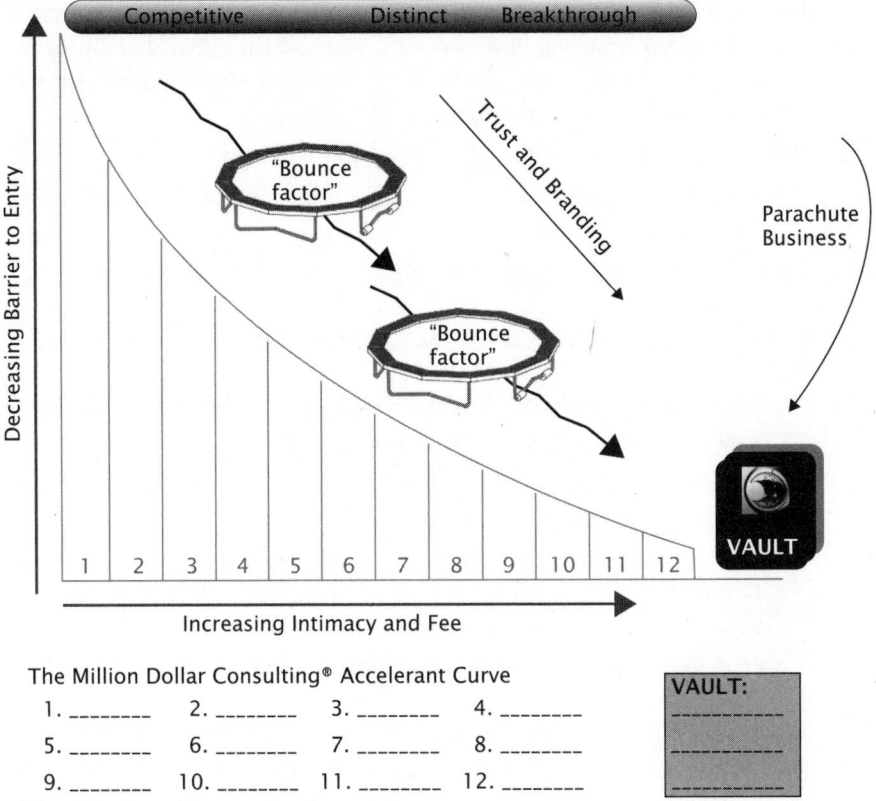

The Million Dollar Consulting® Accelerant Curve

1. _____ 2. _____ 3. _____ 4. _____

5. _____ 6. _____ 7. _____ 8. _____

9. _____ 10. _____ 11. _____ 12. _____

VAULT:
_____
_____
_____

FIGURE 4.4 Accelerant Curve

would involve impersonal purchases or attendance at large events, whereas the right-hand side would include personal coaching, retainers, and so forth.

The Gospel

Think of the fourth sale first. A client is never an event, but part of a relationship that endures as long as you provide value and volition.

The vertical entries (there is no magic number; I've simply used a dozen for the illustration) represent your service and/or product offerings. Given the criteria on the axes, the left third would tend to be seen as competitive, the middle third as distinct, and the right third as proprietary or breakthrough.

Finally, the chart culminates in your personal vault. These are services that are based on a very strong bond between you and the client. Examples:

- A $25,000 per month retainer.
- Licensing your intellectual property to that client.
- Providing private newsletters, audio, video, and so forth tailored for that client.
- Exclusive contracts with noncompete clauses (at significant fees).

Three factors drive clients down the Accelerant Curve:

1. The trust and brand that you develop, so as to encourage the buyer to want to partake of more and more value.
2. No chasms where the buyer would reach a point where there is no next step that makes sense.
3. Bounce factors that impel the client to jump ahead by several leaps. For example, many people who read my books, which may cost $40, immediately enter my Mentor Program for $5,500, and then proceed to my Million Dollar Consulting® College, which is $14,500.

When you view your business this way, you can think of "the fourth sale first," meaning that a client represents a long-term, high-revenue potential *if you can provide long-term, evolutionary value in the form of varied services and products.*

When you achieve a significant brand, you'll be the beneficiary of what I call "parachute business," which is business that "drops in" on the right side without having to proceed down the curve, given the repute and strength of your work and its discussion among your constituent prospects. (That's why we discussed viral marketing earlier.)

You may have an offering—a teleconference, say, or coaching services, or a workshop, or a communications audit—that delivers varied value based on its configuration and delivery and that, therefore, may occupy several points on your Accelerant Curve. (My Mentor Program is available in three dimensions, with increasing intimacy and fee.)

Ironically, as you proceed to the right, to the vault, your labor intensity tends to diminish because:

- Retainer-type work is valuable because of the potential for timely access, but not necessarily presence or usage.
- Licensing intellectual property is by definition remote and subject to the client's implementation, not yours.

So you can achieve nirvana if you use this methodology correctly by providing an incentive for clients to increase their scope of business and commensurate fees while demanding less of your presence. Ten retainer clients at $10,000 per month each is a seven-figure annual income that is virtually all profit.

I'm introducing the Accelerant Curve at this point because it is one of the most important factors in moving from five figures to six, and from six figures to seven. It enables you to discard certain approaches based on their poor fit into the curve, rather than retaining them out of blind affection. As you become more and more successful, the entire mechanism shifts to the right, meaning that even your low-barrier-to-entry offerings may carry substantial fees, since your brand is so magnetic.

A newcomer can start with two or three services in each category, but a veteran should ensure that there are five or six. You can also use the following as a six-point template for your marketing and structure:

1. Do you have free or very inexpensive offerings to lure people and induce them to become acquainted with your value?

2. Are there logical, sequential, evolutionary steps so that people can continue to work with you? (Few people will move directly from a $40 book to a $150,000 strategy project, although it's been known to happen.)

3. Are you differentiating products and services so that buyers realize that a great deal of value is available only from you?

4. As you build the relationship, can you easily maintain the momentum?

5. As you develop products and services, do they fit in your evolving Accelerant Curve, or are they solutions seeking problems?

6. Are you increasing your vault, which is the ultimate and most intimate client relationship?

Take a few minutes to use the chart, and test what you can at present fit into the competitive, distinct, and breakthrough categories. Ask yourself if you've been insufficiently active in creating varied services, or too complacent about the ones you have been successful with.

Buyers can't slide down a theoretical curve.

Shameless Promotion

I've found that when I write a book such as this one, even for an excellent publisher such as this one, I had better be prepared to promote the book myself if I want to see excellent results. After all, the publisher has thousands of titles for which it is responsible and it wouldn't be a prudent business decision to focus solely on my work. However, I put out at any one time a single book, and it's entirely reasonable for me to focus solely on it.

That's because it's my accountability to do so. Anything the publisher does for me helps, but I'm the one accountable.

If that's true for a book, what about your name? Your results? Your intellectual property? Your expertise? Despite viral marketing, technology, referrals, and all such excellent sources, you had better be prepared to promote yourself.

Shamelessly.

People tell me all the time that in certain cultures (and they seem to include every place from the United Kingdom to Japan and Greenland to Antarctica) one cannot do this; in certain parts of the United States (Maine to California, Minnesota to Florida) one cannot do this; with certain markets (banking to auto demolition, chemicals to amusement parks) one cannot do this.

The Gospel

The one guaranteed method to ensure that your name is bandied about and cited positively is to do it yourself.

I have news for all of them: One *can* do it and might as well get good at it.

"Shameless" will indeed depend on who you are and where you are, but mostly on your own volition and chutzpah. But no matter who and where you are, it's almost a certainty that you can promote yourself better than you are doing now. We all have an overt or covert sense of what's proper and decent and appropriate.

But that sense is usually overly modest and baggage from the past. This is an age of reality television, body piercing, and multiple tattoos. I don't think you're running a risk of arrest by the decorum police if you mention more often that you do good work.

Fundamentally, this is a mind set issue.

Poor Mind-Set	Positive Mind-Set
▪ I'm trying to sell something.	▪ I'm providing people with great value.
▪ This is adversarial; one person wins.	▪ This is collaborative; it's win-win.
▪ Others should sing my praises.	▪ Only I can effectively market myself.
▪ Modesty makes others comfortable.	▪ Confidence makes others confident.
▪ I should listen more than talk.	▪ When I do talk, it must be compelling.
▪ No one wants to hear how good I am.	▪ Everyone is interested in being helped.
▪ You have to walk the talk.	▪ You also have to talk the walk.

Remember that existing clients know you. They have a frame of reference about your work. But prospects usually have none of that. That's why you have to talk the walk and turn the hackneyed bromide of walking the talk on its head. Too many consultants complain that their prospects don't seem to appreciate them as much as their clients do.

Duh!

When I entered Rutgers University, some upperclassman decided to create a pickup basketball game in the gym. There were 11 of us, so one person wasn't going to play. I had played varsity ball in high school, so I wasn't worried.

Until I wasn't chosen. I was furious with these oafs. Later that day a friend, listening to my whining, asked, "What did they say when you told them you had played varsity ball?"

"I didn't tell them."

"Well," he said, "there you go."

You need to tell your prospects about your prowess. Here is a variety of ways to do this without being arrested:

Alan's Shameless Techniques

- Make your web site a high credibility area with position papers, print and video testimonials, client lists, and so on. Direct people there all the time. With the advent of iPhones and iPads, they don't have to wait to get back to the office to do this. They can often do it while you're with them!

- Drop client engagements into your conversations. "The compensation issue you're raising is similar to projects I've completed for Boeing and Apple." If you have signed nondisclosure agreements, then you can substitute ". . . for a major global manufacturer and a top-tier computer company."

- Use your name to build your personal brand, as I've described at the top of this list. Do that in your newsletter, blog, and so forth. (My blog is at www.contrarianconsulting.com, but the name on the masthead is "Alan's Blog.")

- Introduce new ideas representing your expertise. In conversation, say, "You keep referring to 'team building,' but in my experience most organizations have committees, not teams, and I've determined the four key principles for committee building." That will rivet attention on you.

- Create visibility almost every day. Record a podcast, create a brief video, post an article, speak at an event, write a letter to the editor—whatever it takes and whatever you're comfortable doing. People cannot hear your name too often.

- Don't assume that posting on social media platforms is the equivalent of doing all this. If you choose social media, then you have to do all the other stuff, as well. Assuming that restricting your promotional activities to social media outlets will result in a sustainable business is like leaving the runway lights on for Amelia Earhart—it's a nice thought, but very unlikely to be helpful.

- Send out press releases weekly. Create them about your new client, accolades, speaking appearances, new model, opinion on current events—whatever. You can do this with a private list of talk show producers, assignment editors, and media people you maintain, or you can use a membership source such as www.expertclick.com. There is also, on the Web, a plethora of free press release sources. (See my blog entry: www.contrarianconsulting.com/press-release-distribution-sources.)

- Finally, tell people how good you are and demonstrate your enthusiasm for working with them. Enthusiasm is contagious, and a quiet reserve is narcoleptic. "One of my clients told me just last week that I'm the best change management expert to ever set foot in her company, and I'd love to show you why she thinks so!"

I've said this before, and I'll probably say it again later because you have to embrace this salient fact: If you don't blow your own horn, there is no music.

Technology Strategies

Technology interacts and intervenes with most of our marketing in one form or another. The key is to not allow it to also interfere.

Wall Street Journal technology columnist Walter Mossberg told a group I was hosting, "Just as you don't announce you're plugging into the electric grid when you use a hair dryer or television, we're also going to stop saying that we're 'going online' because we'll be online at all times." Like most thought leaders, he has a way of succinctly changing one's point of view.

Thus, with iPhones, iPads, Androids, notebooks, laptops, and a variety of personal digital assistants (PDAs) yet to be invented, let's reasonably assume the following tenets will apply to all of us in professional consulting and related areas:

- We will have personal apps that clients can access and that may provide entirely new and separate streams of income.

- The social media platforms will coalesce, evolve, and recombine into much more pragmatic and focused vehicles to create targeted communities, interest groups, development experiences, and so on.

- Web sites will become organic, in that they will change very frequently, perhaps even daily, to reflect recent events, whether a new testimonial, a new economic condition, or reporting on new intellectual property.

- Branding (which we'll talk about in the next chapter) will be harder because of the general noise level but also easier because of unprecedented visibility possibilities, thus making differentiation and unique value the keys.

- Not unlike the 24-hour supermarket, there will be clients and prospects globally seeking assistance and expecting responses on a 24/7 basis. Speed of response will be as important as quality of response, and may be even more of a differentiator.

- You are potentially accessible no matter where you are, which is not necessarily a benefit.

- Work and personal lives are really one life, in which you should expect to deal with a new paradigm of returning calls from the beach if it means a $150,000 contract, and taking Wednesday afternoon off if it means seeing your daughter's dance recital.

- You can become pseudo-isolated, believing that your constant interactions over electronic media constitute affiliation, when in fact it's the equivalent of listening to a recording instead of being in the concert hall.

The Gospel

Use 100 percent of the 30 percent of technology most relevant to you. That will ensure that you control it and it doesn't control you.

If it's more difficult to read the *New York Times* on an iPad than to read the actual paper, *and the newspaper is present*, it would be folly to use the iPad just for the sake of using the technology. If it's easier to look up stock prices on the iPad than by using the paper, *and the iPad is present*, then it's silly to use the newspaper to track stock prices.

You do what makes the most sense for you in terms of time, efficiency, and accuracy.

That rule applies to all technology. Having the latest, largest (or smallest), and best is not necessarily a wise pursuit. Is version 3.0.25b really worth the hour's investigation and installation when version 3.0.25a has been working just fine?

Here are five suggestions for your overall technology strategy and philosophy, above and beyond the tactical advice you'll find throughout the book on virtually all aspects of creating a successful and lucrative consulting practice.[4]

Alan's Technology Philosophy for Nontechnologists

1. Don't confuse conversance with use or investment. Here's an example: I'm active on Facebook and LinkedIn since they are major social media platforms that I'm often asked about. I participate and have many "followers" and "friends" because I wouldn't be in a position to provide appropriate advice (such as you're reading in this book) without having been there and done that. However, that does not mean that I spend more than 10 minutes a day on these activities, nor that they are key components in my own marketing plans.[5]

2. Don't do it yourself. Find an excellent technical guru or company that will build and evolve your Web presence, technology needs, and so forth. The outstanding ones will also proactively suggest innovations and leading-edge projects for your consideration *that are consistent with your value proposition and marketing plans.* Don't waste your time attempting to be your own technologist unless you're also advising prospects not to hire you and to serve as their own consultants.

3. Use the medium appropriately and exploit the uniqueness. If you're going to be merely a talking head on video, then why make a video instead of an audiotape? If you're recording audio that requires people to visualize something, why use an audio and not a video? If you're giving people Web access to certain value, why drive them away by requiring information that may make them fear they'll appear on e-mail lists and be the object of spam?

4. Leading edge is not over the edge. I first heard of a tablet on which newspapers would be printed and "used by everyone" at the American Press Institute in 1990! There was even a primitive working model. It took another two decades and still not "everyone" is using this to read newspapers! Use some moderation and pragmatism, always keeping in mind your prospects and audience. Ask yourself what most people are likely to be receptive to, and how quickly. You can always ratchet up your approach if you've been too conservative, but it's very costly to back away from a major investment made because you were overly optimistic and imprudent.

5. What you do find extremely useful, exploit and learn to use well. If you're using a keyboard daily, then learn to speed type—it's not difficult (far less so than most video game controls). If you're sending out newsletters, find the best, most automated, and most reliable databases. Use professional recording gear.

Technology, like electricity, is part of our daily existence. My advice is to focus on results and goals and then work backwards, employing the technology that is most efficient and effective to speed you to that destination. Here's a caveat: If it comes with two instructional videos and takes hours to learn, either find a professional to do it for you or don't do it at all.

Notes

1. An outstanding resource is *National Trade and Professional Associations of the United States* (Columbia Books). There are similar publications in many other countries.
2. The words you use with yourself—self-talk—inform your behavior. Try to avoid thinking in terms of "pitching" and "price."
3. I don't suggest you do follow everyone who follows you on Twitter, or you'll be pulled into the time dump. There is no etiquette about this, so don't be bullied into a waste of time.
4. For example, if you review the Market Gravity Wheel, you'll see that most of these are dependent on some form of technological involvement.
5. This is the same reason I joined Mensa, because I suspected these were a bunch of smug people who simply can take a test well (or got lucky, or cheated), and I was right. If that's the top 2 percent of the population, as they claim, German shepherds are going to inherit the earth.

Chapter

Presence
How to Be an Authority and Expert

Creating and Nurturing a Brand

A brand is a uniform expression of quality. It may be a work, a phrase, a logo, or a name. Your ultimate brand is your name, as in "Get me Jason Wilson."

The three requirements for a powerful brand are:

1. You identify a market need that:
   - Already exists and is vibrant (strategy formulation).
   - You can create and make vibrant (remote coaching).
   - You anticipate will be vibrant (the Brazilian market).
2. You have the competency to:
   - Create intellectual property and provocative ideas.
   - Trademark and protect proprietary models and techniques.
   - Stand apart from most competitors.
3. You are passionate enough to:
   - Accept the inevitable rejections.
   - Constantly evolve and improve your approaches.
   - Become an enthusiastic evangelist for your results.

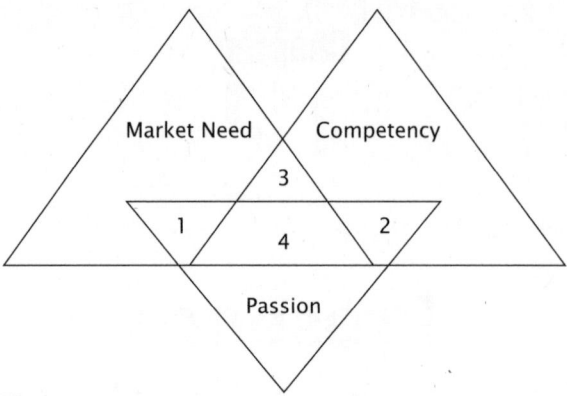

1. Brand is a clever concept, but substance can't be delivered.
2. Brand is ideally suited to you, but market is unreceptive.
3. Brand is potentially effective, but isn't supported.
4. Brand is magic.

FIGURE 5.1 Requirements for a Powerful Brand

Figure 5.1 shows the three pitfalls when even a single one of these three elements is missing. But if you have (or can develop) all three, then you can virally build your brand.

The Gospel

If you are a sole practitioner, the brand has to be about you. If you intend to build a company to sell someday, the brand has to be about the company.

Branding is best accomplished through repetition and consistency. When I was a beginning consultant with no money in my pocket and lost amid the noise and smoke of the profession, I became "the contrarian." I didn't realize I was creating a brand, but sometimes it's better to be lucky than good. I pointed out that the quality movement really wasn't about quality, that team building was ineffective because more organizations actually had committees, and that strategic planning was an oxymoron.

People were skeptical, cynical, aghast—and interested. I was hired to speak, asked to submit articles that led to columns, and emerged from the smoke and noise. On the way to my name becoming a brand, I used Million Dollar Consulting, Balancing Act, Architect of Professional Communities, and a dozen other phrases, which I have protected.

FIGURE 5.2 Networking Your Brand

Once you are consistent and repetitive, you can exponentially spread the word.

This chart in Figure 5.2 is limited by our space here, but is unlimited in a three-dimensional universe. This viral nature to spread your brand is, of course, intensified by technology today, *but it is not sufficient to relay solely by means of technology*. You need to speak, write, appear, network, and generally push your brand through networks such as I show in the chart.

You should initially create brands around your value proposition. If your value proposition is: "We reduce sales closing time and cost of acquisition," your brand might be something such as: "The Sales Accelerator" or "Fast Close."

You can then create newsletters, blog posts, columns, podcasts, videos, speeches, booklets, and so on (think of the spokes in the gravity wheel) to broadcast your brands.

The overall sequence looks like Figure 5.3.

You begin by creating the brand. Consider whether you have traction: Do people respond well, is it cited, are others drawn to it? Then position it with your intended buyers, understanding what they read, what they listen to, what they attend.

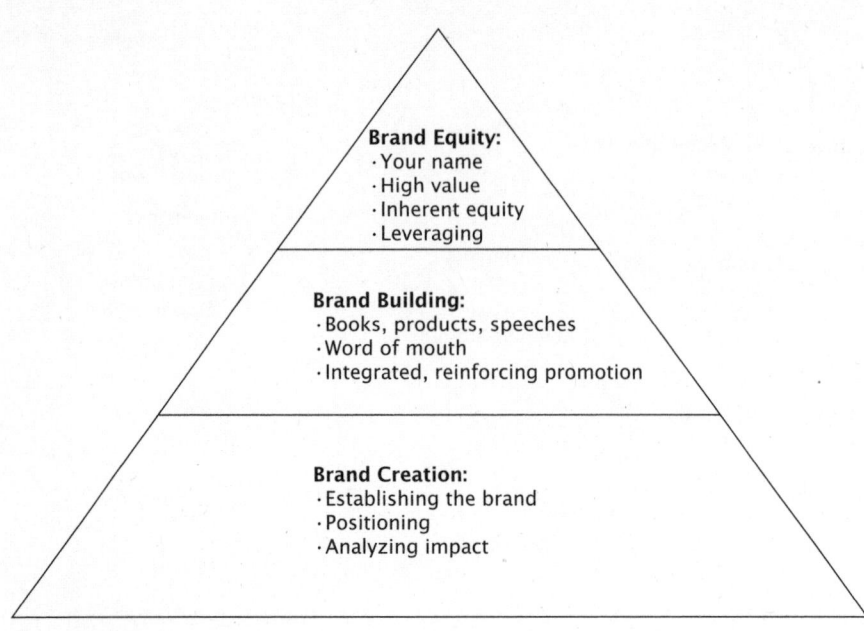

FIGURE 5.3 Brand Pyramid

Build it as I've indicated. Use the gravity wheel to disseminate it in every possible way within your comfort zone (and, perhaps, outside your comfort zone). Finally, appreciate the equity. Convert your brand to your name, while retaining other brands. Leverage it to gain alliance partners and introductions. You won't be surprised to hear that it's far easier to get a book proposal rapidly considered when you have a strong brand, or to get to see that elusive buyer.

And once your brand is strong and recognized, you can increase the leverage through expanded offerings.

Expanding Products and Services

Beware of the dreaded SOSO. It's no accident that the derogatory review "so-so" also stands for "same old, same old."

As I look back on my work, I'm often astounded at the advice and counsel I was giving clients in the late 1980s into the 1990s. But they appreciated it, and it was the best I had to offer. Most of it worked well at the time. But I also used to think that my Corvette and GTO were the fastest cars I'd ever drive, until I purchased Ferraris and Astons and Bentleys. They all were fabulous cars, but are not right for me today. (When I told someone, after my third Ferrari, that I wasn't going to buy another because I had outgrown them, he said, "I never thought I would hear an adult male make that statement, and I doubt I ever will again." But have you seen the gray-haired guys driving the Corvettes? Talk about cognitive dissonance.)

Somewhere between two-thirds and three-quarters of my income these days derives from products and services that didn't exist three years ago. The right side of my Accelerant Curve, and my vault, keep growing, as does the parachute business that lands there. That's what brands do, and they evolve into celebrity, which we address in the next chapter.

For now, let's look at the disposition of your products and services and a rational strategy to develop them in any economy. First, let's agree that there are four basic relationships, as depicted in Figure 5.4.

In normal economies, quadrant 1 is the low-hanging fruit. Clients who trust you and have used your services will be inclined to continue with you—repeat business. The next most likely target of opportunity is quadrant 3, wherein those same clients are receptive to new offerings—new business to current clients.

After than, quadrant 2 is next, taking your existing work, with commensurate testimonials and referrals, to new clients. And the last and toughest is quadrant 4, where you would be attempting to offer new things to new people, a hard row to hoe (and, therefore, the bane of all new consultants, for whom any buyer is new and all products and services are new).

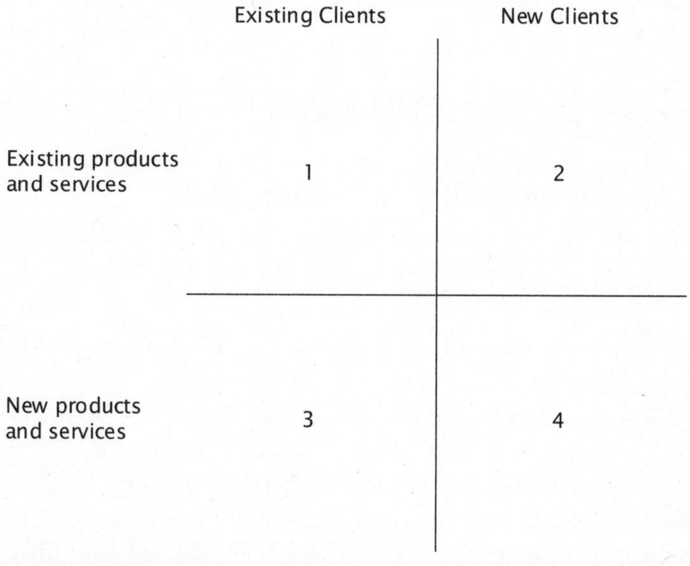

	Existing Clients	New Clients
Existing products and services	1	2
New products and services	3	4

FIGURE 5.4 Market Priorities Quadrants

However, in tough economic times, even good clients tend to blindly cut back expenses (by "blindly" I mean despite the return they're deriving), so the remedy is to start with quadrant 3! After all, they already trust you, and if you're offing new solutions, new innovations, and new opportunities consistent with changing times, they're likely to listen. The second choice is quadrant 2, where your existing products and services *will appear new to new clients*. Then comes quadrant 1, and finally again is quadrant 4.

So you can see that a simple chart like this will aid immeasurably in your expansion strategies, and you need expansion strategies because the following factors will threaten to make your existing offerings SOSO at any given time:

- Economic turmoil
- Competitive entries
- New technologies
- New trends and even fads
- Saturation of your traditional base
- Primary target industry and business restructuring
- Public perception change
- Government regulation

You get the idea. Don't wait to be reactive, acting out of desperation.

The Gospel

You are your own R&D factory, and your clients constitute your laboratory. Always have something cooking on the workbench.

One final consideration: How do you know *which* clients to approach first, or even which prospects have the highest potential? To some extent that's both art and science, but we can focus on at least the science aspect here.

This is a matter of a combination of your diversity—my "cooking" lab referred to in "The Gospel" box—and your client's maturity. (See Figure 5.5.)

The more diverse your offerings and the more mature your client,[1] the more comprehensive your approaches can be. At the opposite pole, the less mature and the less diverse, the more you're a commodity—a one-trick pony.

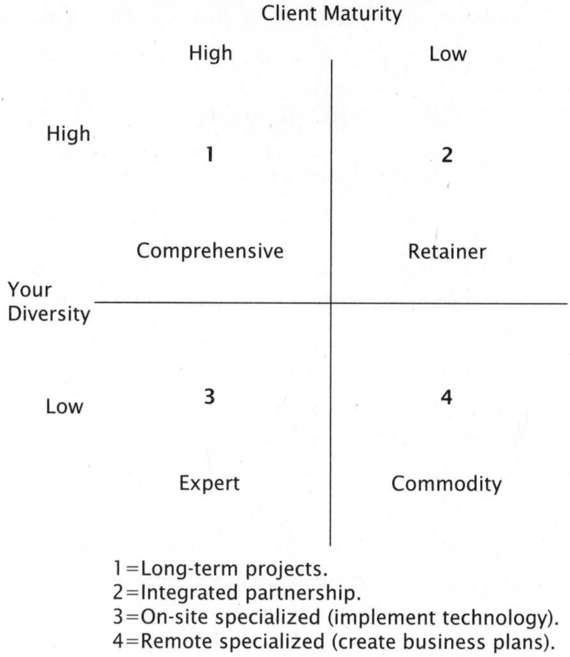
Client Maturity
High
Low
High
1
2
Comprehensive
Retainer
Your Diversity
Low
3
4
Expert
Commodity
1=Long-term projects.
2=Integrated partnership.
3=On-site specialized (implement technology).
4=Remote specialized (create business plans).

FIGURE 5.5 Client Maturity

If you have high diversity and your client is low on the maturity index, a retainer may be the appropriate positioning. And if your diversity is low but the client is mature, the client may choose to use you as a narrowly focused expert.

Figure 5.5 gives examples of how you might make the best of any of these combinations.

Considering Alliances

The discussions among consultants about "getting together" and "joining forces" and "joint ventures" are equal only to the groups that endlessly discuss evidence of the Loch Ness monster, aliens in Hangar 52, and whether the Chicago Cubs will ever win the World Series again: pretty pointless.

Here's your watchword, straight from actor Cuba Gooding and the movie *Jerry Maguire*: "Show me the money."

Any conceptual alliance is a waste of your time and energy. I'm telling you this unequivocally after observing consultants burn up otherwise discretionary time yakking about how they would work together—theoretically. They create intricate spiderwebs of how their methodologies would interlock, integrate, and create synergies, but none of this is within shouting distance of an actual client.

> ### The Gospel
>
> The only time an alliance makes sense is when there is money on the table.

Several years ago a consultant approached me and explained he had a large client of $1.5 billion in revenues. He had been doing leadership and team-building work for a couple of years, but now the CEO had asked him to help with strategy because the top team trusted him, though strategy was not his strong suit.

We agreed that he would introduce me as the strategist, which all but sealed the sale right there. I'd create a proposal, and he would assist in the delivery to learn the process. We would split the $160,000 project 60/40, me/him.

This approach worked splendidly. The consultant continued to work with that client with even more tools in his kit, the client was very well served, and I had business I otherwise would not have obtained. The consultant had approached me with money on the table.

Here are six guidelines for effective alliances, at any stage in your career, which avoid the pitfalls and exploit the benefits:

1. Focus on a clear, short-term piece of business that either party is dealing with. If you can't name the client and the time frame, don't even begin the conversations.

2. Look for $1 + 1 = 160$. That is, your joint participation should exponentially increase the value to the client and, hence, the fees to the two of you. If you would normally receive, say, $80,000, but with your alliance partner your project is priced at $140,000, that means, with a 50/50 split, you're now receiving only $70,000!

3. The best alliances are those in which there are competencies and skills provided that the other party doesn't have. If you are both experts in reducing the sales cycle, why do you need each other and why does the client need both of you? But if one of you reduces the sales cycle and the other is an expert in recruiting sales talent, that might make more sense.

4. Don't mistake your need for affiliation with a need for alliance. This is a chronic error. If you're lonely being on your own, then join professional, civic, social, or religious groups. But don't form a business entanglement just because you don't like being alone!

5. Check out the potential partner as if you were checking out a client. Spend time in various settings, check out the individual's or firm's history, and ask for the client list. *Two red flags:* One is an alliance partner who won't share information about the business, and the second is a partner who is struggling. Don't allow your alliance work to be a cover-up for some kind of consultant soup kitchen.

6. Don't make it legal. Don't go rushing out to form an LLC or create signed agreements and contracts. Legal business relationships are worse than bad marriages to escape from and will compromise your finances, personal life, and clients.

Alliances are peer-level partnerships between two consulting practices and *not a form of subcontracting.* Your partner has to be providing methodology, or business acquisition, or technology, or other important aspects of normal client acquisition and execution. Each of you may deliver, *but if the other party is being paid solely to deliver, then that party is a subcontractor—a pair of hands—not an alliance partner.*

Delivery people are very abundant. These are people who can't effectively market their own services and acquire clients; thus they must depend on others who can market to get them business. Some are paid as little as $300 *a day* by national workshop and seminar firms. Because they are quite easy to find, and despite their self-aggrandizing claims that delivery is everything (it's important but not nearly as difficult as business acquisition), you can find excellent delivery people at this writing for $1,000 per day.[2]

When you do find legitimate circumstances for an alliance and a high-potential partner, consider a formula like this to distribute income:

	Acquisition 50%	Methodology 30%	Delivery 20%
You			
Them			

Example: Let's say that you acquire business, but need my methodology to deliver it, and we split the delivery between us. And let's make it a $100,000 project. That would result in the following:

	Acquisition 50%	Methodology 30%	Delivery 20%
You	$50,000	0	$10,000
Them	0	$30,000	$10,000

That's $60,000 for you and $40,000 for them. You can adjust these percentages to take into account such factors as one person's brand, support staff, or whatever. But never treat the three areas as being equal in importance, and always agree beforehand on the disposition and formula. This obviates the need for legal remedies and keeps things simple.

As you can see, if the other party is 100 percent in the third column with no contributions in the first two columns, then he or she is a subcontractor and all bets are off—you simply agree on a daily rate.

Referral Business

Here is a phrase to memorize: "Referrals are the coinage of my realm. Given the success of our current project, whom do you know who could also benefit from such value?"

And here is the offer that can't be refused: "If you would make the introduction, that would be greatly appreciated. If not, may I simply use your name? But if you prefer, I won't mention you at all."

I think you see the choice of "yeses" at work in the second set of questions!

Referral business is the middle ground between the warmth of people approaching you (Market Gravity) and the iciness of cold calling. It is one of the greatest weaknesses of consultants, because they don't ask in a timely fashion, or they feel it is inappropriate to ask, or they don't have the right language.

Many of us who are successful can trace *all* of our business to less than a half-dozen original sources. That is, our varied businesses share a great deal of common referral DNA.

The Gospel

If you don't actively seek referral business while working with a client, you are not convinced that you provide value and others deserve to have access to it.

There are three types of referrals: client, nonclient, and indirect referrals.

Client Referrals

These should be sought on an ongoing basis. Some criteria:

- Apprise your client at the outset that you'll be asking for referrals later in the project once you're both happy with the results.

- Use language and choices such as I've suggested.

- Follow up with the referral immediately. Sample language: "Judy, I've been referred to you by Tom Lane, who told me he thinks you would greatly appreciate the kind of results he and I have generated together. Tom has never given me bad advice about these things, so I wanted to honor his suggestion and meet with you. I'm available on three different dates next week. How are these days and times for you?"

- Contact all of your present and past clients at least three times a year to request referrals.

- Maintain the mind-set that you are not asking for a favor; you are seeing to *do a favor* by helping mutual acquaintances and professional colleagues.

- With current clients, *always* ask for referrals about two-thirds of the way into your project. Absence does not make the heart grow fonder in business; it makes people forget.

If you follow these steps and utilize this language, you'll have an excellent chance of a meeting with the new person. Ensure that he or she is a buyer, of course, and if not, seek an introduction with the real buyer.

Nonclient Referrals

These come from other consultants, third parties, and serendipity. Criteria:

- It is unethical to recommend someone as a paid consultant to your buyer and not disclose that you have a financial interest. Hence, if there is a referral fee (see next item), that fact must be transparent. Otherwise, the client believes the referral is objective, dispassionate advice, when it is really a business arrangement.

- Use a referral fee formula. Here's my suggestion:
  - Provide me with the name of a buyer who has need for my type of help. I seek the buyer out and close the business. I'll pay you 5 to 10 percent of that project's fee.[3]
  - Introduce me to the buyer, whom I pursue and close the business, and I'll pay you 10 to 15 percent.
  - Introduce me to the buyer with whom you have such a strong relationship that I'm hired on your endorsement, and I'll pay you 15 to 20 percent.

- Literally ask *everyone you know* for referral business. You refer people to your doctor and lawyer, but they don't refer people to you because they usually don't appreciate what results you generate; they only have your business card at best. Reach out to your entire professional, social, and civic communities.

Indirect Referrals

Referral business is hugely important in this work, second only to Market Gravity in developing new business. You can maximize this approach through what I call "indirect referrals" with these techniques:

- If you have permission to use your clients' names (which is normal, though not necessarily their logos), make your client list visible on your web site, in your press kit, and so forth. "You worked with Acme? I have a contact at Omega who would be interested in talking to you."
- Consider a three-dimensional expansion from your existing client contacts. The diagram in Figure 5.6 indicates the potential.

You can see that the potential to reach out to others is much greater than we would otherwise imagine. You can walk those routes, slowly and precariously, or you can fly to those destinations efficiently and quickly on the wings of a strong referral.

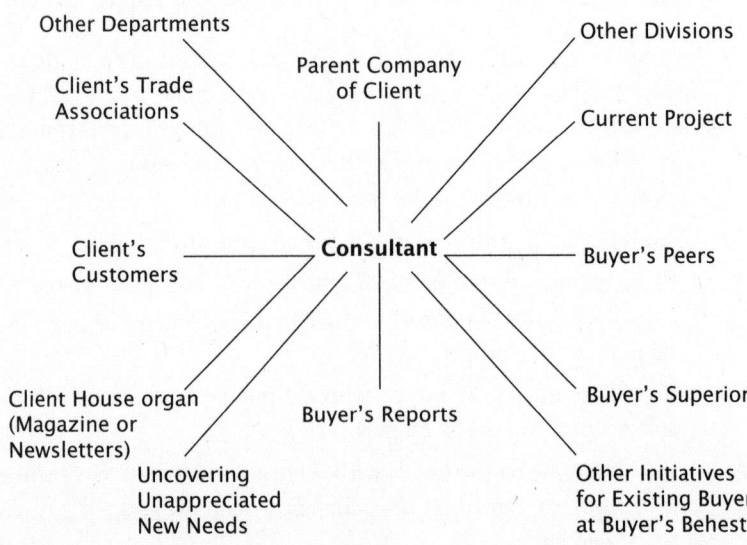

FIGURE 5.6 Expansion Potential

Don't forget that some of your existing clients came through referrals, so remind them with language such as: "Just as you and I came to meet through the recommendation of Sandy Phillips. . . ."

Finally, treat your referrals well through the best kind of reward: Refer them to others, whether a client or a third party. The surest way to maintain ongoing referrals is to reciprocate. Keep a careful data bank of who is capable of doing what for whom. If you make it a two-way street, traffic will increase significantly.

Retainer Business

Retainers are for "access to your smarts." They are not like a lawyer's retainer, where the attorney is simply taking a deposit from which he or she deducts hourly (or six-minute-increment) fees (please bring me the abacus).

Nor are they intended, in my world, to cover a succession of projects in which the consultant actively engages and assists in creation and implementation. In short, they are not for active *involvement*.

Retainers are right-side items on the Accelerant Curve, and often vault items. They are almost always the result of trust and prior traditional projects, and seldom the configuration in which a consultant begins work with a new client. Their advantages:

- You are primarily a remote resource with relatively limited need to travel and meet in person.
- You can take on quite a few retainer clients concurrently. (Ten clients on retainer at $10,000 per month equals $1,200,000 annually, not counting anything else you may be doing while you're up and about.)
- You deal solely with the key person or key people.
- You may be very seldom called upon, creating large amounts of discretionary time.
- The contacts that do occur will tend to be brief and concise.
- Retainer arrangements can be very long-lived.
- You may also take on projects for that same client with separate fees reflecting the value you provide for those initiatives.
- Fees are usually paid in advance and/or have noncancelable provisions.

I was on retainer, for example, to Calgon and its president for five years. During that time I helped out on a half-dozen independent, discrete projects. The retainer alone was $100,000 a year.

You must have an excellent trust level and rapport with your buyer to enter into a retainer relationship, but you also must have excellent personal discipline. That's because a retainer can be a land mine if:

- You feel guilty if you're not accessed frequently, and consequently you:
  - Insist on calling the client and offering help.
  - Roll over the time into the future if you're not used.
  - Take on project work to use up the retainer time.
- You actually agree to a retainer that covers unlimited projects, meaning that you may have accepted $50,000 for independent projects that would have provided fees of $175,000.

The Gospel

There are two equally insidious extremes: scope creep, in which you allow the client to add more and more tasks to your project, and scope seep, where *you* keep adding more and more tasks to your project!

In a retainer arrangement, you are like an excellent insurance policy or high-quality sprinkler system: You're not accessed unless needed; the client is paying for the comfort, security, and peace of mind in knowing that you are there; and your worth isn't dependent on actual use. (You don't want to keep flooding the first floor just because you paid good money for the sprinklers.)

Here are the three criteria for creating a seamless, watertight retainer arrangement for yourself:

1. *Determine how many people are involved.*

   For example, are you dealing with the vice president of sales, or also his or her three general managers? What is the total number of people who have access to you?

2. *Determine the scope of your involvement.*

   Are you to be available during normal business hours eastern time, or also western time? What response rate is acceptable for phone calls (e.g., two hours) and e-mail (e.g., a day)? Are there to be periodic meetings in person? Is it permissible to call you on a weekend or during off-hours?[4]

3. *What is the duration of your involvement?*

> Is this a 90-day, half-year, or annual agreement? (I'd advise you to never agree to month-by-month retainers, which are too easy to cancel and don't provide enough time to prove the value.)

Enter into minimum of 90-day agreements and *always* get paid at the beginning of the period. I actually charged Calgon $10,000 per month, but I gave a $12,000 discount for payment on January 2, which was always accepted. You don't need a typical proposal with objectives, metrics, and value, but you do need a letter of agreement stipulating the conditions raised by my three criteria/questions.

In 25 years of consulting in my own practice, and probably 30 retainers, *I have never, ever had a client who abused the relationship.* Just as in my current mentoring of consultants globally, which features unlimited access to me, includes guarantees of responsiveness, and is, in fact, a retainer arrangement, no one has ever abused the dynamic with excess demands or communications.

If you've ever worked with an executive who truly had an open-door policy, I'll bet that person never complained that so many people were coming through that open door that no work could get done! The offer is sufficient, and occasional use is respected, and the simple comfort that the option is there is of high value.

Ironically, many clients accept that more readily than do the consultants who ought to be providing it!

The keys to making a retainer successful and apt to be repeated and renewed include:

- Be *very* responsive. Try to exceed even what you've agreed is reasonable.
- Demonstrate a real sense of priority. Return a call or e-mail at 8 P.M. if you can. It may not reach your client until the next day, but the gesture alone is very valuable.
- Never, ever feel guilty or unappreciated if you're not contacted for a while.
- Make every actual interaction extremely valuable, and don't be shy about sending a follow-up indicating that "I've been thinking about our phone conversation, and this also has occurred to me. . . ."

With the advent of Skype, GoToMeeting, and smart phones (and probably by the time you read this book holographic representations) providing real-time communication, expert retainer advice is easier and more valuable than ever.

Fortunately, this is also very true in a potentially lucrative, wider market for all of you: global consulting.

Global Work

Global work comes in three basic forms, listed in order of ease of entry:

1. Work with domestic organizations doing business abroad with a local presence.
2. Foreign organizations with a presence in your country.
3. Foreign organizations with no local presence in your country (though their products and services may be represented by others locally).[5]

When you are working with a local multinational—in the United States, Hewlett-Packard or State Street Bank, for example—you should engage in the following:

- If you're traveling overseas for any reason, let your contacts know and ask if they would like you to meet anyone while on your trip. This is a good reason to publicize your calendar in your newsletters or on your blog, by the way.
- When working on your local project, invite anyone from other units to attend any relevant presentations or meetings.
- When you find someone from another country invited to a meeting in which you are presenting *or merely participating,* ask to be introduced.
- Try to remain culturally neutral. That is, demonstrate how your approaches can work in any country and are not locally dependent.

When you are working with a client who has dealings with a multinational that has operations locally—in the United States, say Toyota or Shell Oil or Gucci—ask for referrals. For example, Toyota has a huge credit operation that is available to any auto dealer. Or you may find you or your family doing business with a local Toyota dealership owned by an acquaintance. Some best practices:

- Treat major local operations *as local businesses.* When I worked for Mercedes North America, for example, I had no dealings whatsoever with the German parent and didn't attempt any because of language difficulties at the time.[6]
- Seek out businesses and industries in which you are already well established, giving you content familiarity and operating insights.
- You will usually be in a better competitive position if the local management is hired locally and not imported from the home office. There will be more independence and more willingness to hire local resources.

When you seek to work with an organization that is based elsewhere and has no substantial presence locally—that might be Airbus Industrie or Eni in Italy—then you need some very clear rationales to justify your investment and their interest. These rationales might include:

- You are an expert in their content area, a thought leader whom they cannot afford not to listen to.
- You have a contact who has been hired by that organization, preferably from a current or former client of yours.
- You have some roots or special interests in their home country.
- You will be traveling to that country for some other reason (e.g., work for a client or personal reasons).

Serendipity can provide wondrous opportunities. I was once in Milton Keynes, England, for two separate clients: a food flavoring company headquartered in Cincinnati where I had been brought in on a reference from someone who was a client in another firm, and the British Standards Institute, which had come to me because of a book Michel Robert and I had written (*The Innovation Formula*, HarperBusiness, 1988). The UK immigration officer looked at my jeans and two-day beard and said, "What kind of business are you doing in Milton Keynes?"

"Why do you think I'm on a business trip?" I asked him.

"Because," he replied readily, "there is no other sane reason to go to Milton Keynes."

Use the Internet to stimulate your approaches to overseas work, especially in terms of my third category. Any of us can appear internationally at virtually any time with any kind of information, stimulation, and provocation. I probably have more people in my Mentor Programs and various communities in Australia, per capita, than anywhere else in the world. Short of the moon, it's hard to get any farther away globally, but the business there has justified 15 trips as of this writing, including two vacations with my wife.

Just as in retainer work, you should adjust your fees for global work. Since I need a home base to demonstrate this, I'll use my own—the northeast United States. Here are six guidelines:

1. I add a premium for work outside of the United States, Canada, Mexico, and the Caribbean Islands. My rationale is that it takes no longer to get to Mexico City, Antigua, or Vancouver than it does to Seattle or Los Angeles. I would never add to my fees within the United States based on geography (expenses will change, of course, with distance), so I don't do it with neighbors, either.

2. For Europe and South America, I add a 50 percent premium to my consulting, coaching, speaking, and all related work.

3. For Asia and the Pacific Rim I add 100 percent.

4. I never charge for travel days, since I use value-based fees. However, I do make certain that I arrive at least a full day ahead of any work for acclimation purposes, especially if I'm speaking at a formal conference. Most flights from where I live would arrive in London or Sydney at 7 A.M. or so.

5. I charge business class airfares (though I upgrade and pay the difference to first class). I will not accept coach reimbursement for international trips, and I believe you are personally daft if you sit in a coach seat for 8 to 18 hours and expect to be energized, positive, or even healthy when you land. I have never found client resistance to this *if* the client considers you a partner and not a subcontractor.

6. I insist on payment in advance for everything less than a six-figure engagement, and I ask for 50 percent deposits for those before I depart. I expect my expenses to be reimbursed within 30 days of submission. All funds are quoted in U.S. dollars, no matter what the current exchange rate. I accept wire transfers and credit card payments. (Those of you who want to add on something to cover credit card fees have to learn that this is simply a cost of doing business and you should never nickel-and-dime clients as lawyers do when they charge you for photocopies!)

Working globally will greatly enhance your standing at home, because you will become something of a celebrity with international exposure and clients. One of the reasons I write books like this one is that they are often translated in major markets (so far, mine are in nine languages).

Notes

1. Mature clients have a history of using consultants, are early adopters, partner with consultants responsibly, and are results and not task oriented.

2. By "delivery" I mean for focus groups, interviews, observation, research, workshops, and so on. They will inevitably accept daily rates.

3. All of these are for the immediate project, not repeat business, expanded business, and so on.

4. I would often take a late-night or weekend call from the president of Calgon when he had a crucial board meeting the next day or an eruption of some kind at work.

5. If you're interested in a thorough discussion beyond these several pages, see *The Global Consultant* by me and my co-author Omar Khan, from John Wiley & Sons (2008).

6. Today, as with many global companies, English is often mandated even in home offices.

Chapter

Celebrity

How to Be *the* Authority and Expert

Thought Leadership

A relatively recent construct, "thought leadership" has entered the vernacular to denote expertise and status as a conveyor of intellectual capital. It's as good a term as any, but the concept is fungible—it may be expressed differently by the time you read this.

No matter, the concept is sound: If you want to achieve the equivalent of "super status,"[1] then you can merely be terrific at implementing the tried and true, but you have to create the true, having tried it first yourself.

In a study I was part of several years ago for the National Speakers Association, we found that true buyers of speaking services (not meeting planners or bureaus) primarily sought and were attracted to . . . expertise. If you look at the thought leaders extant today (e.g., Marshall Goldsmith in coaching, Jeff Gitomer in sales, Walt Mossberg in consumer technology, me in solo consulting), you'll find some commonalities.

Thought leaders tend to:

- Create intellectual capital that they translate into intellectual property that can be purchased and accessed and implemented by others.

The process of turning concepts and intangible ideas into pragmatic and tangible approaches is known as "instantiation." In one strategy project, the CEO wanted to know beforehand, "Will you bring your own intellectual capital? We don't need merely a facilitator; we need an active leader for the process."

- Be unafraid of making their approaches public. They don't fear thievery or emulation or plagiarism or knockoffs. That's because their brands are so strong by dint of their leadership that most people will know the origins, and the thieves aren't important and can fool only a benighted few. This will be my 40th book available for the public. I'm hoping there are more to come.

- Never believe that their ideas alone will be enough for people. That is, the books, speeches, postings, citations, attributions, and a plethora of interactions near and far only serve to make the thought leader *more sought*, not less. If you can read one of my books or listen to one of my downloads and improve satisfactorily, that's great. But you're probably also thinking about attending a workshop or participating in my Mentor Program. *All thought leaders have advertent or inadvertent Accelerant Curves, with a heavy emphasis on the right side.*

- Become cited and quoted, and (perhaps inappropriately at times) be considered the final work or authority on a subject. When President Clinton needed some cheering up, he brought Tony Robbins to the White House. Whenever there is an air disaster, John Nance, a famous pilot and aviation expert, is immediately on the media. (This can go to absurd lengths, such as when, during the 2010 oil disaster in the Gulf of Mexico, a congressional hearing took testimony from James Cameron, the director of *Titanic*! Marshall McLuhan anticipated this, calling it the mixed-media effect, where an expert in one area is unjustifiably considered an expert in all areas, which is why so many celebrity entertainers wax not so eloquent on politics.)

- Be unafraid of failing. They pump new ideas and methods into their respective niches and aren't shocked or crushed when some of them fail. If you're not failing, you're not trying. Of course, if you're failing much more often than you're succeeding, your thought leadership decoder ring might just be taken away. That's why there are not thought leaders in meteorology, television ratings, consumer electronics, horse racing, or the stock market. Everyone who tries has a mediocre record.

What does this mean for you? It means that the road to celebrity isn't paved with gold or good intentions, because *it's a road you create yourself.* That's the good news and bad news right there. This is our final dedicated chapter on marketing, so it's appropriate that you understand that you create your own celebrity in this business.

The Gospel

Don't follow in the footsteps of those you respect or try to emulate the obvious successes of others. Instead, pursue what they pursued. There is no royal road, but there is a clear destination.

You need to create intellectual property from your intellectual capital. So much of that will appear in writing that we're going to discuss authorship separately in the next section of this chapter. But for now, here are some alternatives for you to consider in creating your own road, your own leadership:

- What patterns have you observed in your consulting work that represent wisdom to be applied in the future? For example, do companies spend inordinate time on remedial work and ignore their all-stars?
- What regular and constant outlets will you use for the expression of your intellectual property? Will you send weekly press releases, create a teleconference series, write columns, appear every morning on Twitter, build products? Think of the Market Gravity Wheel.
- How will you protect your work, not so much to prevent theft but to ensure it's associated with you and your brand? Will you trademark, copyright, patent? Will you create metaphors, value propositions, taglines?
- How will you balance the short term and the long term? Networking is short-term, a speech is medium-term, and a book is long-term. *But all such plans have to begin today.* What plans are you establishing to keep your ideas in front of your constituency on an ongoing basis?
- Remember that outreach is for instigation and gravity is for investigation. Make your blogs and newsletters provocative and controversial, but make sure your web site is replete with high credibility. Don't confuse these roles. Web sites don't sell your value; they reaffirm it for people exposed elsewhere.
- Are you a member of and immersed in the key associations, informal and formal, of your specialty? Even if there is little worth intellectually,

you must remain apprised of what's happening at all levels. You can best critique from within the tent, not outside.

In an electronic age, thought leadership is more achievable faster than ever before. However, there is commensurately more noise to compete with your clarion call. Hence, you must be prepared to be bold, assertive, constant, and flexible. Use all the media at your command.

And the most powerful of those media may still be the written word.

Authorship

Celebrity consultants appear in print, either hard copy or electronic. That means you have to write something, and often.

The ultimate expression of authorship is a commercially published book. That means a major publisher (e.g., John Wiley & Sons, McGraw-Hill, Simon & Schuster, AMACOM, etc.) publishes and distributes your book in varied forms—book stores, Amazon.com, electronic, and who knows what else by the time you read this?

A few words on self-publishing: I have written 40 books as you read this, 35 of which are commercially published and five self-published. They each have their own objectives. The former group is for credibility with buyers. I have never cared about best sellers, though I've been fortunate enough to have a few. But the main goal is to gain the credibility that ushers me rapidly and unimpeded into buyers' offices, makes me a sole source not subject to competitive bidding and requests for proposals (RFPs) in government and certain organizations, and so on.

The latter (self-publishing) is for higher-priced offerings and higher margins to me, sold on my site, when I'm speaking, or in volume to certain customers. They are often for niches too small to be profitable for commercial publishers.

But don't let anyone tell you that self-publishing has the same cachet or status *with corporate buyers* as does commercial publishing, which has the credibility of an agent (usually), an acquisitions editor, and an editorial committee all believing in the value and relevance of the work *in which they are investing time and money.*

I read most books today on an iPad (even though I buy the hard copy version for my large library, which I'm sure is therapist material), but in 2010, only about 3 percent of all books were electronic. That percentage is going to dramatically change, of course, but don't be satisfied with *solely* an electronic book. There are the advantages of flexibility, appeal to nontechnical people, presence in bookstores and libraries, for instance, that a book in hard copy also provides.

If a buyer-to-buyer referral is the platinum standard for marketing in our business—perhaps the 12 o'clock position on the Market Gravity Wheel—then a commercially published book is the gold standard, at one o'clock. I stated earlier that I, like most other highly successful consultants, can trace most of my business to a handful of originating sources and spin-offs. One of those sources for me was *Million Dollar Consulting*, first published in 1992 and currently in its fourth edition, on the shelves for nearly two decades without absence. This is one of the prime bounce factors on my personal Accelerant Curve.

The Gospel

Everyone can write. "Writer's block" is merely a clever term for procrastination. But not everyone has something to say. That's a key differentiator.

You should start (and continue) publishing in these sources, leading up to a commercially published book:

- Articles—in trade and professional publications, for pay or for free.
- Columns—in publications where your articles develop a following.
- Booklets—self-published, brief focus on specific issues.
- Interviews—responding to reporters and other authors.[2]
- Press releases—which you initiate to the media with your ideas.
- Letters to the editor—stating your expert position on key issues.
- Blogs—be provocative and instigating in your frequent postings.
- Chat rooms—organize your own or take a leading role in others'.
- Web site—create intellectual property for download.[3]
- Position papers—treatments of your value proposition and approaches.

You get the idea. There is a plethora of existing venues and venues you can create to express yourself.

These will give you excellent practice and momentum to write your first book. After that—especially if your book sells decently—the second and third books are far easier. Writer's block is not a factor when you get warmed up through weekly writing among all those categories just listed.[4]

Here is how you write a book, rapidly, powerfully, and efficiently:

The Art and Science of Authorship

  A. Why Write a Book

- Second best credibility source (*if* commercially published).
- Establishes a brand with great effectiveness.
- Creates a downslope for continuous publishing.
- Forces you to connect and configure your own methodology.
- Outstanding source of potential passive income.
- Ego and fulfillment.
- Ongoing learning (understand what you don't know).

  B. How to Write a Book

- First have something to say, or don't read on.
- Think of the reader and audience, not yourself.
- Don't just whine—offer solutions and hope.
- Focus on the pragmatic, not esoteric.
- Use memorable language, phrases, metaphors.
- Do not emulate others' ideas (e.g., *Chicken Soup for the Turkeys*).
- Discipline, structure, and planning:
  - Create calendar time.
  - Create contingency time.
  - Ensure you are undisturbed and unmolested, but above all comfortable.
  - Use a formula (X pages, Y pages per chapter, etc.).
  - Use variants (mini-interviews, case studies, self-tests).
- Don't write everything you know; write what the reader needs to know.
- Attribute meticulously, but don't borrow too much.
- Write conversationally.

  C. How to Commercially Publish a Book

- Create a treatment or proposal.[5]
  - Theme (title and purpose).

- Table of contents.
- One chapter in entirety (any chapter, 20+ pages).
- Two paragraphs about all other chapters.
- Page on your unique credentials.
- Several pages on competitive marketing analysis.
- Description of primary, secondary, tertiary audiences.
- Thorough description of unique marketing assets you bring.
- Distinctions of book (e.g., interviews, self-tests, etc.).
- Estimated length and delivery time.
- Choose an agent or acquisition editor by name.
- Write a cover letter and submit treatment.
  - Multiple submissions are fine.
- Don't jump at contract.
  - If no agent, use a good lawyer (not cousin Louie).
- Understand that you will have to promote.
- Beware of advice from others.
  - One book is an accident, two are a coincidence, and three are a pattern.

In summary, whether you are starting out, at midcareer, or at an advanced level of consulting, it's never too early or too late to write a book (or *another* book). A publisher breaks even at about 5,000 sales in hard copy, and is usually ecstatic at 15,000 sales. We're not talking James Patterson or Danielle Steele in sales here.

For a first-time author, an agent is always a good bet. Agents are paid for performance (15 percent only if the work is sold), and what they submit will be read by acquisitions editors. Find one whom others recommend and who has specialized in books such as the one you're proposing.

Value-Based Fees

A chapter on celebrity might seem like a strange venue in which to discuss value-based fees, but hear me out: Your ability to charge based on your value increases as your brand and repute are respected, *to the extent that your perceived value will actually follow your fees!*

What you're seeing in the diagram in Figure 6.1 is a phenomenon I stumbled upon 20 years ago. The rational position is to assume that the higher your perceived value, the higher your fees can be. *But the lines eventually cross as you achieve celebrity.* The implementation of thought leadership, of manifest expertise, of being an object of interest to others, builds a powerful brand. That brand causes the lines to cross, no less than gravity bends light rays in the cosmos. (Just call me Einstein—I couldn't resist.)

Value-based fees are the practice of charging for your contribution to the value the client derives from the project. The standard language I use whenever I'm asked my "fee basis" by buyers who have been inured to hourly billing is simple:

> "My fee is based on my contribution to the value you derive from this project, which includes dramatic return on investment (ROI) for you and equitable compensation for me."

That's why the conceptual agreement of our earlier chapters concludes with value, based on business outcomes for an economic buyer. That value should always be conservative ("Let's take just half of that projected improvement") but still represents a 10:1 or better return. Including emotional factors, the equation we stated earlier was this:

$$\frac{\text{Tangible benefits} \times \text{Annualized benefits} + \text{Intangible benefits} \times \text{Emotional impact} + \text{Peripheral benefits}}{\text{Fee}} = \text{Value}$$

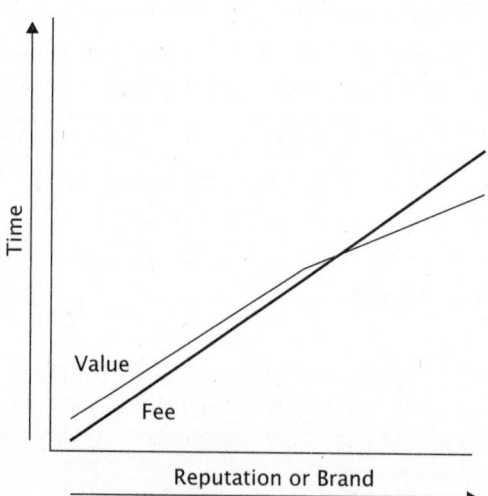

FIGURE 6.1   When Value Follows Fee

However, once you achieve celebrity, people will expect to get what they pay for.

When it's Bulgari, Brioni, or Bentley, buyers aren't shopping for the best price or attempting to negotiate with the salespeople. They want the brand for the pragmatic and practical virtues, but also for the emotional and ego satisfaction. A stunning example of this was Jim Collins's very successful book, *Good to Great* (HarperCollins, 2001). Thousands of buyers and business owners suddenly wanted to go from "good to great" without even realizing what it meant or where they currently stood on that scale! They simply wanted it emotionally, and Jim's speaking and consulting fees simply became whatever he wanted them to be.

If you achieve a high profile, don't waste the success by merely looking at the view. Aggressively increase your fees, because people are not shopping price; they are pursuing value. We all know that people interested in an expensive home who ask how much it costs to heat it, or who are interested in an expensive car and ask how much the insurance would cost, can't really afford either. The heating and insurance costs are less than peripheral considerations.

So I'm including value-based fees for your review in this chapter because, ironically, they don't just result from celebrity; *they can fuel celebrity.*

In the Figure 6.2 you can see the relationship between your fee and the buyer's commitment. That commitment is heightened substantially by your credibility and profile. The more you are a celebrity (in your chosen field), the more the buyer will arrive at rapid commitment to partnering with you. It's the difference between "I've never heard of you—prove to me you can help me" and "I've been very impressed by your approaches—how can we work together?" In the second instance, neither credibility nor fees are an issue.

In the lower right quadrant we have low buyer commitment and a high fee. This, of course, will get you nowhere at all.

In the lower left, there is low commitment and low fee, which is at best an apathetic buyer: "See our HR people—perhaps they'll be interested."

In the upper right, there is tremendous reciprocal value, pragmatically and emotionally; a high fee and high commitment comprise an ideal sale. But

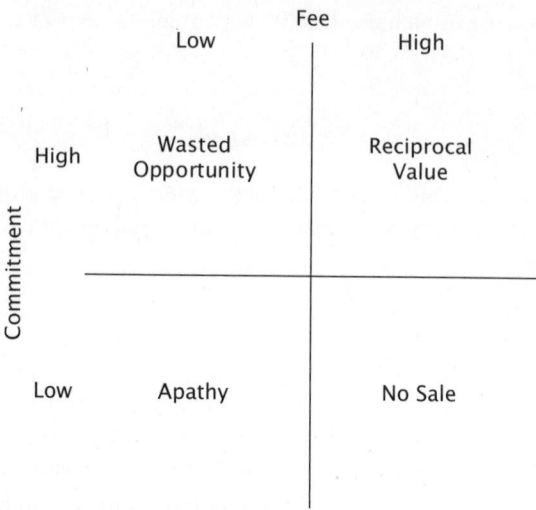

FIGURE 6.2   Buyer Commitment and Fee

in the upper left is the wasted opportunity. Here, your brand and repute have created high buyer commitment, but you have not matched that with high fees. That means that your credibility can erode in addition to the fact that you are leaving six figures on the table each year, *which you will never be able to recover.*

Two keys:

1. When you don't charge enough despite your high credibility, you will be cheating yourself and your family and never be able to recover that lost money.

2. You will also promote doubts with the buyer. Once you're told that the price of the Bentley is far less than you expected to pay, you begin to wonder if the car has been in an accident, has flaws, or is simply overrated.

Subcontracting, Franchising, Licensing

When you achieve the fame and attention that word of mouth, books, highly visible projects, thought leadership, and referrals create, you'll have a pleasant challenge: a filled pipeline. That is, you'll have a great deal of current business and a significant number of leads and signed proposals leading up to your doorstep.

While most consultants say, "I would love such a problem!" it's surprising how many become depressed and uncertain when this largesse appears.

First, here are the criteria as to whether to accept business. Don't forget, we covered earlier that in order to reach out you must concurrently let go, so the bottom 15 percent of your clients should be jettisoned (New York) or gently reassigned to others (California) annually.

- The business is challenging and utilizes or increases your talents.
- There is a high profit margin (not merely revenue—the goal is to keep it, not merely to make it).
- Any travel involved is acceptable or attractive, not onerous.
- You can minimize your personal labor intensity.
- It is consistent with the brand and image you have meticulously developed in becoming a celebrity.

Thus, it's counterproductive to let go of an old but no longer profitable or interesting client just to find a replacement that also is not profitable or interesting.

We are moving toward the right side of the Accelerant Curve for you, personally, and you have four very important options that you now command: subcontracting, franchising, licensing, or doing it yourself.

Subcontracting

This is *not* an alliance partner; these are people whom you pay a time-based rate to deliver what you sell. They are neither employees nor part-timers; they are strictly subcontractors and your relationship should conform to Internal Revenue Service (IRS) (or your country's) rules to ensure they are not considered employees (e.g., you provide less than 80 percent of their total revenues annually).

I suggest that you identify and work with a fixed, small group, so that there are no constant reeducation requirements—they know your approaches, procedures, and policies. You trust each other. Hiring subcontractors is similar to dealing with a prospective buyer in that you must gain trust on both sides first. You can't lead your life worrying whether a subcontractor will steal a client, your intellectual property, or your watch.

There are hordes of people who can deliver well but cannot market themselves. National seminar firms pay $400 per day (that is not a typo) and have no trouble acquiring the talent. If you pay $1,000 per day and use people repeatedly, they will respond well. Find these people in professional trade associations (Institute for Management Consulting, National Speakers Association, Society for Human Resource Management, American

Society for Training and Development); by networking; and through your blog postings.

Many people I mentor have remained solo practitioners with all the benefits, while utilizing a half-dozen consistent subcontractors with all of those benefits. Have your attorney draw up a simple working agreement. (I've placed a simple, nonlegal example that I use in the book's Physical Appendix.)

Franchising

At this level of success, you may want to consider training others in your approaches who *can* do their own marketing in a noncompetitive relationship. This is usually best done in other countries, so that you franchise your business in Italy, South Korea, or Argentina.

You would receive a fee that may be one-time or annual for the right to use your brands, endorsement, intellectual property, consulting practices, workshops, speeches, and so forth within that agreed-upon territory for a given amount of time. The criteria (quality, volume) would determine rights to renew or retain the franchise.

I don't like arrangements where you receive a percentage of the business, since that requires you to audit the franchisee's books, and I'm always reminded of the Hollywood deals where a film making $200 million in revenues seems to never show a profit. Either grant rights in perpetuity if certain criteria are maintained (larger franchise fee) or grant them annually or every two years if the criteria justify renewal (smaller franchise fee, but ongoing).

Variable factors include any translation costs, your personal appearances and support, the ability to resell the franchise, and so forth.

Licensing

I discussed earlier the two kinds of business models: solo practice and the company with infrastructure that can eventually be sold.

For the solo practitioner, licensing is the way to sell a part of your business and gain those benefits. The enabler is your intellectual property, which is why a degree of celebrity is required.

In this format, you license a consulting, coaching, or training approach to a client organization. You formally transfer the skills, copyrights, and supporting materials. You may do this in perpetuity, annually, or somewhere in between. Variables usually include training their trainers, consultants, and coaches; providing updates on your intellectual property developments that are pertinent; performing quality checks and audits; replacing internal consultants as needed; and so on.

If you were to personally deliver what the client required over the course of a year and the fee would be $200,000, then your licensing fee should be a good deal for you and the client, say, $150,000. The client saves 25 percent and you probably save 85 percent of your time, which becomes wealth (discretionary time). You must specify in these arrangements whether the client may use the approaches outside of the immediate organization (e.g., with vendors) or, if it's a trade association, with members.

The Talent Prevails

The fourth option is that you do it yourself, but at an extremely high fee.

You have to recognize that, as the celebrity, *you* are the talent. Most consultants charge more when they bring in subcontractors, using quantity as their metric. You should charge more if you do it yourself, using quality as your metric.

Years ago, State Street Bank wanted me to help with a global effort to implement a more effective communications strategy. I told them they had three options:

1. I could train their people (licensing) to do this worldwide. They told me that this approach lacked credibility.

2. I could use my contacts in their key global cities (subcontracting). They turned this down as the "poor cousin" phenomenon, since the home office would deal with me directly.

3. I could do it myself, but this was by far the most expensive option.

They determined the value of the project was well worth the highest-quality approach, and my wife and I flew around the world on a $350,000 project. The client was pleased and so was I.[6]

Reinvention

The greatest pitfall in your celebrity journey is what I've come to call the "success trap." It looks like Figure 6.3.

In this series of S-curves, a new product or service may have trouble achieving traction but, if it's good, it will enjoy a steep growth curve. (Feel free to substitute your career for product or service in the example!) At a certain point the growth levels off and becomes a plateau. Because of the laws of entropy, all plateaus will eventually erode and decline.

Hence, we need to jump to the next S-curve, the next growth cycle; this segment is reinvention. But the time for that leap is counterintuitive. You don't

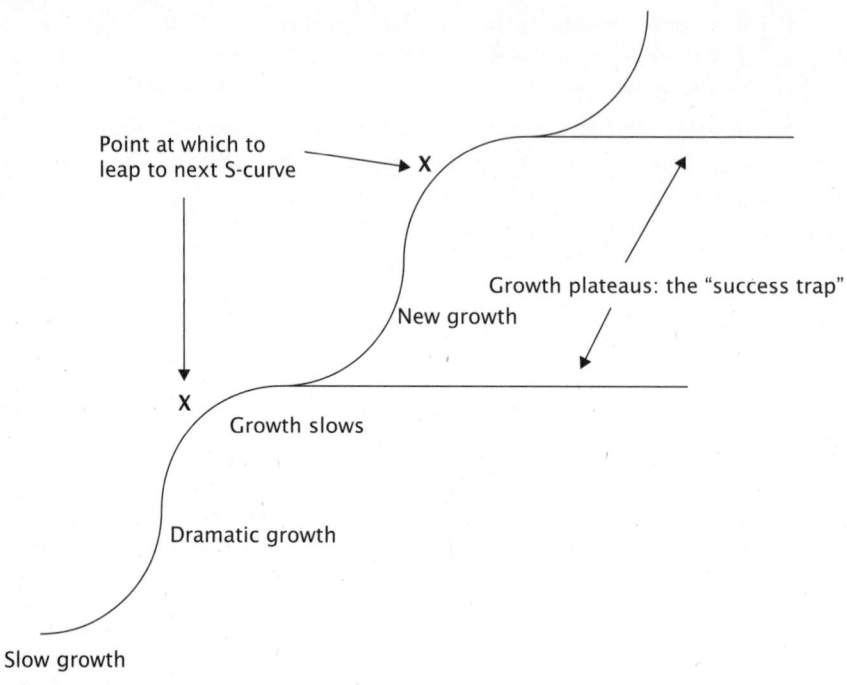

Point at which to
leap to next S-curve ────→ X

Growth plateaus: the "success trap"

New growth

X

Growth slows

Dramatic growth

Slow growth

FIGURE 6.3 The Success Trap

wait for the plateau, because you will have lost acceleration and energy. You leap near the very top of your current growth cycle, perhaps even before you've reached the very top.

As you can see in the graphic, it's far easier to leap to the next S-curve when you have a full head of steam, turbochargers blasting, than when you are coasting on the plateau (the "success trap"). The chances of a successful transition at that point are small.

The Gospel

You build on strength. When you are strong and growing is when you should take prudent risk, innovate, and initiate new offerings.

Even after all these years and at my level of success, about 75 percent of *all* of my revenues are derived from products and services that *did not exist even three years ago.* (The manufacturing giant 3M had a strategic goal that 25 percent of all revenues had to have originated in products created within the prior three years. And that is a $25 billion company!)

I find speakers making the same speeches they did 20 years ago, laughing and crying on cue at the exact same junctures. I see consultants, no different, offering the five-step leadership program or 30-day audit that they originated a decade ago, despite the fact that technology, society, the economy, demographics, and public perceptions have all changed dramatically. I observe coaches who don't seem to have realized that factors such as company loyalty, retirement options, workplace stress, and technological expertise requirements have all radically altered in the years since they began coaching.

Reinvention is also critical to building a sustaining thought leadership. One of the criteria for thought leaders is to *lead*, not merely perpetuate. Peter Drucker was leading well into his 90s. Warren Buffett is another excellent example of the embracing of change and the creation of change throughout one's career.

Here are some of the keys that I've found for highly successful consultants to maintain a consistent path of reinvention and leaping to the next S-curve with maximum torque and horsepower:

- Examine your current services for dimensional shifts. Can you build on your offerings with better and more sophisticated variations? My Mentor Program, for example, can be utilized in a regular membership, in a guided membership, or in total immersion, and in two dimensions: with me directly or with mentors I've trained.

- Anticipate need. The shifts I've constantly referred to in the workplace and society will continue. What is the trajectory that you see and how might you provide value in its path? For example, can you provide help in managing employees who are never seen physically, or in creating applications for professional services firms, or in helping companies build global brands?

- What areas of ambiguity exist or are emerging in which clients and prospects need a light to help them through the dark? Can you provide investment stability in volatile economies? Can you help with strategy formulation that involves technology as a prime reducer of cost? Can you provide committee leadership if most organizations really no longer have traditional teams?

Diversify what you already do, investigate what clients may need, and analyze areas of general ambiguity that are emerging. Here are specifics to trigger reinvention and S-curve navigation:

- *Unexpected success.* How do you build on efforts that succeed beyond your best estimates?

- *Unexpected failures.* Did someone have a great idea that is still valid, and it was only the alternative they chose that was poor?

- *New technologies.* How can you combine and recombine to create new applications and savings?
- *High growth.* What are the greatest growth (and most recession-proof) areas to target?
- *Demographic shift.* Who will have the most discretionary income in the coming years? (It's often not who you think.)
- *New knowledge.* What breakthroughs in thinking and application hold the greatest promise?
- *Perception change.* This one you can actually influence. What beliefs and values are changing in business and society?

At the early stages of your career, building competence and reaching out are key. As you grow more and more successful, and your "gravity" attracts people to you, reinvention becomes a top priority.

Creating Communities

One of my trademarks is "Architect of Professional Communities®," reflecting what I now realize I've been doing unconsciously for years (sometimes it's better to be lucky than good).

Communities today are more virtual than real, although the best ones embrace both possibilities. You can create communities of your peers, your clients, your suppliers, and others. *The major benefit of a community is that the members receive value attributed to you even when you aren't present, by dint of your having established the forum.*

Some years ago, as the Web became a common presence in our lives, disenfranchised and alienated customers formed web sites that sounded something like this: www.acmecompanysucks.com (with no offense intended to Wile E. Coyote). These often justifiably irked customers (or clients) were able to commiserate with each other, consider retribution and legal action, and generally vent, usually discouraging prospects and new customers for the company in the process. Think about what happens when thousands of wronged customers all decide to write negative reviews of a product.

However, the best of these companies, truly concerned about their customers and their own futures, quickly built their own sites and encouraged customers to vent there. That enabled the companies to react to legitimate concerns, squelch rumors, and provide the clear perception that they were listening. They were, in effect, able to co-opt the discontent and turn the energy into a positive.

If you don't believe that works, try this: If a letter to a company CEO doesn't result in a remediation of your problem, post the issue on Twitter or Facebook. You'll find that the company will often respond in the form of someone charged with tracking the mention of the organization's name, usually using something like Google Alerts to inform them. That's the power of the social media community in a very focused manner.

Your communities, at celebrity level, should include the following access and possible interactions:

- Teleconferences (or podcasts) that are periodic and free. You can create these in advance and broadcast at set periods. You should also arrange for them to appear on iTunes and similar sites.
- Chat rooms (mine is called AlansForums.com) where there is a charge for the general public, but community members enjoy participation as a free benefit. This is a prime example of your not having to be present for members to derive value from the experience attributable to you.
- Videos posted periodically accessible by the public, which you shoot with a videographer (see my "The Writing on the Wall" on my site and blog) or more informally with a flip video. These can be posted on YouTube.
- Workshops that you run enabling your community members to meet each other. These can be high value and content for a fee (discounted for the community) or free with little structured programming and a great deal of networking.
- A blog that community members access via RSS feeds and that you keep lively with multiple posts in multimedia every week. You should invite and respond to commentary on your blog to encourage participation.
- An interactive web site where people can take self-tests, download intellectual property, and participate in multimedia learning.
- A substantial amount of publishing so that your intellectual capital is exposed to a wide audience.
- Regular contributions to social media platforms but *not* to talk about your breakfast or quote a well-trod platitude. Instead, post something

of value to your community every day. (At this writing I have 2,000+ followers on Twitter and follow no one. This works very well for my brand, despite the Twitter etiquette fanatics who insist on reciprocity!)

The communities follow a principle analogous to apps on your smart phone. They entice people to join, which creates more value, which attracts other people to join, which generates still more value, and so on. Consider these communities as three-dimensional galaxies moving through space, which embrace additional systems as they move and spin off, within them, subcommunities of planetary systems.

The Gospel

Communities take on a growth cycle of their own, as long as you continually pump intellectual capital into the system.

People in the outer communities may have read your work or heard you speak. As you move inward they have attended workshops, become corporate clients, been personally coached, and so forth. If you think of the Accelerant Curve, the communities and the ties become more intimate and smaller as you move from left to right.

You may be a *member* of a community of peers, but you should be the *leader* of a community of clients, prospects, recommenders, publishers, media people, and so on. These communities should overlap, which is why I use the galaxies example, so that they will have some shared interests and some discrete interests. The Web's ability to enable this 24/7 globally is an enormous boost to community building and sustainability. Where else can your members access a peer in Germany or a prospect in Australia or a potential alliance partner in South Africa?

Before we conclude this section of the book and move on to the implementation side of consulting, I want to place in context the odyssey we've been on thus far (see Figure 6.4).

We've moved from the impulse to attempt consulting, to the participation in the profession, to the adoption of the craft's norms, to implementing new ideas that work for us, finally to realizing that thought leadership and celebrity are a function of continually taking a leading-edge position and not fearing failure—because if you're never failing, you're simply not trying hard enough.

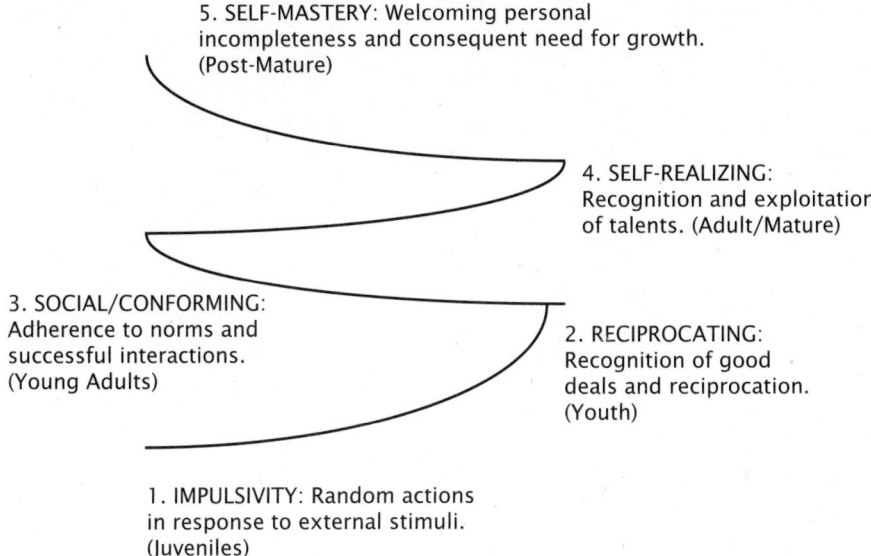

FIGURE 6.4 Configurations of Growth Stages

Notes

1. We are obsessed: supermodels, Super Bowl, supernatural, Super Mario Nintendo—even my car is a Super Sport.

2. See providers such as PRLeads.com and Expertclick.com.

3. Left side of the accelerant curve.

4. If you do draw a blank on some issues, see my book *Breaking Through Writer's Block: Every Business Letter and Template You'll Ever Need for a Thriving Professional Services Practice*, which is on my web site, and which I self-publish.

5. Resource: Write the Perfect Book Proposal: 10 That Sold and Why, 2nd edition, by Jeff Herman and Deborah Levine Herman (John Wiley & Sons, 2001). Jeff is my agent, but I have no financial interest in this excellent resource.

6. Flying from Sydney to Bangkok in the nose of a Qantas 747, my wife was working a calculator. Worried, I asked what was going on. "In actual working hours," she said, since she saw me come and go every day, "you're making $14,750 an hour." "Put that away," I said, "and never speak of this again."

Deuteronomy
Consulting Methodology

The rules for closing business with a client as partner, implementing efficiently and well, delighting the customer, and receiving high fees.

You don't do things to a client. You help to improve the client's condition.

Chapter

7

The Perfect Proposal

How to Write a Proposal That's Accepted Every Time

Assuring Success

I was once hired by a pharmaceutical consulting firm in New York. They told me that they put an emphasis on proposals but the firm was suffering in terms of profit. I found out that they were generating about 300 proposals annually—nearly one per day—and had an entire back-room crew devoted to their production, and rewarded based on . . . drumroll, please . . . numbers of proposals sent to prospects.

They were focused on input (production) and not output (resultant business). And they were consultants!

The first part of implementation of a project—and the bridge from your marketing efforts of Section II—is to create a proposal that's accepted every time. My hit rate over the years has been 80 percent. I send out far fewer proposals than many other consultants, but the proposals have been for larger projects and accepted more readily.

The proposal process begins with your doing everything possible to assure yourself of success. That's before a word is on paper, before you've determined your methodology, and in many cases, before you even have a hint of the route to proceed down. At one point, addressing a group of consultants at a national conference, I asked what their objective was in the first meeting with a prospect.

"To come out with the signed contract!" shouted one, reminding me for all the world of the used car dealer who goes to the manager for a better deal and then rings a bell when the customer signs.

"Then you're a better man than I," I told him.

Here are the environmental and psychological conditions that are instrumental in ensuring that the proposal has every chance of success when that time finally arrives.

Find the Economic Buyer

This is the greatest continuing tactical error that consultants commit. They are not diligent enough in pursuing the true buyer. If they enter at a low level, they content themselves to remain there, where it is relatively unthreatening and comfortable; yet it is impossible to make a sale, because there is no budgetary approval. When people can't say "yes" but can say "no," they usually say "no" eventually. Providing a proposal to people in human resources, training, or other low-level support areas is like sitting on the lakeshore awaiting the Loch Ness monster. Your patience is impressive, but your family will starve.

You must learn to ask the questions intended to determine the economic buyer (cited earlier) and deal with low-level people only so long as they can introduce you to (or minimally, identify) the true buyer. You are not in this business to make friends.

> ### The Gospel
>
> You must accept rejection and reject acceptance. This is a relationship business, and you will not always be successful. But do not align yourself with those who can't say "yes" but can say "no."

Establish a Trusting Relationship with the Economic Buyer

Trust means that you honestly believe the other person has your best interests in mind. If that's true, you will accept challenging and even negative feedback, because you recognize it's for your own good. If that's not true, then you will tend to reject even compliments, because you suspect there may be a hidden agenda behind the accolades.

Here is how you establish trust with a true buyer:

- Provide value. Don't be afraid to offer ideas and best practices. Note that I'm not talking about *solutions* and I'm not suggesting how but rather what. That differentiates marketing from free consulting!

"Here are four methods that my best clients use to manage remote people." "How are they applied?" "Well, that depends on your culture, and I'll figure that out when you hire me!"

- Never assume the client is damaged. An astounding number of consultants reach the bizarre conclusion that the person smart enough to want to talk to them is simultaneously stupid enough to have caused or perpetuated the problem. And never think that you can solve in 12 minutes what the prospect has struggled with for 12 months.

- Drop instances into your conversation, without disclosing confidential information, of how you've helped major firms (or organizations similar to the prospect's). Paint the buyer into the picture that you've created in your consulting work for significant results.

- Take your time. Ironically, the more time you take to develop a trusting relationship with an economic buyer, the faster you will be able to provide a proposal and secure the business.

Demonstrate That You Are a Peer of the Buyer, Not Lower-Level People

Even if you were introduced or referred by subordinates, immediately stake your claim as a peer of the true buyer. Techniques:

- Wear very good clothing. This isn't "dress for success" but an expression of taste and your frame of reference.

- Use fine accessories. Don't take out a 50-cent pen to take notes. Use a Cartier or Mont Blanc pen.

- Don't appear like a pack mule. Leave your luggage in a closet with the receptionist or in your car. Don't lug a computer bag around; it's the modern equivalent of pocket protectors and phone holsters.

- Use a subtle, modest business card. When was the last time you saw a bank or manufacturing executive with his or her picture on a business card?

- Watch your language. Don't dumb down, but do learn to be conversant in the prospect's profession of industry. If you're in a bank, for example, you should know what a loan defalcation is, and in a hospital what capitation means.

Always Create a Definitive Net Time and Date

Never allow the relationship or conversation to be based on "Let's talk again once I've reviewed this," or "Get back to me in about a month." You *must* create next steps that are on both your calendars. The buyer's time is no more important than your own, and the time to set the next date or meeting is before the end of the current one.

If you attend to these factors, you'll create an environment, relationship, and mind-set that will produce the most likely acceptance of a proposal. Take the time to set this up, no less than you'd prime a wall before painting it lest the paint run and not adhere. Never be afraid of a powerful buyer.

But always be patient.

Conceptual Agreement

Let's review where we are in our basic business model (see Figure 7.1).

Only after establishing a trusting relationship, and assuring that the conditions are optimal for success, can we pursue conceptual agreement. If I don't trust you, I'm not going to share my goals with you and I'm going to be somewhat suspicious of any professional—and certainly personal—questions you pose. That's why I maintain that the longer you take to create a solid, trusting relationship, the quicker you'll acquire quality business.

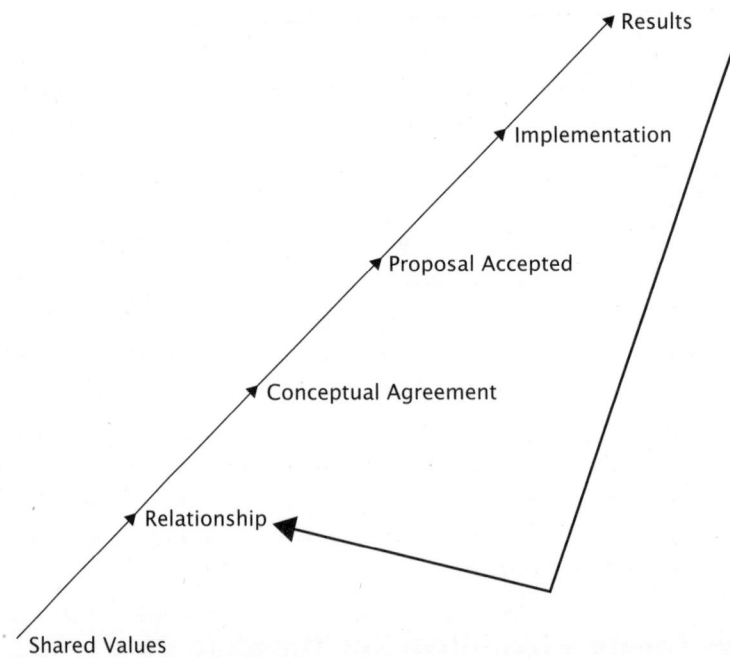

FIGURE 7.1 Consulting Model

Conceptual agreement is a phrase I use to encapsulate three vital elements in formulating proposals that stand the strongest chances of acceptance. I want to summarize them again here, because they are that essential to business acquisition: objectives, measures of success, and value.

Objectives

These are business outcomes. They are not tasks, deliverables, or activities. You can almost always tell a nonbuyer because you will be asked about "deliverables," and "how many days?" and "what do the materials look like?"

Here are examples of inputs (deliverables) turned into outputs (results):

Input	Output
▪ Run a focus group	▪ Gain employee commitment to change
▪ Observe workplace behavior	▪ Validate management interventions
▪ Standardize the sales process	▪ Decrease costs of business acquisition
▪ Improve advertising	▪ Increase top-line revenue growth
▪ Debug technology	▪ Improve competitiveness

You get the idea. Even rubrics such as "improving communications," "building morale," and "lowering stress" are not valuable unless the consequent results of increasing time to market, reducing involuntary turnover, and lowering absenteeism are considered.

Measures of Success, or Metrics

These are indicators of your progress toward achievement of the goal. Even if the goal is much longer-term and is expected to be fully realized long after your involvement is over, you need metrics to indicate that while you were there your contribution mattered and achieved the shorter-term objectives.

An indicator is just that—you have to be able to know whether something is apparent to others. Lousy indictors include statements such as these four points:

1. The workforce will be better informed.
2. Customers will have greater loyalty.
3. Management will be more confident.
4. The workplace will be greatly improved.

How do you know (and prove to a third party) that these supposed indicators demonstrate any changes at all? Typically, metrics come in two varieties:

1. The factual and objective. Using the four points:
   1. Service representatives will forward less than 10 percent of calls to technical experts. (This is easily documented.)
   2. Repeat business will grow over the next six months.
   3. Managers will reduce their average week from 60 hours to 45 hours through delegation to subordinates.
   4. There will be fewer grievances filed about privacy violations and fewer accidents reported monthly.
2. Subjective with an acknowledged source. Examples:
   - The buyer will report that about half the prior time is spent on serving as referee for teams every week.
   - The sales vice president will report that customers no longer complain about the uncomfortable and unappealing surroundings in the executive offices.
   - The director of R&D and the marketing vice president will report that they are meeting at least once a week with harmonious and shared responsibilities emerging.

Metrics are vital not merely to show progress and/or completions, *but also to demonstrate your role in their accomplishment.*

The Gospel

Value is the basis for return on investment (ROI). If you can't establish the value of the results with the buyer, do not proceed to a proposal.

Value

This is the most misunderstood of the three elements. Value comprises the impact of meeting the objectives.

You may say that an objective such as "increased profits" demonstrates significant value by itself. But ask this: What is the total impact of increased profits? It could include:

- Higher dividends for shareholders.
- Higher equity for sale of the business or an exit strategy.
- More income for ownership.
- Greater investment in expansion.
- More favorable terms from investors and lenders.
- Greater ability to be philanthropic and help the community.

You can see the point. The value of this project is far greater than merely meeting that one objective, and when you multiply this action by five or six key objectives, then you create huge value *and commensurately high ROI and fees*. Don't forget that most value is also annualized for your client.[1]

Objectives, metrics, and value—the elements of conceptual agreement—also represent the central three points in your actual proposal.

The Nine Components

My proposals are all about two and a half pages and have nine components. That's it. There are no resumes, company histories, or obsequious love notes to the buyer.

The Gospel

A proposal is a summation (of conceptual agreement), not an exploration (of a relationship).

We cover the peripherals and what's *not* included in the next segment, but for now, let's focus on the heart and soul of a proposal that will usually be accepted by an economic buyer.[2] You can find proposal examples in the Physical Appendix and the Virtual Appendix.

1. Situation Appraisal

This is a brief (one- or two-paragraph) description of what the issues are that prompted you to discuss this project and reach the agreements and conclusions that follow. The intent is to cause the buyer to nod in agreement, "Yes, that's what we discussed," right from the outset.

A *poor* situation appraisal: "Acme is a company that sells explosive devices to predators in order to facilitate the capture of wild prey." This is useless. Acme already knows that!

A *good* situation appraisal: "Acme's position in the provision of explosive devices for wild prey has become endangered by the reliance for 90 percent of its business on a single customer, a coyote with no permanent address."

Or: "Acme wishes to expand its market penetration from the American West to the savannah of Africa, expanding from coyotes to lions."

Note that situation appraisals can reflect either a problem to be solved or an opportunity to be gained.

2. Objectives

This is the start (#2 to #4) of a repeat of the conceptual agreement already achieved. I prefer bullet points.

Our objectives for this project include the following, as we've discussed:
- Expansion to occur within 18 months.
- Use of internal resources only—no subcontractors overseas.
- [and so on]

3. Measures of Success

Same format:

Our measures of success, previously agreed upon, include:
- Monthly sales reports indicate growing percentage of foreign sales.
- No net increases in employment on monthly payroll.
- [and so on]

4. Value

Same format:

The value we discussed that will accrue from meeting the objectives include:
- Diverse customer base to help offset domestic economic fluctuations.
- Attracting more investors and increased stock price with global presence.
- [and so on]

5. Methodology and Options

Here we list the choice of "yeses" for the buyer, who has not seen them in detail before (you may have generally discussed them). You do *not* cite fees here.

> *Option 1:* We will conduct a study of the highest-potential, most lucrative, and easiest markets to enter and will create a strategy and tactics for the top five choices.
>
> *Option 2:* In addition to option 1, we will develop introductions with the key governmental, trade, banking, and political figures to accelerate speed of entry [and so on].
>
> *Option 3:* In addition to option 2, we will serve on retainer for up to one year to be your sounding board and fine-tune the implementation in the longer term.

Note that options escalate, and that each new one embraces the preceding one(s). These are not add-ons or phases of the project.

6. Timing

The client deserves to know the extent of the disruption, change, and interventions, and also when you will disengage. (This is consulting, not codependency.)

Thus: "For option 1 the timing will be 30 to 45 days; for option 2, 45 to 90 days; for option 3, 90 days up to a year, depending on the extent of the retainer."

7. Joint Accountabilities

Since this is a partnership, not something you do to the client, you have both separate and joint accountabilities. Here are generic examples:

Our accountabilities include:
- Signing nondisclosure agreements.
- Monthly or more frequent debriefs as requested.
- Response to questions within 24 hours.

Your accountabilities include:
- Personal e-mail and cell phone access and 24-hour response.
- Documentation for employees and clients as needed.
- Security clearances, company IDs, office in headquarters.

We jointly agree:
- To immediately inform the other if any situations develop that could materially affect the outcomes and success of this project.

This last category is included because I've found myself knee-deep in a project when the buyer announces that there is a divestiture or acquisition and I couldn't be told earlier because the deal was pending. That's unacceptable, and places you in the position of possibly lying to company employees.

8. Terms and Conditions

My favorite part of the proposal: This is the *first time* the buyer sees the fees. It's very simple:

The fee for option 1 is $65,000.

The fee for option 2 is $98,000.

The fee for option 3 is $35,000 per quarter.

Fifty percent of the fee for option 1 or 2 is due on acceptance, with the balance due in 45 days. Alternatively, we offer a 10 percent professional discount when the full fee is paid on acceptance. Fees for option 3 are due on the first day of each quarter of the retainer.

Expenses are billed monthly as actually accrued, and are due upon presentation of our invoice. We charge for reasonable travel, lodging, tips, and meals. We do not charge for copying, courier, administrative work, phone, or other communications.

It's important to let the buyer know you are not nickel-and-diming like an attorney (for an attorney's bill of $4,517.44, $17 is for copying and $.44 is for a stamp). It's also important to charge reasonably; that is, you're free to stay at the Four Seasons, but you should charge your client only Marriott rates. I fly first class all the time. I charge domestic clients unrestricted coach fares and charge international clients unrestricted business-class fares, and I pay the difference.

You should have your fees paid quickly, never stretched out and never at the conclusion of a project. And then this:

The quality of our work is guaranteed. If we do not meet your objective within these time frames and that fault is ours, we will refund your full fees. However, otherwise this contract is noncancelable for any reason, though you may postpone and reschedule. The original payment dates must be met.

The quid pro quo is that you'll guarantee your quality (but never results, which are subject to far too many variables you can't control), but the contract is noncancelable *for any reason.*

9. Acceptance

My proposals also serve as a contract, since I don't want a formal contract going to the client's legal department, where people are paid to obfuscate and delay. Here are the words:

> Your choice of an option below and your payment constitute accept-ance of the terms and conditions herein. In lieu of your signature, we will proceed solely on the basis of your payment.

The rationale here is that many buyers can authorize six-figure checks, but can't sign contracts without legal department scrutiny.[3] Thus, an oral "yes" and a check will make me a working consultant.

How to Submit

So you now have a great act, and it's been well received out of town. How do you ensure it will play well in the big city, with major critics and a much more sophisticated public?

You make sure that your masterpiece is displayed well, you rehearse what needs to happen, and you plan for both preventive and contingent actions. In all candor, no matter how good a proposal you create and no matter how tight the conceptual agreement, if you simply hit "send" on the keyboard or toss it into the mail, you're going to encounter problems and a much lower accept-ance ratio.

Here are the key considerations, which you can control or highly influence.

Never Suggest Phases

An option, as we've discussed, is an "additional yes" because it embraces the prior, lower value and lower fee option. With a new car, you may choose the sports option and the interior option, but in any case you're buying that car.

With phases, you're suggesting that the project be done in part and piece-meal. This is usually because consultants wrongly insist on "needs analyses" or "information gathering," or "preliminary diagnosis." You might as well insist on lowering your income.

You'll *never* have enough information at the outset, and I've never been involved in a project in which I didn't find surprising new elements as I sailed along, and had to adjust accordingly. The problem with a phased approach that calls for multiple buying decisions is that after the information retrieval:

- The client can say it doesn't appear to be as bad as they thought.
- The client can decide to do it internally.
- The client may put it up for bid.
- You may make an error casting you in a bad light.
- The client may hire you.

That's 20 percent good, 80 percent bad. Are you beginning to see my point? ("We don't pass the ball more," said legendary Ohio State football coach Woody Hays, "because three things can happen when you pass, and two of them are bad. Why would we want to do that?")

Suggest the largest project you can to improve the client's condition using a choice of "yeses," not a series of buying decisions. (The greatest competition you'll ever face is internal, not other consultants.)

The Gospel

Think of the fourth sale first. Try to create a seamless relationship long into the future. That is not helped by constant buying decisions and reviews.

FedEx the Proposal

If a client insists on an electronic copy, provide it *but also FedEx the proposal.* (I could say "courier," I realize, but FedEx simply is the most reliable alternative. Don't be penny-wise and pound-foolish.) The hard copy will stand out above the noise, have the benefit of your letterhead and expensive paper, and be easier to sign and return. Send two copies, with your signature already executed. Don't create wasted time by insisting the buyer sign two, return them, and you return one. This is a trusting relationship, remember?

Create a Time and Date Certain to Review

Tell the client, "You'll have electronic and hard copies this Tuesday morning before 10:30. Can we talk the next morning at 9:00 eastern time and discuss the option you prefer and how soon we can start?" This is called an assumptive close, and at this point in the process, it's not assuming too much.

Never accept "I'll get back to you when I return from this trip" or "Give me a week." You're passing the ball, and too many bad things can happen.

Don't Add Bling

This is a summation, not an exploration. *It is not a sales document or a negotiating document.* It does not require biographies of you or your team, promotional literature, testimonials, or neon lights. All of that should have been a part of the marketing process that got you into the buyer's office, if it were even needed then.

Don't put every page on letterhead, just your cover sheet. There are no photos, graphs, charts, or hyperlinks needed. This is a straightforward summary of the conceptual agreement, and the only thing new are the fees, since this is the first time the options have been formally presented, once you've had a chance to think through the project and process.

Before Submitting, Ask One Key Question

While you are with the buyer, and before you assemble the proposal, ask, "Is there anything we haven't discussed that might be an obstacle to our proceeding as we've agreed to this point?"

The buyer may say something about fees, but you can then say, "Of course, but I'm also sure that a dramatic ROI will overcome any concerns about the fees, correct?" (If the other person is overwhelmingly concerned about cost no matter what, you're probably not talking to an economic buyer, so jump off this train.)

But the buyer may say, "There is the busy season ahead," or "We are replacing the vice president of sales," and so on. Find this out before you create the proposal and work out with the buyer how to overcome the obstacle: "Wouldn't it be best to implement this in your busiest season, when you'd have the most dramatic immediate return and assurance it was working no matter how hectic the conditions?"

Even with a solid relationship, the buyer may not have surfaced something obvious to the buyer but hidden from you.

Be Prepared for Success

If the buyer says, "Yes, let's go with option 2," then be prepared to start. We cover that transition to launch next, but try this: *Include an invoice for each of the options in your FedEx package and electronic submission.* The client can simply choose the relevant invoice and begin the processing. (Don't forget, at least 50 percent of the fee is due on acceptance, not launch.)

Don't view this as overly aggressive. View it as a convenience for the buyer and an accelerator for the project. My policy is to always accept an oral approval, ask that the buyer forward payment, and then begin to pour cement for the foundation.

How to Close and Launch

Well, we're almost there. The buyer with your proposal in hand is about to make a decision. You've prepared the culture and set the expectations, and given the buyer choices based on conceptual agreement.

However.

When I ran the sprints in track, the coaches admonished us to "run past the tape." That meant that runners had an unconscious tendency to slow down at the finish, seeing the race was about to be won. It was at that point that someone behind them would lunge ahead and win by a couple of inches.

So we were told to visualize the tape as another 10 yards down the track. That way we'd be running full speed and in our finishing kick as we crossed the actual finish line. I won my share of races using that technique. I didn't so much get faster at the end as others seemed to let up a little.

Now we have to run past the tape with the proposal, because so much now hinges on the buyer's reactions, and we should be hitting at least 80 percent of these projects (many of the people in my Mentor Program have documented close rates of over 90 percent consistently using the format I've described in this chapter).

So here is the finishing kick to run past the tape.

The Buyer Wants to Meet

I don't advocate meeting with the buyer when the buyer sees the proposal for the first time. It's too simple for the buyer to say, "This has been very enlightening; let me have some time to read it carefully and we can talk next week." You want the buyer to *already* have read it carefully when you follow up. Since you have conceptual agreement, there really is no need at all to meet in person.

If the buyer insists and it's not a huge inconvenience (the client isn't nine hours away), then insist that the buyer read the proposal and give you a summary of any questions or concerns so that you can prepare and make the best use of your collective time.

The Buyer Says That Some More People Will Look at the Proposal

There are two considerations here:

1. This is a real buyer who is enamored of consensus decision making or just afraid to discomfort anyone. Remind the buyer that projects like these often make key subordinates uncomfortable and that they will normally raise objections, especially because they weren't involved in the conceptual agreement stage. Also remind the buyer

that these are strategic, not tactical, decisions, and rightfully only the buyer should be making them.

2. This is not a real buyer, and you've blown it. If the "buyer" says, "I need approval from my board/partners/members/superior," you were either lied to or missed all the signs. In this case you say the following: "You'll be asked questions about things the others weren't party to and you'll be in an unfair position since only I can answer some of those questions. Can you set up the meeting for me to be present also?" Then you can just try to hope for the best, but your odds are not good.

The Gospel

You won't win every proposal or overcome every objection. But to not be prepared for what you know may be raised is simply malfeasance.

The Buyer Loves Option 3 but Only Has Budget for Option 2

You don't fold here, or the buyer will wonder how much more can be asked for no matter how strong your relationship. Explain that the reason for three options is to provide just these kinds of choices in terms of ROI; then turn the discussion to the considerably higher ROI on option 3 and away from the fee itself.

If you're discussing fee and not value, you've lost control of the discussion.

Tell the buyer that you can start with option 2 and always upgrade as the project unfolds.

The Buyer Attempts to Negotiate Price

Be aware of two tricks of the trade here:

1. Many companies have internal policies that mandate that all discounts offered must be accepted. Therefore, when you offer a 10 percent discount for full payment in advance (as noted earlier), the offer must be accepted. That both provides a better bargain for your client and eliminates the urge to negotiate.

2. Negotiate terms, but never fee. You can accept 25 percent instead of 50 percent in advance, or the balance in 90 days instead of 45. (Never accept payment at the conclusion or you run the risk of never being fully paid.) This will demonstrate flexibility but preserve your fees.

Never allow the buyer to tell you that there are purchasing or accounts payable policies. You have your policies, too. The point of dealing with a true buyer is that support units can be read the riot act. Exceptions are made all the time. (If you're ever experiencing late payments, *never* argue with accounts payable— *always* go to your buyers and say, "We have a problem," with the emphasis on "we." Every business in the world can draw a manual check, and computers take only a few hours to provide one. When someone says, "It takes 30 days," that means your invoice sits on some low-level person's desk for 29 days.

Case Study

Always find the causes of your successes, not merely your failures. When one buyer within Merck, George, accepted my offer of a 10 percent discount every January on $250,000 of business, I finally asked if that percentage was the key, or if it should be slightly higher or lower.

"I don't care about the discount," he said.

Stunned, I stammered, "Then why do you pay in advance?"

"Because," he explained, smiling, "then my projects can't be canceled."

In any large organization there is always someone (the CEO) or something (recession) that can cancel projects if the money hasn't already been spent. You can sue over your contractual provisions of being noncancelable, but that can be exhausting with a huge organization.

Lesson learned: Always ask what's in the buyer's self-interest, not just your own, if you want true commitment!

Finally, when the buyer says "yes" and chooses an option, which will happen most of the time, be prepared to proceed. The sooner you start some action, whether on-site or remotely, the more acceleration the project will experience and the faster you'll be paid.

If anyone objects, especially subordinates, the buyer will simply say, "We've already started."

Notes

1. See the full fee equation in Chapter 3 and Chapter 6.

2. Once again, for maximum depth and templates, see my book *How to Write a Proposal That's Accepted Every Time* (Peterborough, NH: Kennedy Publications, 2002, 2008). I will be publishing *Million Dollar Consulting® Proposals* in 2012.

3. At the New York Federal Reserve, the legal department delayed our start by 60 days, changed my two and a half pages into 45 pages of indecipherable gunk, yet didn't change a thing about the relationship at all. All they did was delay the benefits by two months.

Chapter 8

Implementation
Magic Formula: Rapid Results with Low Labor Intensity

The Role of the Buyer and Champion

We'll talk in Section IV about methodologies and intervention techniques. I want to focus here on the nature of the intervention once the proposal has been accepted.

Just as we should prepare the environment and culture for the acceptance of a proposal, we should do the same for acceptance of our intervention. Probably the most critical factor in the eventual success of our implementation is the role of the buyer.

With rare exceptions, the buyer should be the champion of the project. The buyer may delegate accountabilities to lower-level subordinates, and you will take on many as the consultant, *but the buyer must be the point person who is leading the charge.* In the American Civil War, when massed brigades marched in eighteenth-century style across fields into the fire from nineteenth-century weapons, there was every reason to believe that the soldiers would find shelter or hit the ground for safety. But they didn't.

The brigadier general leading a brigade would get on his horse, draw his sword, and yell, "Follow me!" And they did.

He didn't say, "I'll meet you there," or "Let me know when you get there." He was in the front, the main target for enemy sharpshooters.[1]

When firefighters arrive at a conflagration today, the most senior officer present, even a chief, leads the firefighters into the flames (unlike police, by the way, where senior officers set up a command post and remotely direct patrol officers or SWAT teams). Firefighters know that they are never asked to endure danger that senior officers would not.

Your buyer isn't going to be subjected to enemy fire or flames (one would hope). But he or she will have to be the point person, leading the charge. What does that mean?

The Buyer Must Exemplify the Desired Behavior

The single most effective factor for changing organizational behavior is that of the avatar. People want to see the leader, visible, on the "horse," leading the way. If the desired change is use of technology, the leader should be the first to demonstrate how the company has integrated it. If the change is a more interactive and nonsilo workplace, the leader should abandon the formal office.

If the new culture calls for "immediate response to customers" and the leader is seen telling an assistant that a customer will be called back because the leader is chatting with other managers, that doesn't create the right environment.

Case Study

When I asked a bank's executive vice president how he was leading the new project to integrate technology into every transaction, he proudly showed me a new computer on his credenza.

"But how do you actually use it?" I asked.

He pushed a strange button. Nothing happened to the computer, but his secretary immediately walked in and said, "Yes, sir?"

"Margaret," he said, "please show Mr. Weiss how we use this computer!"

You can't make this stuff up.

The Buyer Must Enforce Subordinate Accountability

Projects don't work with people watching; they work with people *doing*. And people best *do* when they are being monitored and evaluated.

Each of the buyer's direct reports and key subordinates must have a role in the implementation that includes accountability for its success. That may be something as minor as ensuring certain training activities or as major as changing a customer service or R&D relationship.

Many subordinates will otherwise tend to hang back or test the wind with any venture that is new and involves even prudent risk. The buyer can't allow them to do that. These are the colonels who must keep reminding the troops to follow the brigadier. As the battle is fought, and once the battle is over and the objective gained, the buyer needs to be looking around and seeing which people are keeping up with him or her, and which are lagging behind.

There should be at least monthly, informal evaluations of each subordinate's role and how well it is meeting the project's needs.

Buyers Must Use Their Clout Where Needed

As a consultant, always be aware that you have accountability but not responsibility. That is, you are an independent operator who can advise, but you can't command or direct. (That's why I maintain that it's *never* appropriate or even ethical for a consultant to temporarily become the director of sales or CFO for a client. You are not an employee, you are not vested in the firm's future, and you have no right to be making daily or long-term decisions for that organization.)

Therefore, when another department, or a customer, or a recalcitrant manager is an obstacle to progress, the buyer must step in and use either personal influence, hierarchical authority, or peer-level connections to resolve the conflict and remove the barrier. You should never take political sides, and you can never threaten someone's job. But you should set up the expectation and accountability that the buyer may have to exercise such legitimate responsibility as matters progress.

The Gospel

Implementation is a partnership. If the client and especially the buyer are not pulling their own weight, you will sink with them.

The Buyer Is Your Partner and Must Act like One

Partners are accessible. When consultants tell me that their buyer isn't reachable or isn't available, I know they've blown the relationship.

You wouldn't dream (I hope) of not immediately returning a buyer's call or e-mail message, and you should expect the exact same prompt treatment in return. You should have the buyer's personal e-mail address and cell phone number. None of your communications should be monitored or filtered by a secretary. If the buyer is traveling, I have news for you: Phone and computers work internationally.

Never abuse the privilege, but you're going to have to provide regular debriefs and updates, report victories, and get support for setbacks. (They happen.) You can't do that if you have no one to talk to.

Occasionally, your buyer may not be your champion. The CEO of a Fortune 500 company may hand things off to a highly visible and powerful lieutenant. But that's rare. Prepare your buyer for the role of champion.

And then help the buyer onto the horse.

The Key Stakeholders and Influence Points

I know that "scope creep" sounds like a geek with binoculars, but it's a ubiquitous term for a project that, like the great old science fiction movie, *The Blob*, just keeps slobbering all over everything in sight.

This happens to all kinds of professional services firms, not merely solo consultants. When I worked with the consulting arm of Hewlett-Packard (HP) years ago, they referred to a condition known as "undocumented promises." Since my job was to help them move from hourly billing to value-based fees, I thought I had better understand what I thought was a technical software term.

It turned out that undocumented promises were those informal agreements reached between HP implementation people and lower-level client people, who would say things such as, "As long as you're here anyway, could you take a look at . . . ?" and "You're going to have to take care of this issue before you can get to your own project, because it's in the way." The last thing the implementation people wanted to do was to have to say "no" and have the client personnel report to their superiors that HP people had refused requests, and those client superiors would talk to HP superiors—well, you get the political picture.

The trouble was that once you added up all these undocumented promises and the labor and work that they consumed, *the project's margins were being squeezed out of existence.* It took the company quite a while to determine that being polite (or being afraid to rile superiors) paled in comparison to losing profits. If there are enough of these seemingly minor requests, your profits evaporate. Termites can bring down a house. The typical termite is one-quarter inch long.

Do you ever wonder what's gnawing at you?

For solo practitioners, scope creep is deadly. Many of these gnawing requests can originate with the buyer, since you should be regularly interacting with the buyer, and may seem like part of your job.

They are not. That's why the proposal has established objectives, metrics, and value, along with optional methodologies from which the client has chosen the preferred alternative. The proposal is an organic document, driving and regulating the engagement. Hence, never be loath to point out that what you're being asked to do is not consistent with what you agreed to do and produce.

How do you say "no" to your buyer? (You say "no" to nonbuyers by simply explaining that the request is not consistent with what you and the buyer agreed upon, so it should be taken up with the buyer to see if it makes sense to amend the project to include it.) You give the buyer a choice of "yeses."

Sample dialogue:

BUYER: Alan, while you're here today, would you carve out an hour to attend one of my staff meetings? I know it's an hour taken away from the compensation project, but I'd like an independent and objective view of why my people don't participate at these meetings.

ME: Joan, I'd be happy to, so let's discuss the alternatives. First, I could simply do this as a one-off request, charge you for my observations and report, and send you an invoice with my next expense statement at the end of the month. Or, if I find that some work needs to be done and you agree—perhaps coaching, or meeting reconfiguration—I can write you a new proposal with the fee benefits of my being on-site frequently anyway. Or, we can let this wait until the current project is complete and then attack it with a fresh start. How urgent is it?

BUYER: I hadn't planned a budget for this, which is why I thought you might be able to simply squeeze it into your schedule. It's important enough for me to want to stop wasting time with these unproductive meetings.

ME: Ah, but it's clearly of high value to you, and it demands my full attention and careful consideration, and probably talks with you and with at least some of the people in that room. I know you don't want me to guess at causes, and I know whatever action you take you want it to be of the highest quality.

BUYER: Fair enough; I see your point. Attend the meeting and send me an invoice, but let's use that as a deposit if you and I both agree that more intervention is needed on your part. [We shake hands.]

Obviously, that's a true story. And that's how you prevent scope creep, even from your buyer. Let me review some ground rules here, because consultants have a horrible habit of undercharging and overdelivering. This is akin not merely to carrying a flamethrower on thin ice, but to turning it on and pointing it at your feet.

Avoiding scope creep:

- Tell nonbuyers to take their requests to your buyer, since you're not authorized to expand the project unilaterally.

- Separate a favor ("Would you look at this new logo design and just give me your immediate reaction?") from a project ("I'd like you to watch my sales director present at the corporate meeting and tell me how she can improve").

- Don't feel inferior. You are partners with the buyer. You wouldn't say to the buyer, "Would you mind if we didn't meet that fourth objective? And I'd like to add $15,000 to my fee." Partners don't talk to each other that way. Don't feel as if you'll lose the business by saying "no" or suggesting alternatives. You have in place a proposal, the parameters of which are quite clear, which is why you structured it that way.

- Just because someone else has done something that's not optimal, or you could do something faster and better that someone else is charged with, doesn't mean you should do it. If you want to impress your client, do so through superb work on your own project, not by cleaning out the client's metaphorical garage.

- Demonstrate that what's being asked can easily be accommodated by client personnel, and make some quick recommendations for how to do so and why it makes sense (internal skills building, familiarity with the culture and politics, and so on).

- Finally, if something *is* in your way and no one else is removing it, tell the client, "Look, you obviously didn't anticipate this, and therefore I never prepared for it, but it must be done or we won't be successful. I'm willing to take it on if you're willing to reimburse a reasonable additional fee." (See "Midcourse Corrections" later in this chapter.)

Scope creep is *the* major cause of profit erosion *and* loss of wealth for solo consultants because it dramatically and exponentially increases labor intensity. The good news is that the consultant can absolutely prevent it. The bad news is that too many consultants don't have the courage to do so, or are under the misapprehension that doing everything but taking out the garbage adds to their luster.

All that adds to is their long days and time away from home.

Unfortunately, there is even a more insidious time waster and wealth eviscerator.

Avoiding Scope Seep

Welcome to the most invidious and potentially damaging aspect of consulting intervention dynamics: scope seep.

I coined this phrase a decade ago when I realized the (quite appropriate) focus on scope creep was not sufficiently remediating consultants' excel labor intensity or the pressure on margins. When I began to coach more closely and observe throughout the project, I determined that what I thought was scope creep was, in fact, scope seep, meaning that corrective actions were not addressing the correct cause of the problem.

Scope seep occurs when the consultant, without impetus or request from the client, enlarges the project unilaterally without changing the proposal, agreements, or fees.

Please read that again, think about it, and then we'll proceed.

The Gospel

Every rational client I've ever met will accept free work. If my plumber said that he'd caulk all the bathrooms in the house as long as he was here, I'd readily accept at the original fee. However, my plumber has never, in my memory, offered that service, because he is a good businessman!

Here are some conditions that prompt scope seep from otherwise intelligent and rational consultants. Beware—it can be like crack cocaine (or at least a chocolate addiction), so be strong. Indicators:

The perfection over success trap
- You find someone doing something that you know can be done either better or faster and you want to intervene. Remember you are after success, not perfection.

The tidy-up detour
- You can't resist fixing a meeting's agenda, or reconciling conflict among some peers, because you don't like to ignore anything out of order. You need to tuck your anal-retentive urges away.

The mine is bigger than yours pitfall
- You have a methodology you love that is not needed on the current project, so you actually spend time desperately trying to find some place to use it, whether or not you get paid for it (and whether or not anyone cares). Don't carry all of your toys around with you.

The "oops" belly flop

- You find that both you and the client have made an error in your assumptions about the project, and it's a major one, but instead of treating your buyer as a partner, you decide just to take care of it. You need to treat your partner as a peer, and not as a parent or child, and figure out how best to address the new challenge.

The ego catch wire

- You just can't resist sharing the wealth, and once one person pays you a compliment you decide to teach anyone who isn't actively engaged on the phone all that you know. You can't pay your mortgage with acolytes.

Scope seep is entirely the consultant's fault and problem. Once you submit to it, you create a subtle slide into bankruptcy because the client *will soon assume that you find these practices normal and acceptable,* and will soon add scope creep to your burden. After all, if you're suggesting that you take on additional goals, then why can't the client add to them?

In football, this used to be called "piling on," then "unnecessary roughness," and today a "personal foul." No matter—they are all 15-yard penalties.

Here is a useful template to view your own ability to empower yourself to resist overdelivering, which is also useful in helping clients avoid their own powerless work environment:

Powerlessness versus Power

Powerless	Empowered
▪Create bureaucracy.	▪Do the right thing.
▪Are insecure.	▪Are self-confident.
▪See "them and us."	▪ See "us."
▪Focus on task.	▪Focus on result.
▪Follow rules.	▪Think.
▪CYA.	▪Take risks.
▪See win-loss issues.	▪See win-win issues.

You need to focus on doing the right thing *for you* and not on docilely following your own inflexible rules (e.g., you have a six-step strategy approach and the client must receive all six, whether paying for them or not). Even one-person firms can be bureaucratic when focused on task and not output. *I've worked with many Fortune 500 giants that are entrepreneurial and agile, and coached many solo practitioners who were sclerotic and ossified.*

If you are self-confident (we're discussing self-esteem at every turn in this book), then you will be secure enough to resist scope seep's siren call. When you view the relationship as a true partnership ("us"), you'll happily accept the client's role and not insist on your constant involvement (interference).

The most powerful antidote—the true antivenom serum—to scope seep is to focus strongly on results and how to achieve them best, fastest, and most efficiently, thereby necessitating that you don't stop along the way to repave the parking lot or reposition the watercoolers. You're an entrepreneurial consultant because you're paid to think—remember, you're *not* a pair of hands, but a brain—and you're a refugee (in all probability) from a larger organization, so stop trying to create and follow rules. Instead, create actions and outcomes.

Take prudent risks, don't worry about protecting yourself (CYA: cover your "assets"), and engage your buyer in a win-win collaboration.

My point throughout this book is that the buyer and the client organization are best served by quick results, the faster the better, which is why time-based billing is unethical aside from being simply stupid. But to engage in that speed, you can't allow the client (scope creep) or yourself (scope seep) to place barriers, obstacles, and detours along the path. You'll have plenty of those as it is without the extra exertion.

Don't become your own worst enemy. Occam's razor[2] posits that the simplest route is usually the best one. The simplest route in consulting is not to accept or seek tasks outside of your commitments to the client specified in the proposal.

Success, not perfection.

Midcourse Corrections

One of the reasons I strongly discourage phases and needs analyses is that we seldom have all the information (let alone knowledge) that we need *even after conducting these huge wastes of time!* Fortunately, we have effective adaptive actions.

Every program, project, engagement, and assignment will have speed bumps and detours. Learn to recognize them and adjust. Here are some typical *causes* of the need for midcourse corrections:

- The buyer has made some bad assumptions, which you have now verified as incorrect.
- The buyer has inadvertently overcommitted in terms of support and is not investing the time needed to be the champion.

- Key people are on vacation, ill, responding to emergencies, or called away by client demands.
- The competition makes a dramatic, unexpected move.
- A new technology emerges suddenly, or an existing one fails.
- Key customers of your client desert.
- There is an unanticipated rush of new business for your client.
- Lower down in the organization, people are resisting the project because of rumor or competing self-interests.
- You made some bad assumptions (e.g., that a model you used elsewhere would work here).
- Suddenly, two of your largest clients demand your immediate attention.
- You become ill or face a family emergency.
- The economy goes south, fast.

You get the idea! *All* of those things have happened to me during the course of my career, though thankfully not at once. Here are some keys to help with your adaptive actions.

First, be aware of what I call the Thermal Layer (see Figure 8.1).

Despite the best efforts of the client and your own intent, there is a key layer of middle management that controls the daily work and oversees the operating values of the organization (which may or may not be congruent with the core values—those wonderful statements you see in the annual report and on plaques on cafeteria walls[3]).

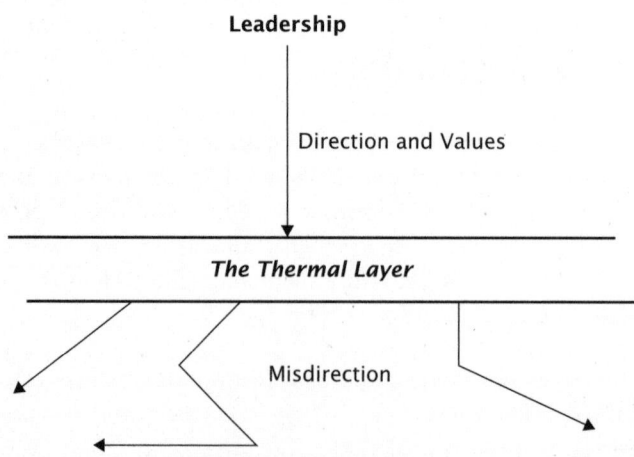

FIGURE 8.1   The Thermal Layer

One of my clients provided vans on snow days so that people would not have to drive and wouldn't clog up local streets. But the vans departed from work at 5:30 P.M., and when a few people would rise to meet them, a supervisor would say, "Sure, leave the rest of us with all this work." We fixed this by providing staggered van departures, from 4:30 to 7.

The Thermal Layer will refract and distort senior management intent unless you achieve goal congruency and mutual self-interest.

The Gospel

Even GPS in your car allows for detours and alternative routes. You need CGPS: Consultant GPS.

Second, prepare your buyer for the inevitable terrain. Let the buyer know that one of the features of your regular debriefings will be new information, verified and/or nonvalid assumptions, instances where the buyer's clout is needed, and so on.

Third, and as a corollary to the second factor, provide your client with *a lot of good news*. You will have an opportunity, as I'm highlighting, to provide bad news. So as to place the latter in perspective, do *not* only debrief or communicate with your buyer when something unexpected or rotten has occurred. If the buyer is inured with good news, the bad news can be accepted in proportion.

Fourth, never take it personally. When you meet resistance or obstacles or simply intransigence, face it as a fact of the project, completely expectable, and not a testimony on your character or talent. People won't oppose you, per se, unless you give them reason to. (See the following point.) Thus, handle these issues objectively (observed behavior and evidence in the environment), don't use slander ("They are not team players"), and don't go running to the buyer for bigger guns right away.

Work it out.

Fifth, never, ever take sides in political or turf battles. Nor should you believe that, within the context of an unrelated project, you can cure long-standing internecine strife and family feuds. You're after success, not perfection. Once you take sides, you'll lose the other side and you will permanently damage your credibility and effectiveness.

Sixth and finally, bear in mind that the confidence factors that work for you as a consultant will almost always work for your client, as well.

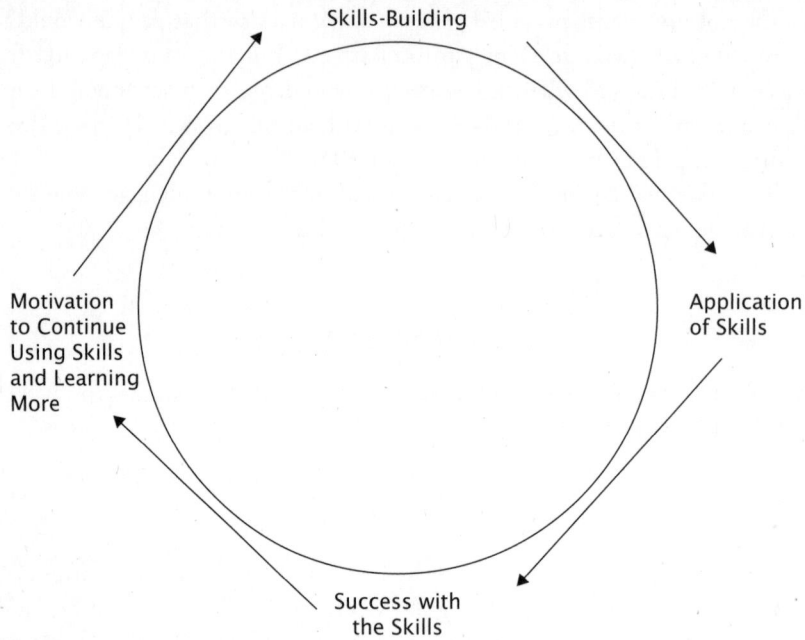

FIGURE 8.2 Building Skills

Help the client personnel build skills and apply them for success, and they will gain confidence in themselves and you, encouraging them to pursue and embrace more of the changes inherent in the engagement (see Figure 8.2). Paint them into the picture; don't try to rub them out.

If you've followed this implementation advice, you've been paid. Now let's see how you leave on the best possible note.

Notes

1. And, in fact, brigadier generals in the Civil War had the highest percentage mortality rate of any rank, a phenomenon never duplicated since, as you might well imagine.

2. After the fourteenth-century logician and Franciscan friar William of Ockham.

3. "We respect our people." Oh, well, that's wonderful. I hadn't thought of that.

Chapter

9

Disengaging

It's Been Nice, but I Really Must Be Going

Demonstrating Success

There is a profound difference between consulting (or coaching) and codependency. At some point, you must leave.

Now, leaving may mean moving on to another project and repeat business with the same client, but all individual engagements must end. (Which is why I've taken pains herein to differentiate retainer arrangements and ongoing access to your smarts. But even retainers end, seldom lasting beyond a year or two.) Sometimes leaving means departing, packing your tent and collecting your souvenirs, and going. That's particularly true with smaller clients, highly specialized projects, and so forth.

Formal disengagements also reduce the risks of ongoing scope creep and scope seep, reduce your labor intensity, and create clear indications that you can now increase other priorities, such as marketing, research, self-development, and so on.

In any case, the first aspect of departing is to have demonstrated success.

> ### The Gospel
>
> The entire point of our profession is to improve the client's condition. Make sure the client recognizes and endorses the improvement

Your project's conceptual agreement includes metrics—measures of progress and success—and a central element. When you are ready to disengage, one of two dynamics will be present:

1. *The project is completed and objectives have been met.*

   This may be the case of a new hiring system, or reduction in staff conflict, or restructured call center. The metrics will indicate the completion and objectives having been met.

2. *The project is completed but the results will require more time.*

   This would be the case in terms of increased sales per telemarketer, or higher long-term retention rates, or stronger word-of-mouth sales. Your contribution toward creating the environment and elements is completed, but it could be a year or more before the final results are evident. (For example, the objective may be to increase retention rates beyond the two-year mark, and you've identified and changed the elements that will be supportive of that within three months.)

In these cases, you ensure that the buyer—with whom you should have been debriefing on a regular basis anyway—acknowledges that you're at the terminal; the project is completed and objectives have been met according to the metrics (and the value, the third aspect of conceptual agreement, will start to accrue); and people can get off the train.

Or the buyer will acknowledge that you made good time, you're on schedule, and this is the proper station for you to disembark while the train and the rest of the crew and passengers continue on to the desired terminal.

Here's what you should do to ensure a successful and positive disengagement, and to maximize the chances for leveraged business internally and externally, which we'll discuss in the rest of this chapter:

- Schedule a personal meeting. This should never be done by e-mail or by phone or by nonpersonal interactions yet to be invented (like mind melds).

- Don't agree to a formal, large presentation. Meet individually with the buyer. (If the buyer wants a more formal staff presentation later, that's fine, but after you two have met privately.)

- Don't send anything in advance. You don't want a copy in circulation, and you don't want questions raised inadvertently when you're not present.

- Do bring an executive summary in hard copy that you will leave with the buyer, and that you will also send later electronically. Mark everything "confidential" and "private," and where appropriate put your copyright on it.

- Be clear about trademark, copyright, and general ownership provisions. Talk to your attorney if necessary, but in general, what you walk in with you walk out with; what's uniquely the client's before you walk in remains solely with the client; and what you and the client create together belong to both of you.

- Include recommendations about what the client should be doing to exploit and build on current progress internally. You're leaving but the results are staying, and should be nurtured.

- Tell the client what your agenda is, which in addition to the final debriefing is to set up the remaining segments in this chapter.

The formula for return on investment (ROI), similar to the original formula we used for value, should be stated here, for your good and the client's acknowledgment. The client's "good deal" looks like this:

$$\frac{\text{Tangible outcomes} \times \text{Expected duration of outcomes}}{\text{Fixed investment required}} = \text{Client's good deal}$$

This requires that you articulately and carefully detail the client's tangible, intangible, and peripheral benefits at this point, *and include any additional ones that have surfaced during the tenure of the project*. In many cases, benefits in addition to those stipulated at the outset will accrue. For example, the client may have identified the true, emerging all-stars who took the project and ran with it, or have discovered an entirely new type of client who responds well to the changes that were implemented.

It isn't inappropriate in any way to suggest the financial benefits and ask the client to verify them. Don't forget, when you originally established the conceptual agreement, you were *conservative* in these estimates ("Let's cut that in half"), but now you have the actual results and project results.

Remember that most results are annualized and grow over time, not unlike compound interest. Include that calculation as well.

Finally, share credit with client personnel and anyone else who deserves it. Make it clear, however, what your specific role was. Ironically, the better you are as a consultant, the more the client will tend to believe what you did was easy (not unlike watching a good shortstop make a play) and perhaps not that different from what anyone could have done, even internal people. You have to disabuse the buyer of such notions.

We all know that what the shortstop makes look easy is one of the hardest positions in all of sports.

Obtaining Referrals

Referral business is the coinage of the consulting realm. Yet so many consultants seem to disdain this particular windfall.

Prior to disengaging, you should fill your referral hopper. You establish the process early in the project by using language such as this with your buyer:

> "As this project progresses and begins to provide the value that we both foresee, I'd like to request some referrals from you for further business, which is a discipline I pursue with all of my clients. Is this acceptable?"[1]

If your buyer tells you early on that referrals are impossible or unlikely, then you can pursue other benefits (e.g., serve as a reference, provide a testimonial, and so on). But in all likelihood the buyer will say, "Sure, let's talk about it later."

So, while you're still there and in the early stages of the disengagement (because this is much more likely to be successful when done in person), raise the issue again:

> "I asked you two months ago if it would be permissible to seek referrals from you when the project started generating the value we both expected, and that time has arrived! I'm seeking the names of potential clients like yourself who would profit from the value I provide."

It's as simple as that. Change my words to reflect your own style, but don't change the timing or assertiveness.

> ### The Gospel
>
> Referrals are a win-win-win dynamic, enabling your client and you to help still more people. That's the focus you must have, and it's the key to the combination of the vault.

You should provide criteria for referrals, because you need quality, not quantity, and that's why I use the language "like yourself" in my request. For example, you may suggest:

"The most successful referrals are to people with significant profit-and-loss (P&L) responsibility who manage at least 100 people and who can make decisions and implement these types of leadership development efforts on their own."

Or:

"I'm most successful in helping small business owners who run a $25 million to $100 million business, have multiple sites, and have at least 200 employees."

You can give your buyer a choice of "yeses":

"I would love a personal introduction, but if you prefer that I simply use your name, that's fine. Of course, if you wish that I not use your name I'll also honor that."

Here are the most typical responses you'll hear and what to do with them:

BUYER: Can you give me some time to come up with some names for you?

YOU: Of course. What time is good on your calendar tomorrow, and I'll give you a call (or stop by)?

BUYER: I know some people who could use your help, but I don't know them personally.

YOU: That's fine, because they'll know of you. May I cite the work we're doing in general terms?

BUYER: Here are some people whom my people provided.

> **YOU:** Thanks, but I really need your peers. As you know, these kinds of projects aren't determined by your direct reports. And when I'm introduced from lower levels in the organization it's tough to reach the true decision makers.

Many of you will consider this approach to be very assertive, bordering on aggressive, and you may be right. But so what? You have a happy buyer, with whom you have developed a trusting relationship, and you're trying to enlist the buyer's aid in helping still more people. There is nothing at all wrong in being assertive in that pursuit.

Besides, the alternative of trying to bring in new business on your own requires a great deal more assertiveness and has a far lower success rate. So when you consider the alternative, the choice isn't so difficult.

> **BUYER:** I'm not sure I know anyone appropriate.
>
> **YOU:** Let me suggest some sources for you to consider:
> - Internal peers
> - Peers at other companies
> - Subsidiaries
> - Parent company
> - Vendors/providers
> - Members of trade associations
> - Customers/clients
> - Civic colleagues
> - Social acquaintances
> - Former colleagues who moved on
> - Former employers
> - Peers at social and professional clubs

When you do get referrals, follow up with them promptly. Ideally, you'll want your buyer to make the introduction, in person, by phone, or by e-mail. You may have to simply call and say, "Joan Davis suggested I give you a call."

What you immediately want with the referral is a meeting, making sure that you're talking to a true buyer. Then you can build the next trusting relationship.

Keep your prior buyer informed of your progress. "I called Tim, but haven't heard back yet," or "Talked to Lorraine and I'm seeing her next Thursday at 10." You never give gifts to corporate employees for referrals (you can see my guidelines elsewhere for referral fees to third parties), but a written thank-you note is always appropriate, whether or not the referral becomes a client. (Beware: Most major organizations have policies about gifts from anyone doing business with the company, so don't put your buyer in an awkward position.)

Finally, reciprocate. Send your clients customers, and let it be known that you sent them. Send your client talent if they're looking to hire people. Send your client other providers who don't compete with you but fill the client's needs. If you do this in advance of your actual request for referrals, you will have already established an informal obligation for reciprocity.

You can obviously obtain referrals from other sources—friends, family, professional colleagues, and so forth. But we're addressing here specifically the components of disengagement and what you must make sure is accomplished. If you're walking away from a happy client without any referrals, then you've left money on the table that you will never recover.

Obtaining Repeat Business

Disengaging needn't mean disappearing. As a very general rule of thumb, mature practices should have about 80 percent repeat business and 20 percent new business. The latter is important to create fresh approaches and challenges, to replace departing business (voluntary or involuntary), and to learn.

But since new business acquisition is the most difficult part of the business, and the most expensive, referrals and repeat business are key links to smooth the continuing growth of the business. We've covered the referrals, so now let's see about repeat business.

My definition of repeat business includes:

- More work for the same buyer of the same kind.
- More work for the same buyer of a different kind.
- Work for other buyers within the same client of the same kind.
- Work for other buyers within the same client of a different kind.

It's important to isolate these types of possibilities to maximize your repeat business potential. I want to reiterate that repeat business is with the same client, not necessarily the same buyer. Thus, your disengagement may be with the buyer while staying with the client, or merely disengagement with the old project as you begin a new one with the same buyer. But you must end your old project if you are to take on new ones—you must let go in order to reach out.

The chart in Figure 9.1 can give you an appreciation for your options.

	Same work	Different work
Same buyer	Expansion	Addition
Different buyer	Transference	Exploration

FIGURE 9.1 Options at Conclusion

Expansion

When you continue additional, virtually identical work with the same buyer, I term this an expansion mode. You are taking the new technology implemented with one unit to another unit under that same buyer. Or you're training another 200 people beyond the original 200, or coaching an additional five direct reports.

Expansion demands that you do a great job for the current buyer, make fairly rapid progress, and manage the project so that great feedback and tangible results (according to the project metrics) are obvious. Expansion often occurs when the buyer has not taken your second or third option in the proposal, but has started more modestly.

In my experience, about 40 percent of all repeat business is expansion business.

The Gospel

You must plan for repeat business in as many categories as possible. Waiting for the client to instigate it is like sitting home waiting for your phone to ring. You wonder if they've lost your number.

Addition

As you work with a buyer, you have an ideal opportunity to discover other areas of high impact where you can play a role.[2] Keep these in mind and do some investigation as you're on-site or working with the client remotely. It's usually premature to offer help for new projects early in your existing one, but it's appropriate about two-thirds into it. (Or more quickly if there is urgency or a critical window of opportunity.)

Addition demands two things:

First, the client must be acutely aware of the range of your capabilities, so that you're not pegged as a one-note wonder and can readily be accepted in a new role with a different type of project. So you may move from a compensation project to a succession planning project, or from a strategy formulation project to leadership coaching.

Second, you must raise the issue or respond to it if the client does. Don't be bashful. The more you have a trusting relationship, the smoother this should be. My experience is that about 30 percent of all repeat business is addition-based.

Transference

Transference becomes possible when you take your existing project to a new buyer. It means that your existing coaching or focus groups are embraced by peers of your buyer (or nonpeers who are buyers in their own right).

When presenting to the senior management group of a large financial institution in Boston, I was introduced to the visiting executive vice president of European operations, based in Paris. I invited him to attend my meeting, along with his domestic peers. He accepted, realized that his colleagues loved the results and that the processes applied equally well to him, and engaged me to replicate the work with him.

Combining some referral techniques, ask your buyer whom you should be speaking to within the organization. Introduce yourself to senior people in other areas. Learn the hierarchy and organization chart. Your restructuring project or telemarketing techniques will tend to travel quite well internally.

Transference accounts for perhaps 20 percent of all repeat business.

Exploration

Exploration entails the provision of different offerings from your current project to new buyers within the organization. It accounts for only 10 percent of repeat business, but can work wonderfully if you're alert for it.

Keep your eyes and ears open, and find a way to be introduced to new buyers with new needs, using a combination of the techniques for addition and transference. Ideally, involve your current buyer to learn about political and cultural realities in the new areas, and, you can hope, gain an introduction.

Repeat business is more nuanced and subtle than you may think, but this four-part approach will help you set an ideal strategy during the disengagement process.

Creating Testimonials and References

A senior vice president at Revlon once happily agreed to provide me with a testimonial. It never arrived. I followed up. The cycle continued: promised, didn't arrive, followed up, promised, ad nauseam.

On a follow-up visit, I asked his assistant for a piece of his stationery. I printed up a testimonial that would make my mother blush, forged his name, and sent it to him. "If you don't provide me with the testimonial you promised," I assured him, "I'm going with this one."

A few days later I had my (legitimate) testimonial.

Some of you (all right, *most of you*) are not that aggressive, but you get the idea. You can't convince a prospect or pay the mortgage with a promise. Part of disengagement is to ensure that you maximize the residual benefits of the successful project—call these your peripheral benefits, beyond the fee, learning, and so forth.

Here are some techniques to guarantee your success is such matters.

Prepare the Buyer

As noted earlier, let the buyer know you'll be asking well in advance. When it is so far in advance the buyer will usually absently agree, figuring there is plenty of time to think about it. So document it in writing along the way:

> By the way, thanks so much for agreeing to provide a testimonial and references as the project progresses. I'll be raising this again in about 45 days.

Always Provide Options

The choice of "yeses" is very important here. Ask the buyer if he or she would be willing to:

- Serve as a reference.
- Provide a written testimonial.
- Provide an endorsement for a book or other publication.
- Provide a video testimonial.

- Co-author an article.
- Provide referrals.

This menu approach will raise your chances of getting *something* by at least 50 percent, and often results in your acquiring several of the items on the list. Personal preferences or company policies may prohibit some, so keep your options open.

Seek People Other Than Your Buyer

Testimonials and references can be highly effective from nonbuyers if they are intimately familiar with your work and the results. A salesperson dealing with major customers explaining how much easier it is to close business and a call center agent describing your help in creating sales out of complaints are highly valuable sources.

Use Multimedia

There are few testimonials as effective as brief (30- to 60-second) videos, extemporaneous and not staged, where a client is describing how powerful your results are and how professional your approaches have been. You can do this with a modest camera, you don't need a polished product for this, and you can even ask clients to shoot it themselves and simply forward the file.

For shy clients, an off-camera interviewer works very well.

Provide Examples of What You Need

Send your client prior testimonials so that precedents are set. Explain why they are useful (e.g., specific examples, on company letterhead), and how they can be generic and not disclose confidential information (e.g., "helped our efforts tremendously").

Guarantee Nonabuse

Tell your client that you will only use his or her name as a reference with a buyer (peer) and only at the proposal stage. The client will never be contacted by lower-level people or screeners. Have sufficient references so that you can alternate, and let clients know they won't be called more than once a quarter at most.

For a written testimonial, explain where and how it will be used. If you're going to put it on a web site, the client might not expect it to also be in a promotional piece unless you specify. Provide reasonable guarantees and comfort so that you can stay out of the legal department if at all possible.

> ### The Gospel
>
> If you've done a great job for your buyer and have maintained a trusting relationship, you should expect continuing support as long as you provide optional ways to provide that support.

If Requested, Write It Yourself with Options

Some clients will say, "Put something together and run it by me." When that happens, never provide a "take it or leave it" ultimatum. Provide three or four different versions of the testimonial and let the client choose or combine. I prefer not to do this unless asked (I'd rather provide others' testimonials, as noted earlier), but when asked I want to maximize my chances of success.[3]

With References, Stipulate What's Expected

Help the client understand that he or she is expected to merely state:

- You worked with the client on a project or projects.
- Your work was very well received.
- The client's opinion of the working relationship.
- How well conditions, promises, and terms were met.

There is no expectation that the client would reveal confidential matters or proprietary information. If the projects differ, the client can merely attest to your character and work ethic.

In athletics, the best performers finish and follow through. They continue their swing, align their bodies, maximize their leaps, anticipate the next action. The same kind of all-star potential exists here.

Don't merely complete a project and pat yourself on the back. Consider disengagement to be the juncture that leads to new engagements, internally or externally. Make sure that you have the discipline and confidence to follow through with the proper actions, and ensure that you have the knowledge to have anticipated them and set up the correct expectations.

You're not looking for a favor. You're looking for ways to most expeditiously help others with your value, to leverage your success into their success.

Long-Term Leverage

The final aspect of disengaging, which has heretofore been rather short-term in focus, is to think of the longer term. What leverage can be created by this successful engagement over the long haul (beyond the lasting impact of what's been discussed)?

The first and easiest advantage would be the client organization name on your client list. Ordinarily, you may use a client organization name, citing it as a client, as long as you have not been prohibited from doing so. Many organizations do not allow their names to be used, but that information will usually be included in a nondisclosure statement or as feedback at proposal time. (My habit is not to inquire. I simply assume I can use it unless directed otherwise.)

However, you may *not* automatically use the client's logo, which is proprietary. You need express written permission to do that. So, although it looks great to have that Exxon or Boeing or McDonald's logo on your web site or letterhead, the legal departments of those entities might not be so jubilant about your use of their property. Always seek permission. Sometimes your buyer will tell you right off the bat that it's never allowed.

A brief digression here on my definition of *client*, since I've found what I consider the obvious isn't always so. A client pays you. I do not consider the beneficiary of pro bono work to be a client unless that entity has paid for some other work at some point.[4] A client transaction has a quid pro quo: value to the client and equitable compensation for the consultant.

But even there I have some reservations. I don't consider a barter deal to be a client. If you do business with American Airlines in exchange for free tickets, calling the airline a client would be a problem for me. I know you may consider it equitable compensation, but my belief is that a client thinks enough of your value to find the money to pay you for it. Otherwise you could consider the government your client, since you spend a good part of your year working to support it in acknowledgment of services rendered, such as defending the coasts. You get the idea.

Don't fudge the facts. Clients pay. In specie.

The Gospel

Whether clients are currently active or not, they have still been clients. This is one business where a past client, no longer active, may simply indicate an extremely happy client.

Second on the long-term leverage list is keeping track of key contacts and their movement. You'll find some important dynamics evolving:

- Former nonbuyers have become buyers.
- Former buyers have become more powerful buyers.
- Former buyers have moved to new organizations.

- Buyers from other clients have moved to this organization.
- Needs develop similar to ones you once addressed.

You can track these changes and evolutions by:

- Dropping notes and holiday cards to all contacts periodically.
- Using Google Alerts.
- Reading the trade press.
- Attending industry and professional conventions and conferences.
- Subscribing to house organs.

This kind of movement creates ample opportunities for you to reengage with old buyers and provide logical premises for meeting with new ones. These techniques are far better than cold calls and stand a much higher chance of leading to business. Bear in mind that, despite your best work, key buyers leave and your memory leaves with them in many cases. Hence, that final bullet point in the first category: Return to remind new buyers that they don't need to reinvent the wheel—you invented it for them two years ago.

Third, develop case studies from your experiences at the client. These can be used in your collateral material, or speeches, or interviews, or formal position papers and articles. There are three types:

1. Blind case studies, since you don't have permission to use the client's name or particulars due to confidentiality. That's fine, and you can often make an amalgam of several. "In a major, international financial institution. . . ."

2. Gain the client's permission to use a case study that shines favorably on the client. This will almost always require the legal department's imprimatur, but it's worth waiting for. You often see these in professional journals.

3. Co-author a lengthy case study with your buyer or other client executive. That often plays nicely to the ego of the buyer, will gain you a solid hearing at respected publications (such as *Harvard Business Review*), and creates a powerful statement.

You should be creating a dozen blind case studies a year, and several named examples, as well. Remember, you don't get if you don't ask.

Fourth, develop your model and methodology. I'm constantly surprised by how stupid I was two weeks ago.

Every client is a personal lab that allows you to practice your craft, modify it as needed, and experiment with new approaches. Since you're not dealing with hazardous materials or new forms of life, your experiments are tame but vital to your growth.

- Can you shorten your implementation time?
- Do you need more strategic or tactical tools?
- Can you move into additional markets or industries?
- Can you move more of the labor to the client?
- Can you work better remotely?

You do your best with every client, but your best has to constantly get better! (Otherwise, you're in the success trap.) Evaluate every engagement after you leave to determine what you've learned and how to institutionalize it into your model in the future, and what didn't go as planned and how to better anticipate it in the future.

As your career progresses and you say to a prospective buyer, "I've worked with Mercedes-Benz, JPMorgan Chase, the Federal Reserve, General Electric, Hewlett-Packard . . ." and you take a breath at that point, the prospect is likely to simply respond, "That's fine. Let's talk about our operation." In other words, you don't need further credentials, testimonial, or references. Just those names make the difference.

Until you reach that point, use the techniques in this chapter. Once you do reach that point, continue to use them economically, as I've indicated in the preceding paragraph.

All client engagements come to an end. Otherwise, instead of a consulting relationship, you'd have a codependency and you'd be paying someone else to get out of it!

Notes

1. If this client came to you by way of referral, be sure to point that out in this sentence!
2. Note that I never talk solely of "problems to be solved" since the best clients are best served by exploiting opportunity and raising the bar.
3. I do this all the time when I endorse books, and my testimonial is almost always chosen for the jacket because I've provided the author and/or publisher with options from which to choose or to be combined. No one else does.
4. And never provide *pro bono* work for a for-profit organization.

Acts of the Apostles

Implementing Consulting Methodologies

How to improve the client's condition.
First, you may have to do some harm.

Chapter 10

Interpersonal Methodologies
People First

Coaching

In this section I'm faced with the daunting task of showing you around the waterfront without allowing detailed inspection of the boats!

I've allocated three chapters to the methodologies of consulting, because the book's mission is to cover all aspects of consulting: entry, marketing, proposals, implementation, ethics, life balance, and so forth. So what follows is an oxymoronic "detailed overview." Buckle your seat belts.[1]

Coaching is something that all consultants have always done. When you are implementing a project, you are virtually always helping your buyer and others in the actions and behaviors required for success. Any consultant on retainer is a coach, perforce. The movement in the past decade to set coaching aside as some sort of specialty is bizarre. The best coaches are those who understand organizational dynamics, change management, team building, and so forth. Most coaches, with their degrees and certifications from so-called coaching universities, have a very limited view of the organizational universe, sort of like driving a car through one of those peepholes in the hotel room door.

Besides, who certifies the certifiers?

Coaching is not mentoring, the latter being a reactive, sounding board type of relationship. Coaching is assertive and proactive.

You can coach individuals or teams, but it's a distinction with little difference since teams comprise individuals.

The key thing to immediately sort out is whether your buyer is also your client. Your buyer is that person authorizing a check for your value. The client is that person or company whose condition you're trying to improve. Thus, the buyer may hire you for personal help or to help a subordinate.

If the latter, immediately establish which of these two options obtains:

1. The coaching is completely confidential between client and coach, and the buyer is merely paying the fee and will benefit from the success of the client.

2. The coaching is to involve the buyer in terms of progress and feedback, and is not confidential solely between coach and client.

Once you do that, make sure all three parties are crystal clear on the rules of engagement. In the first situation, you must deny any buyer's request about specifics or discussions. In the second, you must caution the client that what is discussed will be shared with the buyer.

Digression

My habit in all organizations when someone says "I'd like to tell you something in confidence" is this: "Before you do, be aware that I will determine whether the matter materially affects the well-being of my client, and I reserve the right to inform my client if I deem it necessary. Do you still want to tell me?" I would also suggest that there are no true secrets in any organization once two people know something.

The proper way to set up a coaching assignment, once you've identified buyer and client, is:

- Establish behavioral objectives; for example, run meetings on time with preestablished agendas, allowing participants to speak freely, and summarize the next steps before adjourning.

- Create metrics for success; for example, meeting agendas will focus on results, not tasks, and will be distributed at least 48 hours in advance.

- Establish the value of meeting the objectives; for example, meeting duration and frequency will decline by at least 20 percent, and complaints from participants will cease.

See what we have? Conceptual agreement!
Then establish your methodologies, which can include:

- Observation and shadowing, where you participate in the daily schedule.
- Initiation of 360-degree assessments, where you interview peers, subordinates, superiors, customers, and others, looking for facts and patterns.
- Rehearsals and role-playing of evaluations, presentations, and so on.
- Observation and feedback of specific events, such as sales calls, board meetings, or even taped situations that you can't attend.

The Gospel

Your goal is to improve the client's condition within a reasonable time frame and so that the client can sustain the improvement. Disengagement is even more important in coaching assignments so that you don't create codependency.

Note: I'm not a big believer in random tests and feedback. Even most validated tests have their roots in identifying aberrant behavior, not in distinguishing among healthy behaviors. There are too many tests that place labels on people. (She's a high 5, compulsive opportunist, with green overtones, a real HCOG.) Unfortunately, there are too many inexpensive and inaccurate tests that are merely meant to enhance coaches' revenue streams. Caveat emptor.

Here are eight things you need for successful coaching:

1. Clear support from the buyer.
2. Positive chemistry with the client.
3. Reasonable expectations for improvement over a reasonable time frame.
4. Access to the conditions and situations that are the keys for improvement.
5. Candid and frequent debriefings and feedback.
6. Specific growth suggestions (as opposed to "Be more of a team player").

7. Rapid responsiveness on both sides.

8. Identified and respected disengagement.

As a coach you are *never* a therapist (even if you have the credentials and training). Don't become immersed in personal issues (life coaches rarely have any credential other than that so-called university certification).[2] Focus on these critical elements:

- Observe behavior; do not guess at motive.
- Look for examples in the environment, not hearsay.
- You change behavior through appeals to enlightened self-interest, not coercion.

Facilitating

The fundamental and key aspect of facilitation is agreeing with the client as to whether you are providing intellectual capital.

When I was talking to the CEO of a $1.5 billion company about helping to run a strategy retreat, one of his first questions was: "Will you provide intellectual capital?" I was happy to hear it.

Let's define facilitation for our purposes here:

Facilitation is the act of organizing and conducting a meeting with the intent of reaching the objectives for the meeting, including next steps, dates, times, and accountabilities.

That meeting may be formal or informal, about tactical matters (the need to create better communication between field reps and marketing) or strategic matters (what markets have the highest expansion potential). As a consultant, you are the ideal person to perform this function, since you are (or should be) impartial, familiar with best practices, an expert at the process of facilitation, and trusted.

There are two conditions that may prevail in terms of intellectual capital:

1. You are simply expected to run the meeting; ensure that everyone is heard (see step 5, rules of engagement, in the next list); organize the inputs and suggestions; and summarize agreements and remaining disagreements. You can do this by knowing the *process* of facilitation, and need know nothing about the *content* of the issues or about the client. This is the least valuable form of facilitation.

2. You perform the preceding duties but also provide your own insights on the validity of the suggestions, what you've seen work or not work elsewhere, risks that haven't been discussed, and so on. You are an active member of the conversation. You need be conversant, not expert, in the client's issues. This is the most valuable form of facilitation.

You may be facilitating in the course of a larger project, or simply be engaged for one purpose alone. In either case, make sure your client (and, eventually, the participants) are agreed on your role. If it's the first condition and you seek to insert your own suggestions, there will be friction. If it's the second and you merely expedite the discussion, people will feel that you have little value. You should charge far more for the second, so make sure you and the buyer agree, and then you explain your precise role under the rules of engagement for the session.

The Gospel

Facilitation should involve debate, disagreement, and even argument. One of my clients called this "putting the dead rat on the table." That's inelegant, but also quite apt.

Here are nine steps for excellent facilitation:

1. Agreement with your buyer as to objectives for the session (what are the desired outcomes) and your role, as discussed earlier.

2. An agenda circulated in advance of the meeting with the objectives for results, which may be one item or several.

3. A proper facility, with refreshments, sufficient room, and the required audio/video aids.

4. Agreement on time frames, not to allow disturbances or interruptions, no use of cell phones or checking of e-mail, enforced break times (you can't run back to your office).

5. Rules of engagement:
   - Your own role.
   - Everyone will be heard, with no interrupting, but no speeches.
   - Focus on facts, not personalities. Observed evidence and facts are required.
   - What the end result will look like: next steps, accountabilities.

- If a recording is being made, how it will be used. (I always advise against recording because it dampens participation. Write things on easels where everyone can see them.)
- How much time you intend to devote to varying issues or phases (to prevent circular or unending conversations).
- What constitutes final decision:
  - Leader will listen to debate and decide.
  - Group will decide based on consensus. (Consensus is something you can live with, not something you'd die for.)

6. Handle any questions and then begin.
7. Enforce time frames assertively.
8. Number or otherwise organize notes for collation later.
9. Summarize agreements and next steps.

Many clients will provide an administrative person to collate the notes and easel sheets or transcribe the recordings. You should always request that, since it hugely reduces your labor intensity.

Here are some tips for the most common facilitating challenges:

- The leader takes charge. You must reach prior agreement with the hierarchical leader or leaders that they are peers in the room as far as interactions are concerned. You may need to interrupt and say, "Tom, as I understand it, this is your point. Let's hear how others react to it."
- If people won't let go of an issue, ask the group, "It seems as if Lisa and Laura are the only two who believe we should go left. Am I right that the other 10 of you want to go right?" *You are after consensus, not unanimity.*
- If no one wants to accept accountability for certain steps, turn to the group and ask, "Who would be most effective in accomplishing this?" Alternatively, you can then ask the hierarchical leader, "Perhaps you should choose someone. Who's the best choice?"
- If time keeps running short, separate the issues into phases or sub-decisions and tell the group you've allocated 15 minutes for each. Prolonged discussions seldom increase the quality of the decision, and are usually just procrastination. Enforce the time frames: "Another 15 minutes is not going to change things."

Facilitation requires an absolute objectivity on your part, keeping the client's best interests in mind, not the interests of a faction or a bloc. Sometimes you'll find someone you personally dislike, or with horrible interpersonal skills, to be absolutely right! You're the judge, not the jury.

Keep the court in order, rule when someone is out of order, but help them to reach a well-considered and fair verdict.

Conflict Resolution

In my experience, on an organizational level, 98 percent of conflict is over one of two things: objectives or alternatives. There are the few occasions when there are interpersonal problems, behavioral disorders, and bad chemistry.

But the *causes* of most conflict in the workplace that you'll be called on to resolve (since you're there as neither psychologist nor therapist) are as follows.

Objectives

People are in legitimate disagreement over the destination, the output, the goals, or the results. The sales and human resources staffs and leadership are at odds over the degree to which salespeople should be rewarded on performance no matter how poorly the rest of the salaried staff is paid in an off year. Executives disagree on whether to reinvest in the business or pay larger bonuses.

Alternatives

People are in legitimate disagreement over the route to the destination. They agree with the goals and intended output, but not the methods. Senior management disagrees on whether to meet expansion goals by putting resources into Europe or Asia. Call center management is divided on the type of technology needed to put customer information on the screens of service representatives.

Note that by "legitimate" I'm excluding the political and turf battles that you'll inevitably find. That's because when you follow the techniques I'll outline, you force your client's people to deal with observable behavior and evidence in the environment.

The Gospel

Conflict over the best interests of the organization is common, healthy, and desirable. Never try to eliminate it. Resolve it so that positive results ensue.

Conflict over Objectives

This type of conflict is identified by argument and debate about what will result and the importance of the results—about what is to be done.

Typical areas of conflict for a small business would be:

- Size of the company
- Ownership and succession
- Adding products and services
- Expansion

Typical areas of conflict over objectives in nonprofits include:

- Size and use of volunteers
- Earned versus unearned income percentages in income
- Merging with other groups
- Role in the community

Typical areas of conflict over objectives in large organizations are:

- Acquisition of appropriate technology
- Customer service levels
- Intent of incentive and merit pay plans
- Branding and positioning

Here are six steps to deal with conflict over objectives:

1. Establish who owns the decision and will be the final decision maker. This is almost always a person, not a committee. This cannot be a consensus or group decision.
2. Gather the key stakeholders and contributors to the decision as a group.
3. Try to gain agreement on the "musts" that are to be met. What absolutely has to be accomplished to represent success?
4. Seek compromise where possible.
5. Work with people individually after the meeting if necessary to create further compromise without egos at stake as they are in a meeting.
6. Allow the decision owner to make the final decision.

Conflict over Alternatives

This type of conflict is identified by people arguing about how to do things. Typical areas of conflict for a small business would be:

- Advertising alternatives
- Compensation practices and options
- Which products and services to perpetuate, terminate, and/or add
- Choosing funding sources

Typical areas of conflict over alternatives in nonprofits include:

- Candidates for the board and advisory committees
- Ways to solicit donations, subscriptions, and memberships
- Numbers of events to support, produce, and create
- Use of volunteers' time

Typical areas of conflict over alternatives in large organizations are:

- Promotions and assignments
- Direct and indirect sales techniques
- Methods to best commercialize product development and R&D
- Expansion and growth options

Here are six steps to deal with conflict over alternatives:

1. Establish who owns the decision and will be the final decision maker. This is almost always a person, not a committee. This cannot be a consensus or group decision.
2. Assemble the key stakeholders and reconfirm agreement over the goals and objectives (which are not the conflict in this case).
3. List the alternatives with the advantages and risks (*all* options will have attendant risks), and determine if any clearly outscore others when looked at objectively.
4. Seek to combine and compromise on the alternatives to capture the best traits and avoid the worst traits of each.
5. Where necessary, create a new alternative that everyone can live with.
6. Allow the decision owner to make the final decision.

In the case of conflict over alternatives, the decision owner can some-times allow the group to reach a consensus conclusion and implement it, since the goals or the organization are not in danger—everyone agrees with the pre-sumed intent and outcome. But where conflict is over the objectives—where individuals may not have congruent goals with the organization—that decision can never be made by the group.

This simple system will force people to objectively and rationally study benefits, risks, facts, and evidence. Any attempts to railroad or force a decision will become clearly transparent.

Obviously, you're acting as a facilitator here when a group is involved, so you can determine whether your intellectual capital is appropriate to include. The biggest mistake consultants make in this area is to chalk up every conflict to personality problems. Don't do that.

Negotiating

Ideally, negotiating should produce two happy people (or sides, or factions, or blocs). Of course it seldom does, because people don't understand the process.

The absolute key in negotiating is to identify "musts" and differentiate them from "wants," and never to confuse the two. The former are to be pre-served, and the latter are subject to compromise.

Musts

A "must" has three characteristics:

1. *Critical to the success of your mission or decision.* If it's not achieved or protected, you will fail. Obviously, very few items are actually musts if you abide by this definition. Taking a certain route to get to the theater may be nice, but it's hardly critical in terms of enjoy-ing the show, unless other routes will not get you there in time.

2. *Measurable by all parties.* This is important to acknowledge and to recognize whether it exists and/or its conditions have been met. "I have to feel happy" or "People will seem more confident" is not a measurable goal, unless you specify the means (e.g., fewer items that require senior management approval).

3. *Realistic.* It may be critical for you to sing at an event if you're play-ing the lead in *South Pacific* or *Rent,* and we can certainly measure

tone and memory of lyrics, but if you don't have the voice, then the expectation is unrealistic.

Wants

A "want" is something not critical, but desirable. Wants vary in importance.

- *Highly important wants are usually the inverse of musts.* For example, if the must is "not to spend more than \$10,000," the want may be "to spend as little as possible." If the must is "available in two weeks," then the want is "available as soon as possible," *unless* having it sooner is a burden, not an advantage (e.g., space isn't ready—did you ever land at Chicago's O'Hare Airport early, when you have to sit on the plane in the penalty box because your gate is still occupied?).
- *Moderate wants are desirable, relevant elements.* You may choose to also enhance your repute, or improve aesthetics, or attract more talent to the firm. Note that wants do not have to be measurable.
- *Low-importance wants are strictly peripheral,* and might mean that you also meet some interesting people or learn a new skill.[3]

I think you can now see the method in my method. You want to help both parties to preserve their musts while sacrificing or even abandoning certain wants. The abandonment is best at low-level importance, the compromise or adjustments best at middle-level importance, and the preservation of interests best at high levels of importance.

But even highly rated wants can be sacrificed to preserve musts.

The Gospel

Your role as a consultant is often to help others negotiate successfully, and sometimes to negotiate for yourself successfully!

On some occasions you may be negotiating with people to help speed along the implementation of your project, because even the clout of your buyer wouldn't help, and the people who are resisting have legitimate opposing interests. On other occasions, you may be called on to assist in what seems like intractable opposition.

(Note that facilitation, conflict resolution, and negotiation all overlap significantly on many occasions. That's why you need to focus on results and not on any one particular methodology. Never be a one-trick pony.)

Successful negotiation methodology usually entails some combination of the eight steps in this approach:

1. Determine who the decision makers are and involve them actively in the process. It's frustrating and time consuming to use people who are middlemen and can't commit to a course of action themselves.

2. Talk to both parties independently and understand clearly their musts and wants. They probably aren't accustomed to thinking or articulating in this manner, so help with the definitions and categorization. There should always be relatively few musts.

3. Help to sort out high-, medium-, and low-importance wants.

4. Bring both parties together and facilitate the discussion. Create the ground rules and help maintain order. Contribute your own intellectual capital but *never* take sides. (If you are one of the parties trying to get your project implemented, focus on the other side's musts and high-importance wants.)

5. Plan to spend several meetings if necessary. Keep each one of them brief, because after 60 to 90 minutes fatigue will affect judgment and patience.

6. Seek to combine musts and high-importance wants whenever possible.

7. If the two sides are unable to reach compromises, point out your own suggestions about how to compromise, without taking sides. If that fails, point out the adverse consequences for both parties if they fail to reach agreement and an approach is forced on them (e.g., senior management wearies of the delays, and simply imposes an alternative everyone hates and that undermines all musts).

8. When compromise is reached, put it in writing, and include the accountabilities of all key stakeholders to maintain the compromises necessary for success.

Negotiation is a daily informal aspect of all organizations ("If you get the coffee, I'll make the copies") and is healthy when formally undertaken to resolve impasses. It tends to produce far greater commitment to the new course of action, however imperfect, than mere coercion (hierarchical clout), which at best creates compliance, which is usually temporary and observed only in the breach.

Negotiating parties should be peers, or at least see themselves as peers for the purposes of the negotiation. Never assume one side is damaged just because they are in disagreement. People will follow their own self-interests, which are not necessarily in opposition to others' or the organization's, but may become so.

In that case, don't get into a fight about it.
Negotiate.

Skills Development

In many cases you'll be called upon to improve the skills of client people in groups (not by coaching as discussed earlier). This is typically called training.[4] The writer Maya Angelou said once, "You train animals; you educate people." There is a tendency among schoolteachers today to turn their noses up at teaching, and call themselves "educators." There is a common and ridiculous rubric in the training profession going back decades that there are somehow four levels[5] of training measurement, when, in fact, the only thing that really matters is results.

No matter what you call it, the results had better be improved performance. And, no matter what, training is a noble pursuit and profession. That's because its legitimate intent should be the same as a consultant's: to improve the client's condition.

In this case, the methodology for that improvement is via the acquisition of skills. Note that you can train people in new skills, but not in behaviors. You can coach people for behavior modification to a relatively limited degree (e.g., a shy and retiring, nonassertive person is not going to be become an aggressive salesperson 40 hours a week—the change is too stressful), but you can train people in skills improvement in a major way.

World War II was a pivotal point in training improvement, because trainers had to help millions of workers produce equipment and munitions on a large scale; they had to train large numbers of women in the workforce for the first time; and they had to train millions of new recruits who were primarily from agrarian, rural roots. (Most had never traveled more than 50 miles from home in 1941.)

Postwar business adapted many of the principles that worked so well to improve human performance in organizations. The training profession grew, as did separate, discrete training firms. As consultants, we have the option of providing training ourselves or, recognizing the need, employing others to do so via subcontracting or referrals.

To place training in context, the diagram shown in Figure 10.1 may be helpful.

There are three components to most jobs:

1. *The physical capabilities required,* which can often be compensated for in the form of automation or mechanized aids. A bank teller needs to move money across a counter, a reporter needs to use a keyboard, and an airplane pilot needs to use a throttle and stick.

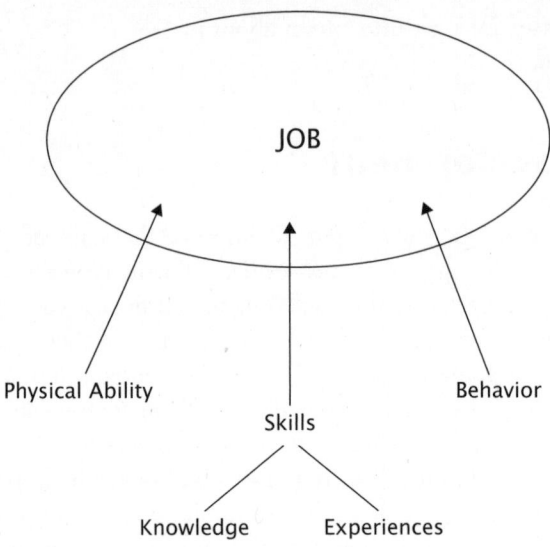

FIGURE 10.1 Job Components

2. *The appropriate skills*, such as making change and doing math for our bank teller, grammar and questioning for our reporter, and navigation for our pilot.

3. *The requisite behaviors.* The teller must have a high degree of patience for the repetitive; the reporter must have high assertiveness to get answers from politicians; and the pilot must remain calm under pressure when there is bad weather or a mechanical malfunction.

All three components are vital for success, and change according to the job. That's why mindlessly making the top salesperson the sales manager or the best photographer the photo editor is ridiculous, even though it is happening as you read this. The skills and behaviors change as one moves up the hierarchy.

The Gospel

Past performance is not a reliable indicator of future performance. People must be evaluated against the future skills and behavior required.

Note that you can't train people in calmness or patience or assertiveness. Training is different from coaching. Bob Mager, one of the finest authorities on training and development I've ever met, uses a classic example: "Can the employee do the job if the employee's life depended on it?" If the answer is no, the person can't do it, then you have a training/skills problem. If the answer is yes, under those conditions the person could do it, then you have a behavior/attitude problem.

Here are four steps that will help you employ appropriate and effective training when needed:

1. Ensure that you have an issue that can be remediated or improved by the acquisition of new skills, the improvement of existing skills, or the introduction of new experiences.

2. Determine what the outcomes should be and what you and the client will measure to determine the efficacy of the training.

3. Create the briefest program possible (or acquire it by using other resources) that combines these elements:

   • What the trainees are to learn (content) through discussion, demonstration, and/or experiences.

   • Why it is important to acquire these skills (self-interest and commitment) and how they contribute to the organization.

   • How it is to be done, with specific techniques, application, support, and so on (including technological aids as appropriate).

   • Examples of the proper results.

   • Practice in applying the skills on case studies, role-playing, tests, low-threat opportunities, and so on.

   • Feedback on performance with advice on further improvement.

   • Application on the job itself, with ongoing feedback from superiors, peers, trainers, and so forth, until mastered.

4. Evaluate the results by asking superiors, customers, and other interested parties for evidence of performance after training compared to before training.

You may choose not to seek to include training as a personal delivery option (do you have the skills and behaviors to do it?) since it can be highly labor intensive. But on a consulting basis, keep in mind the strategic relationship depicted in Figure 10.2, regardless of whether you are personally involved in execution.

The secret to effective training is to work *backwards* from the organization's business requirements. Never indulge in training for training's sake, or because it seems like it's beneficial in and of itself. Business and industry typically spend over $60 billion on training annually, and most of it is unmeasured with no return on investment (ROI) calculations.

Don't waste your client's money or your time.

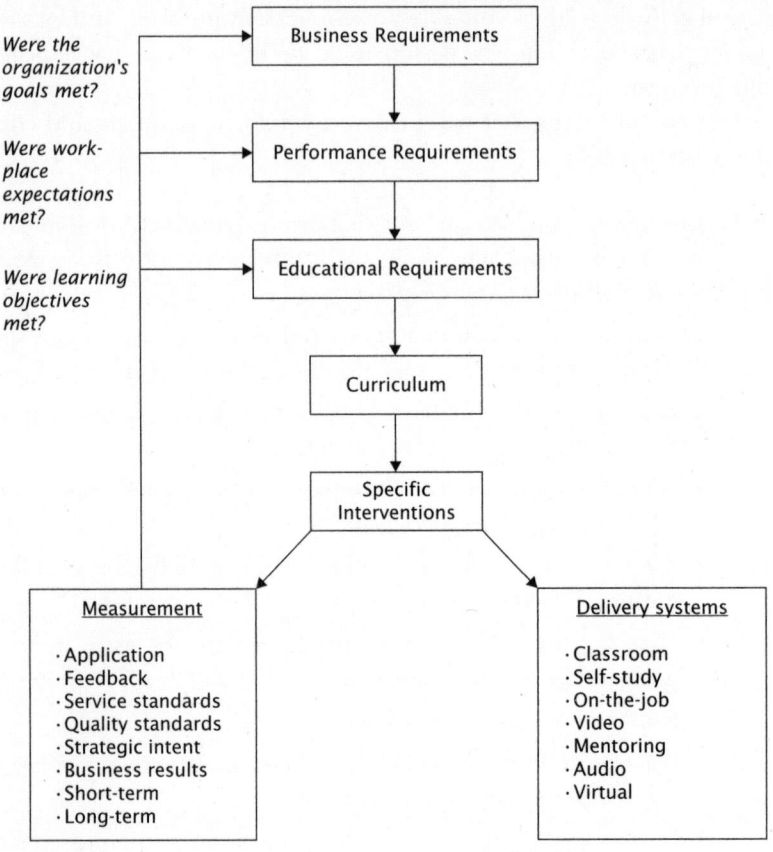

FIGURE 10.2 Organizational Education Tied to Strategic Business Goals

Notes

1. For book-length, in-depth learning, try my books: *Process Consulting* and *Organizational Consulting*, both from John Wiley & Sons. From IDG/Macmillan: *The Unofficial Guide to Power Management.* You can find them all on my web site, as well. Finally, see my *Million Dollar Coaching* from McGraw-Hill.

2. An actual Internet ad offered "Life Coaching Certification in One Day" for $495.

3. For an excellent discussion of this process, see *The New Rational Manager*, by Chuck Kepner and Benjamin Tregoe (Princeton Research Press, 1997).

4. A widespread neologism today is to refer to "a training." You can have a training session, or workshop, or seminar, but "I'm having a training" is like saying "I'm going for a running."

5. Donald Kirkpatrick, an academic, first wrote about these ideas in 1959.

11

Teams and Groups
No One Is an Island

Leadership

We develop individual skills, as covered in the prior chapter, in order to enable people to work better together, which is the subject of this chapter. One plus one must equal 164 in organizational life. That is, the whole had better be *way* better than the sum of the parts.

If that's not true, there is no need for supervisory or management positions at all, because they would not be adding value. Unfortunately, in many organizations that is the case, and it's our job to fix it or prevent it.

When people ask me (as they have 765,000 times over the years), "What is the greatest single influence on organizational performance?" I always choose the same factor: leadership.

The Gospel

Leaders are always sending two concurrent messages when they act. The first is the content of their decision or plan. The second is the process by which they have made it and are communicating it. The latter is usually more important than the former in terms of lasting implications.

What would you say the most desired trait in a leader is if you were to survey subordinates? Would it be assertiveness, or courage, or honesty, or receptivity, or decisiveness, or inclusion?

What people have most consistently told me is: consistency.

Let me put two rubrics to rest right here:

1. *Leaders are made, not born.* While some people may possess behaviors and experiences that give them an advantage (see Figure 10.1 in the preceding chapter on the three elements of a job), most people can acquire the skills and competencies necessary to be a good leader or even a great one. The truly heroic examples (e.g., Lee Iacocca during the Chrysler years, Lou Gerstner at IBM's resurgence, P. Roy Vagelos leading Merck to five years of "America's Most Admired Company" in the *Fortune* magazine polls, Jack Welch running what really were 12 separate companies at General Electric) rely on the right time, right place, and right temperament. But every day, millions of leaders globally are doing fine jobs as they continue to learn how to do so.[1]

2. *There is no perfect leadership style.* The best leaders adjust to the situation, other performers, degree of urgency, and so forth. They are not locked into a doctrinaire set of behaviors. They provide consistency in how they treat others and react and plan, but that consistency is within a finite set of behaviors, not produced by rigid and narrow thinking.[2]

As a consultant (and probably often acting as a coach), never begin by assuming the leader is damaged or at fault, no matter what level of leadership you're engaged with, from front line to executive suite. Don't immediately accept the complaints and accusations of others, who may simply be seeking an obvious target for their own frustrations and poor results. It's easy to point at the guy on the horse.

Here are three keys for working on leadership issues:

1. *Leaders must take account of the following factors in making decisions and involving others:*
    - Is the decision important? Do various outcomes have significantly different results, or will any result be equally acceptable? If the decision is important, the leader must stay involved. If not, it can be immediately delegated.
    - Is there enough information to act unilaterally? If so, independent action is fine. If not, independent action is folly, and other inputs are necessary.
    - Is commitment required, or is compliance sufficient? Do people have to buy into the decision in order for it to be supported—which

demands their involvement—or will they act as you intend with simply a directive, requiring no involvement?

- Will people probably agree on the alternative and will they probably agree on the objective? (See "Conflict Resolution" in Chapter 10.) To what degree does this require formal reconciliation or merely informal support?

Thus, leaders may sometimes act independently and authoritatively, and sometimes collaboratively and collegially. They may sometimes control the decision and sometimes delegate it to an individual or a group. The determining factors should be importance, sufficiency of information, need for commitment, and alignment over objectives and alternatives.

2. *Time is a critical issue that is usually apparent, but not always supported.*

The more you involve others, despite the salutary effects of doing so, the more time is required. Individual meetings and interviews take more time than independent decisions, and interviews that require full disclosure of the issues take even longer. Similarly, group meetings and consensus building require significant time investments.

The time invested makes sense when information is scarce or commitment is required or there is disagreement about goals. But meetings and teams and committees make little sense in the absence of these needs, and simply prolong the process.

3. *Subordinate development is often neglected, unwisely, in leadership style choices.*

We'll discuss succession planning next. For now, understand that the more a leader makes independent and authoritative decisions, the less subordinates can learn about the issues and the processes of resolving them. The more that people are involved, the more you help to develop other leaders.

This, even when decisions can be made alone, if time is not urgent, it's sometimes better to choose to involve others for the purposes of skills development and requisite experiences. Remember: Leaders are made, not born. This is how you help to make them.

Leaders are the avatars in organizational life. People will tend to mimic their behavior because it usually represents successful behavior. When you coach and counsel leaders, you are maneuvering the key change agent in the organization, merely by dint of the leader's public actions. Warring leaders create warring silos. Collegial leaders create collegial organizations.

If you want to create rapid progress in any project, co-opt the formal and informal leaders, demonstrate their options for behavior, and create public examples of how everyone should behave. This may be your greatest leverage point in any consulting project.

Succession Planning

Years ago the Chase Manhattan Bank was a client, and in its headquarters there was a locked room to which, as the story went, only a handful of top executives had the key. In the room, photos of the bank's top talent were strategically arranged to indicate who would succeed whom, and what further development and grooming were necessary.

The name of the place was "Rockefeller's Room," after the CEO at the time.

Succession planning is one of the most vital elements of any organization's growth and prosperity, and one of the most misunderstood and poorly implemented elements. We noted earlier that past success is not a valid indicator of future success, so the ancient relic of "climbing the hierarchical ladder" makes zero sense. When you promote an excellent salesperson to the sales manager's job, you've probably ruined two positions in one stroke.

Are there any further questions why this is such a sensitive and pivotal discipline?

The Gospel

Promotion is not a reward for a job well done in the past. It is a strategic action for the future of the enterprise, attempting to match those behaviors required with those resident or being developed in top talent.

In some organizations, you can see the process done beautifully. At one point, if you weren't given an overseas assignment (considered vital to prepare for higher-level positions) in General Electric by age 40, you probably were not going to ascend much higher in the organization. When he was CEO, Jack Welch insisted on removing the bottom performers each year, even if they would be considered excellent performers in other companies. He wanted to make room for more talent. And when top people such as Larry Bossidy were passed over for higher positions, GE had the bench strength to withstand their departure. (Bossidy went on to superb leadership at Allied Signal and Honeywell, and published a highly regarded business book.)[3]

Figure 11.1 shows what you should be considering as a consultant involved in this area. In the chart, you can see that some people are ready now to move ahead. That means:

- They must be kept challenged and retained. They will probably be attractive to search firms and rivals.
- They should have significant input to their career development to meet personal needs. (See the next section.)

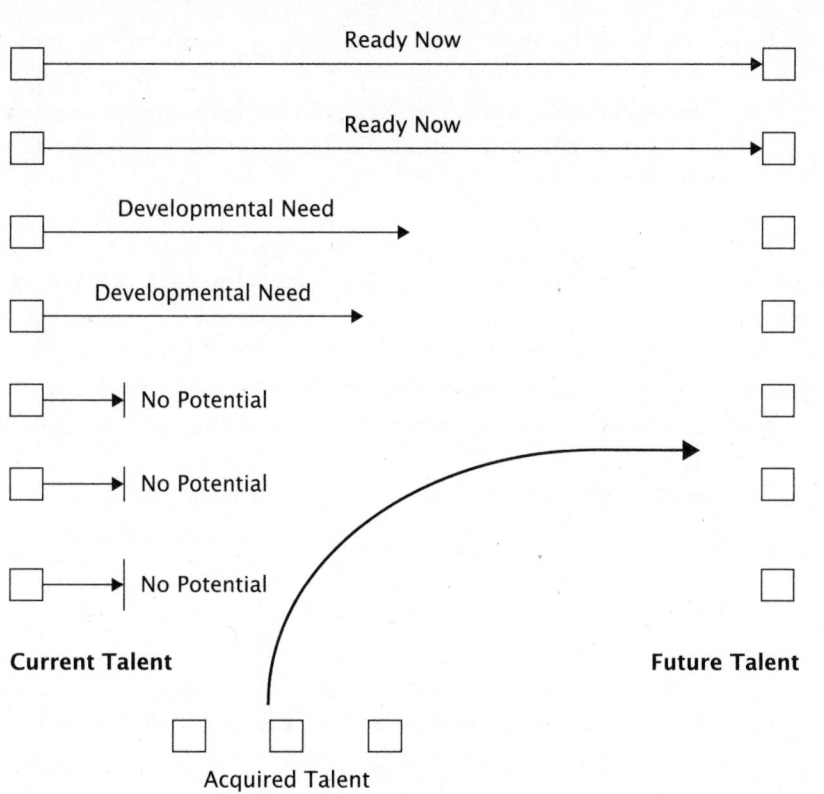

FIGURE 11.1 Succession Planning Scenario

Some people can be ready in the future but require additional development. That means:

- They must receive a choreographed developmental plan that combines the skills, experiences, and behavioral coaching required.
- They must be evaluated frequently and within fixed time frames to be moved to the category above or the one below.

Some people do not have the potential to move on. That means:

- They must be dealt with truthfully and respectfully.
- The organization should expect and welcome turnover among this cohort.
- They should never be promoted as a reward, or to prove inclusion, or for any other nonperformance factors.

Some people will be needed from outside the organization. That means:

- The organization should be recruiting well in advance of the projected needs, either with internal capability or through contracts with search firms.

Most organizations relegate succession planning to the human resources division or department, which is a cardinal sin. Succession planning is one of the most important strategic decisions that any enterprise engages in on a continuing basis, and is an executive accountability, never a staff function (and certainly never a function of an area with as little respect and clout as HR has in most organizations).

As a consultant, consider the following approaches to succession planning:

- Convince the buyer of the executive responsibility required.
- Assess *future* job needs in terms of skills, experiences, and behaviors.
- Establish the triage approach just described: high potential, probable potential, no potential, external potential.
- Insist that the development plan for each person in the succession planning process be the accountability of that person's direct superior, and hold that superior accountable in his or her evaluation review for the fulfillment of the subordinate's development plan.
- Install at least quarterly reviews of the progress systemically and of the individuals within it. (Many organizations feel that succession planning is like a fire extinguisher—you place it on the wall and it's there if you need it. But even these have tags indicating they are inspected and will work if needed!)

Finally, succession planning *must* be married to career development, and that's where we turn next.

Career Development

Career development should mean the following is taking place:

- Everyone is receiving training, coaching, and other options to become as good as they can be in their current job.
- Those with the potential are being developed for future jobs.
- People have the option to select programs for personal enrichment, even if not directly job related.

- The highest-potential people have development tracks that are in sync with their places in the succession planning process.

Building a succession system without integrating career development is like building a bridge by assigning two different contractors to each side, requiring that they use different materials, and forbidding them to talk to each other.

That bridge is not likely to meet in the middle.

This is the fundamental reason why you cannot entrust career development to the human resources department. It lacks the clout, the understanding of the organization's strategic intent, and the competence to create and manage the system. It can be a provider of relatively low-level options (e.g., training vendors), but when you see the HR people tasked to find coaches or develop leadership programs, you know that senior management has abdicated its responsibility. (And this is why I admonish you to never see the training or HR departments as your buyers and to resist being delegated to those dungeons. When you ask anyone in the organization where you can find the best and the brightest, no one is going to point you toward the HR offices.)

Here is where you can play a role in the creation and integration of career development in the categories listed earlier:

- *Everyone is receiving training, coaching, and other options to become as good as they can be in their current job.*

All jobs, from receptionist to president, should have results outputs that determine whether they are being done well and consistently with the organization's needs. Beware: 98 percent of job descriptions are about tasks and inputs. ("Incumbent will process phone orders and complete reports on deviations for the marketing manager.") Many people can do a better job if they have the proper tools, such as performance aids and tutorials. Others need a better understanding of how their job contributes.

Some people need coaching: "Here's how you can better deal with a customer who is screaming at you over the phone." "Here's how you can encourage more input from your subordinates by not cutting off their sentences in meetings."

Your job here is to help ensure that all positions have measurable outputs; the performers understand what they are; they have the tools, skills, attitudes, and experiences to fulfill them; and they receive regular feedback on their performance. This applies to 100 percent of the organization, it is easy to understand but not simple, and a good consultant can make a huge difference in productivity by focusing on this one simple aspect of career development.

> **Most job outputs are measurable; even St. Paul had clear key effectiveness areas, though Judgment Day does represent a long performance feedback loop.**
>
> —*W. J. Reddin, Effective Management by Objectives*
> *(McGraw-Hill, 1971)*

• *Those with the potential are being developed for future jobs.*

Most people in organizational life have aspirations to do better. Many of them have the potential to do so. They may not be a formal part of the succession planning system, but they could qualify someday. In any case, they represent the key bench strength that is available in the case of involuntary attrition, acquisitions, long-term illnesses and disability, and temporary assignments.

The competition for advancement today is unprecedented, and the typical pyramid type of ascension is narrower than ever since organizations are trying to do more with less and generally avoid overpopulating the enterprise. But it's a pragmatic and ethical requirement to develop people who demonstrate the potential and volition for higher assignments and more responsibility. (Increasingly, firms are providing this not through inflated promotions and senior positions, but through the lateral increase in accountability.)[4]

Help in this area by creating a process whereby these people are regularly identified and they receive targeted development for future jobs, not just the present position. In some organizations, all managers are responsible for identifying and nurturing people who can take their place if and when necessary, right down to supervisory level. (Many talented people lose out on opportunities in organizations because there is no one to replace them in their current jobs.)

• *People have the option to select programs for personal enrichment, even if not directly job related.*

While I'm not talking about dentistry or the cello, nor a job with a competitor, it is increasingly common as a key retention component to allow people access to personal improvement. This is sometimes in the form of group learning: a lunchtime program on the arts, for example. It's often in the form of individual improvement: a tuition-refund program for someone studying for a degree or a special certification.

The point is to keep people happy and fulfilled with the company's blessing and support.

Help your client to create a system of options and choices so that employees whose talents and interests are not completely met by the employer can have them met with the help of the employer.

• *The highest-potential people have development tracks that are in sync with their places in the succession planning process.*

Finally, your key area of assistance is what we discussed at the beginning of this segment, ensuring that the bridge meets in the middle. Help the client set up a steering committee of key people who assess whether the succession planning high-potential people are receiving the skills, coaching, and experiences they'll need for key assignments. Ensure that someone is accountable and evaluated in every instance.

Once you've accomplished this, career development becomes an integral part of organizational development, which we'll discuss in the following chapter.

Teams versus Committees

Team building is one of the most overused, overrated, and misunderstood dynamics in organizational life. It's usually done poorly, the salutary effects (such as they are) seldom last for long, and people's expectations are seldom met.

Other than that, it's a great intervention!

Teams aren't built! You don't go on a ridiculous retreat for two days, have some facilitator organize competitive sand castle building or mountain rappelling, and expect to have a more finely honed team. Just because you catch me when I'm told to fall backwards doesn't mean you'll support me on the job. It simply means you don't want to seem like an uncooperative ass in front of the boss, who's standing there terribly uncomfortably as a member of the "blue team" or "Roger's Rangers" or some such goofiness.

I recall a team-building picnic, where all the employees stood around and watched the owner and his wife play gin rummy. That must have really boosted productivity back at the ranch!

Most so-called experts will tell you there are:

Family teams: People who work together as a normal part of their day, and are expected to do so.

Stranger teams: People who come together only for special purposes, like a distinct client response or a community fund-raiser.

Interim teams: People who work together daily until a given project is completed, such as the move to a new building.

Task forces: People who work together until a given objective is met, such as expanding into a new country.

The problem with all of this isn't the type of team, *but the definition of team.* Most organizations have very few true teams. What they do have in abundance are *committees.*

As you can see in Figure 11.2, here are the distinctions:

Committee (top graphic): People who work together but still may succeed or fail independently of their colleagues. They may share resources, information, insights, and other assets, but only insofar as doing so does not undermine their own efforts or place themselves at a competitive disadvantage.

Team (bottom graphic): People who work together and succeed or fail as a unit. They freely and proactively share resources, information,

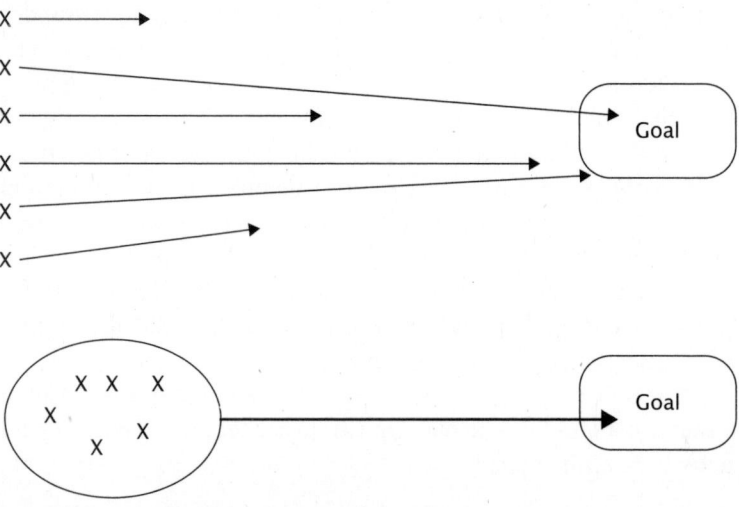

FIGURE 11.2 Committee versus Team

insights, and other assets so that every component of the team can make an optimal contribution to reaching the goal.

Typically, a committee is manifest in a company's executive committee (note the name), executive council, operations committee, customer response committee, and so on.

Typically, a team is manifest as, for example, the customer response team or the new product development team.

Think about it. In your organizational experience, are most groups of people working together as a team or as a committee? Are they evaluated and rewarded as a team or as a committee? My experience indicates that about 75 percent of organizational groups are committees, which is why they don't always play together well (e.g., share resources and information) and why you can't engage in team building with them! You wouldn't try to coach tennis players who play singles to work with a partner on their side of the net in practice, or a golfer to expect someone else to play his or her next shot.

Acid test: Coming out of the meetings, are people talking about how best to support each other and provide resources, including people, to others? If so, that sounds like a team. Or are they talking about how to protect their resources, others being incompetent, and how to resist certain elements in the group? If so, that's a committee for sure.

Most people's pay is not linked to their group, and even if the unit earns a certain amount of bonus, it's usually distributed according to individual performance by a common superior.

Teams don't always make sense. They are not inherently better than committees. You have to decide where they do make sense, and whether the people working together or being assembled constitute a real team.

Here are the characteristics and needs of true teams, by the definitions I've established:

- Teams are self-directed. They set their own rules of engagement and create their own systems for decision making.
- They share accountabilities and hold each other responsible for delivery.
- They create their own "sunset." Few teams should exist ad infinitum. Family teams, described earlier, usually don't meet the criteria in this list and aren't true teams.
- The members report through the team to one person. If they come together reporting to different superiors not on the team, they are probably on a committee.

- They determine their work habits, hours, interactions, and how any incentive pay will be allocated.
- The team is evaluated by a superior responsible for it, but the members are self-evaluated and team-evaluated.
- Periodic 360-degree assessments tend to work very effectively with teams and are quite useful.
- Teams often require external facilitation, skills building, coaching, and other elements that an objective external consultant can bring to the table.

Don't be lulled into the superficial thinking that so-called group experiences constitute team building. Groups are seldom true teams, and the experiences are seldom relevant to the workplace.

The last time I looked, no one treads on hot coals to go down the hall, or rappels down the side of the building to go to lunch, or gives themselves a motivational pep talk before a client meeting.

Communications and Feedback

"What we've got here is failure to communicate," the prison warden famously told Paul Newman in *Hud*. In most organizations you'll hear that there are communications problems; this seems to be a universal dilemma.

But that's because it should be!

I tell my clients who seek to survey their employees that they should expect to receive feedback about how communications can improve. That's good, not bad. People who seek to learn more and to be heard are very positive, constructive people. (It's the ones who don't respond and are apathetic who are the problems. Remember that every complaint or objection is a sign of interest. It's indifference that will kill you.)

The executive vice president of a huge insurance company that was in the midst of devouring an equal-sized insurance company under the guise of a merger decided to interview five consultants whose reputations justified consideration to help with a communications strategy.

I was the final one (perhaps because my last name begins with *W*), and I met the executive in a conference room with five of his subordinates at the equivalent of parade rest. He began his interviewing drill once he had apprised me of the situation about the merger.

"What do you think we should be telling the employees of the two companies?" he asked.

"Nothing," I said, and shut up.

After a brief silence and subordinate eye-shifting, he said, "Are you trying to be cute? What are you talking about?"

"Do you know which executives will lead which divisions, postmerger?"

"No, that's a board decision."

"Do you know which compensation and bonus system will survive, or will you merge them?"

"No, there is a compensation task force working on that with outside consultants."

"Do you know which offices you'll close and which will remain open?"

"No, that's a marketing decision scheduled for 90 days from now."

"Well, you don't have anything to say, do you? If I were you, I'd simply *listen*. Run focus groups, interview people, create surveys, use your intranet, establish a hotline. Once you find out what's on people's minds, answer what you can, and promise to get answers for what you can't as soon as possible."

I got the job: $250,000. Every other consultant had provided detailed subject matter and sound bites.

The Gospel

Anyone who tells you that "the only thing you can do about feedback is to listen to it" is a dolt. You can do something else. You can ignore most of it.

Here are some rules to make some tangible sense out of communications breakdowns or problems or issues.

A probably apocryphal story tells of a British visitor to the caliph's court of the Ottoman Empire in the eighteenth century. On a Saturday morning he notices a long, serpentine line extending a quarter mile from the palace. He asks his escort about it.

"It's the morning to hear petitions," the escort explains.

"The caliph hears each person himself?" responds the visitor, stunned.

"Of course."

"Does the caliph help each and every one?"

"Ah, that is not the issue. Most people just want their story to be heard."

Alan's Communications Criteria

- Listen more than talk. Hear what people have to say. Don't interrupt. Ask clarifying questions if you need to.
- Use examples when making a point. People relate much better to examples than they do to acres of text or hours of speech.
- Do it often. There is so much noise that you may not reach your listener the first five times.
- Use varied media. People learn in differing ways.
- Never ignore the grapevine and watercooler. This type of communication is dignified these days as "viral" but it's the exact same thing: Informal avenues of communication are usually much more efficacious than the formal ones.
- Keep it simple. Never talk in jargon. Tell listeners or readers what they need to know *and not everything that you know.*
- Use a what, why, how, example format. "Here's what we are seeking to do, why it's important, how we intend to proceed, and an example of your role and our support."
- Respond quickly. The speed of your response, even to say, "I'm not sure I'll get back to you," is as important as the content of your reply.

Obviously, I intend these for you, the consultant, as well as your clients.

Elicit and integrate personal feedback only from those whom you ask. Unsolicited feedback is almost always for the sake of the sender, not the recipient. Advise your coaching clients of the same ground rules. Otherwise, if we listen to every bit of random advice we're offered, we begin to resemble the ball in an old pinball machine, getting battered by bumpers and flippers before eventually falling down a drain.

Even with solicited feedback, never generalize from a specific. Once is an accident, twice a coincidence, three times a pattern. Whether positive or negative, never go running off to market your electric fork or burn your potential *Gone with the Wind* because of a few random comments.

Having dealt with individuals and groups, let's move to the organization itself.

Notes

1. Best sources: John Gardner, *On Leadership* (Free Press, 1993), and Warren Bennis, *The Unconscious Conspiracy: Why Leaders Can't Lead* (Jossey-Bass, 1998).

2. Best source: Victor Vroom, *Leadership and Decision Making* (University of Pittsburgh Press, 1973). My points in this segment are reliant on his work. I've known Vic for nearly 40 years.

3. The telltale sign of an organization with excellent succession planning is that people who leave acquire top jobs elsewhere.

4. The primary exception has always been banks, in which everyone is a vice president, including the person opening the door, but not one of them has the authority to actually help you, much less get you a loan!

Chapter 12

Organization Development

All the King's Horses, and All the King's Men . . .

Strategy

Ask six different people about a definition of strategy and you'll receive nine different responses. People use the term wrong all the time: training strategy, strategy to bring on new people, client response strategy—they're really seeking tactics and plans.

Despite titles, and despite senior managers' claims that strategy is their purview ("Why would we hire a consultant when *we're* paid to develop strategy?"), remember that *virtually no one in senior management or executive ranks was trained to be a strategist*. That's a fact. It's not as if elevation to a certain office or executive dining room privileges creates strategic DNA, sort of like a brevet, where field promotion creates a new rank.

That's why you hear so many definitions, or a too-often default position of the dreaded, feeble, ludicrous SWOT nonsense (strengths, weaknesses, opportunities, threats), which is to true strategy what kick the rock is to rugby.

Because of this ill-preparedness (which is even worse in nonprofits) and definitional confusion, strategy keeps getting clobbered. You hear phrases (and even titles) such as "strategic planning." Let's address that term here:

Strategy is the creation of a future picture of the enterprise—what it should look like, feel like, sound like, and smell like—from which you work backwards to determine viable routes to that destination. *Planning* is the extrapolation from the present to predict future goals. It is always limited by conservatism and deliberate underreporting (to preserve bonuses, keep accountabilities low, and so on).

Hence, "strategic planning" is an oxymoron.

Here's a working definition for strategy that can apply to any business, from my favorite source:[1]

> *Strategy is a framework, within which decisions are made that establish the nature and direction of the business.*

As a consultant, you can use whatever definition you like, but you need to be able to explain and defend your positioning, as I've done just now. Most organizations suffer through the following flaws when setting strategy:

- They favor an event—usually a retreat—rather than a process and ongoing work. (Some companies have retreated more than the Confederates in front of Atlanta.) You don't create strategies over a long weekend.
- They place strategy in three-ring, tabbed binders, which are distributed to the top team and then left to gather cobwebs and dust mites on remote shelves.
- They ignore the implementation part, which is the only part that matters.

The Gospel

Most strategies do not fail in formulation, which is always ideal and theoretical. They fail in implementation, which is in the trenches and demands accountability.

- They actually believe they can see five years (or even further) into the future, estimating small issues such as technologies, demographics, politics, regulatory bodies, culture, economies, and so on.
- They don't provide for flexibility and opportunism.

Strategy work is rife with process visuals and diagnostics. Figure 12.1 shows an easy one taken from the Tregoe and Zimmerman work.

Ask those people responsible for strategy which quadrant their company, or division, or subsidiary, or product line is in. Have them write it down. You'll

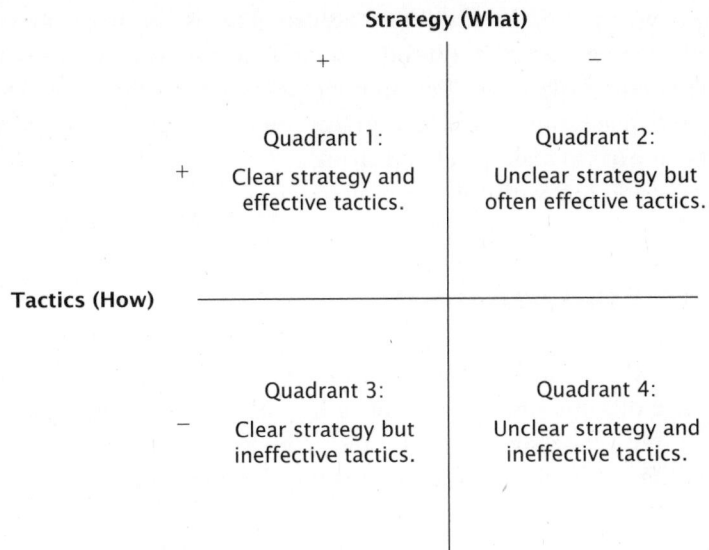

FIGURE 12.1 Strategy Quadrant

find that there is often a major difference of opinion as to the position, which helps underscore the need for an objective consultant even more.

Finally, look at these 10 driving forces—strategic areas that may dominate the organization. Every enterprise has a driving force (and it's seldom profit), but it's often unconscious, unspoken, and by default due to competitors or technology.

1. Products/services offered
2. Customers/user groups
3. Markets served
4. Technology
5. Production capability
6. Natural resources
7. Method of sale
8. Method of distribution
9. Size/growth
10. Return/profit

How do you choose which driving force makes sense for the organization in the future? How do you decide how to get into the top left quadrant (or remain there if you are already there)?

That's why great consultants are needed. This isn't a book on strategic consulting.[2] I simply want you to understand that just because this is a high-level need doesn't make it any less appropriate for your help to be absolutely required. Just make sure you have a process and a rationale that make sense and can be utilized to make profound change.

You can't do that with SWOT.

Change Management

I debated whether to include this segment, since virtually everything we do is about change of some sort and it's not really a separate discipline, but then it seemed that was the very argument for including it.

You'll see in the next segment, on cultural change, that people really are quite adept at change in terms of accepting new tomorrows, but they are leery about the journey leading them from the comfortable nest of today. Here are the conditions needed to help people to make that journey of change:

- *Focus on the macro, not the micro.* If the goals and bigger picture are in focus and clear, then the inevitable convoluted details will fall into place.
- *Emphasize long-term thinking.* If you're worried about next week's sales or this quarter's quotas, you're not going to be focused on the need to overhaul the customer response center or the brand.
- *Use a telescope, not a microscope.* Think of the future and work backwards; don't try to gradually inch your way forward from today.
- *Innovate; don't fix.* You need to raise the bar, not merely restore past performance. (See the segment on innovation that concludes this chapter.)
- *Change the culture along with the processes and procedures.* The next segment deals with this in detail. You can't speak Latin in a Greek-speaking world.
- *Maintain your priorities.* Key issues such as daily customer needs must have support to be addressed through the change process.
- *Avoid fads.* If you try to change with every new book, speech, or social media posting, you're going to capsize the ship from all the rocking. (What does it *really* mean to the average enterprise to go from "good to great"?)
- *Assign a champion.* Someone in a key leadership position has to get on the horse and say "Follow me!" The larger the change, the higher the leader and the stronger the horse must be.

- *Focus on output, not input.* Change has to have an improved effect on your customer, member, client, and so on. Any change not perceived by your customer is highly questionable.
- *Don't be silly.* No one knows what's going to happen in five years, so creating five-year plans is like leaving the landing lights on for Amelia Earhart: nice touch, but highly irrelevant.

Basically, you should define the new reality and reward those who create it, reinforce it, and arrive at it. You must empower people to create and accept change. I use the term *empowerment* not as the New Age buzzword, but as meaning "enabling people to make decisions that influence the outcome of their work."

Creating empowered people requires that management (your clients) understand that power does not corrupt, but *powerlessness* corrupts. When people don't have real power, they make it up, which we traditionally call bureaucracy: the triumph of means over ends. (You're in the wrong line, you used the wrong form, you called the wrong number, your hair is combed the wrong way—we can't help you.)

Here's a quick comparison for you and for your clients:

Powerless	Empowered
▪ Create bureaucracy.	▪ Do the right thing.
▪ Are insecure.	▪ Are self-confident.
▪ See "them and us."	▪ See "us."
▪ Focus on task.	▪ Focus on result.
▪ Follow rules.	▪ Think.
▪ CYA.	▪ Take risks.
▪ See win-loss issues.	▪ See win-win issues.

Don't be bashful about setting the stage for change by asking your client where the organization falls on the powerless/empowered continuum. Is it more like FedEx or more like the division of motor vehicles? Do people go the extra mile or try to not move an inch?

Then, when you're ready to launch the change effort, pay close attention to time investment versus effectiveness (see Figure 12.2).

The Gospel

Success always trumps perfection.

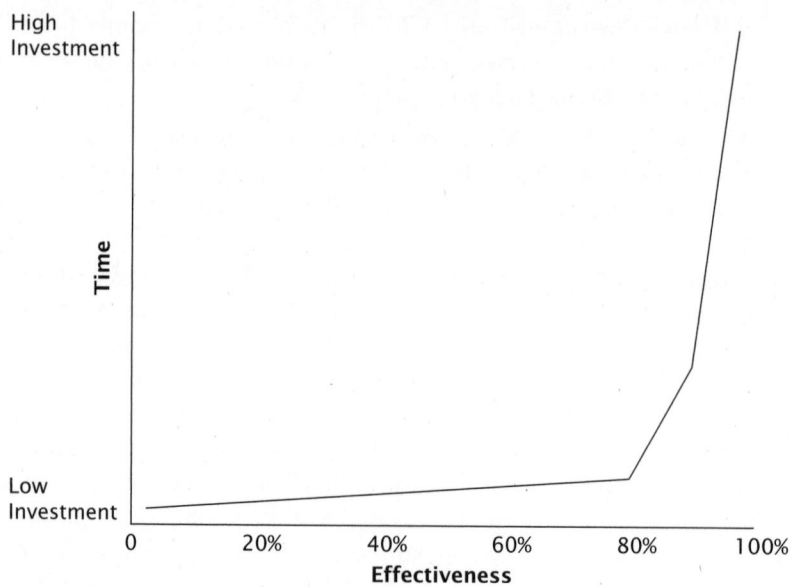

FIGURE 12.2 Time Utilization and Effectiveness

I call this the "80 percent ready: move" principle. There will never be a perfect time to launch, initiate, or implement. When about 80 percent of the factors (people, systems, culture, finances, support, and so forth) are in place, then move.

One of Zeno's paradoxes states that if you make 50 percent progress toward your destination every single day, you'll never arrive! We are after success, not perfection.

Even airplanes have redundant systems, and aren't expected to work perfectly every day—in fact, every single plane you fly in has something wrong with it, somewhere. But that doesn't prevent it from doing its job and achieving the results expected of it.

People change every day. They find new routes to their place of work when there is construction or an accident. They respond to unexpected customer requests accurately and rapidly. They change plans, appointments, and expectations if they must.

People don't fear change, and the assumption that they do is a toxic starting point for a company and a consultant. But people do expect that planned change will better their work and their lives, and that the journey will be neither fatal nor crippling.

Whether organization-wide or localized, change (and even volatility in many businesses) is the new normal. We face it every day, and we might as well get good at it. That means you need to get good at helping in that journey.

Cultural Change

Let's define *culture* for our purposes, always an intelligent first step:

Culture comprises that set of beliefs that governs behavior.

Thus you can readily encounter (and be a part of) neighborhood, organizational, civic, social, departmental, and recreational cultures. If you don't believe that, insert yourself into an experience that others partake of regularly but you do not.

Rarely, I take the commuter train from Providence to Boston. It's a 45-minute trip, and for the regulars on any given train, the procedures and rules and expectations might as well be etched in stone. They are as complex and religiously observed as a golf rule book (which I find only somewhat less puzzling and rigid than the blueprints of a power plant). For example:

- You don't put your coat on one of the hooks provided; you put it in the overhead rack.

- Some seats are always occupied by regulars, which, of course, there is no way of knowing if you're not a regular, and you draw dirty looks and comments if you sit there.

- You place items on the seat next to you and do not establish contact with new arrivals at later station stops, so that you maintain maximum room. You move your items only if the conductor insists.

- The conductors are greeted in familiar terms, and tickets are made available in a certain way, usually just showing a monthly pass that's in a wallet.

- People are never asked to lower their voices.

- You're expected to not look at someone else's computer screen even if it's inches away.

- At the Boston terminal, you file off in a certain manner, join the crowd headed for the terminal, and use a narrow strip near the tracks if you must pass people.

You get the idea. There was actually a fatal heart attack on a Boston commuter line, and help wasn't summoned until several stations had been passed. The conductors claimed that they stopped at the station where they felt the best medical care would be available. But they had radios. I think they didn't want to disrupt the normal culture of the train.

This same regimentation can exist when cultures are ossified, are not accepting of the few outsiders who enter, and create comfortable (though boring) existences for people who are merely trying to get through the day.

Here is the sequence you're dealing with in terms of culture changes:

Beliefs

Attitudes

Behaviors

We all have beliefs, which create attitudes, which are manifest in behaviors. If I believe that the better the organization performs the better off I am, my attitude will be to help others and make sure customers are happy. That may be manifested by my creating ideas for others to improve their operation, assiduously following up on customer requests, and making sure they've been well served. Conversely, if I believe that I'm being passed over for promotion because I don't publicly compliment our egomaniacal boss, then my attitude may well be to hope that the boss fails, and my behavior may be to spread rumors or deliberately fail to meet deadlines important to the boss.

Now add this to the mix:

Beliefs:　　　　　Enlightened self-interest

Attitudes:　　　　Normative pressure

Behaviors:　　　　Coercion

In many cultures, we see the behavior so we try to change it through force, coercion, punishments (or rewards for good behavior). Prohibition tried to do that on a massive scale to end the consumption of alcohol. When it began, there were 80,000 or so bars in New York City. When it was finally reversed, there were an estimated 140,000 illegal speakeasies operating in New York City! Coercion works only briefly, as long as you are present with a big stick, and as long as no one else comes along with a bigger one.

We try to attack attitudes with peer pressure: "Be one of the in crowd," or "Don't be the only one preventing 100 percent participation in the blood drive!" Normative pressure is fickle and seldom long-lived. The drive to conform works when people choose to participate (as on the train), not when it is a forced and phony compliance.

To change the attitudes that are producing the behaviors that we seek to alter, we need to attack the basic beliefs generating those attitudes. By "enlightened self-interest," I mean no appeal should be immoral or illegal. But we've reduced tobacco use by huge percentages over the past two decades because we've educated people that as smokers they may not live to see their grandchildren, or they are hurting ones they love through secondary smoking, or they can't engage in the lives they would like.

The public restrictions and large taxes on tobacco products, like Prohibition, would be circumvented or ignored if the belief systems hadn't been altered. (Remember the films of the 1940s and 1950s? It was sophisticated to smoke; all the leading actors did. "Doctors" on television promoted the cigarettes that were the "healthiest" for you. Today, the TV show *Mad Men* does a great job of re-creating the smoking and boozing nature of the smart set in a competitive world 50 years ago.)

The Gospel

Cultures can change. The change requires that people see their self-interests met in the changes. Those that don't, despite everyone's best efforts, are not part of the future.

"It's just our culture" may be true or false, but it's not an excuse in any case. You're not dealing with a centuries-old Mayan culture, and not an inflexible set of standards created by some higher power. You're dealing with beliefs that govern behavior, and those beliefs are subject to change.

In fact, one of your most valuable roles as a consultant is to ensure that your client isn't the victim of a default culture created by veteran employees (work here five years, then arrange to go out on long-term disability), the competition, advances in technology, or a volatile economy.

You should not have an alien culture taking over your company, like some science fiction movie where pods are growing in the closets or certain people have peculiar bite marks on their necks.

Though I have to tell you, I'm very suspicious about those Boston commuters.

Crisis Management

Sometimes you'll be called in to help with a crisis, and sometimes one may erupt while you're with a client (not due to your being there, one hopes!). In any case, this is where clients really need external, learned help.

We tend to view the BP Gulf disaster, Three-Mile Island, the *Exxon Valdez*, the Tylenol crisis, and any number of CEO firings for inappropriate behavior as iconic examples of the good, the bad, and the ugly. But there are patterns even amid the chaos.[3]

Some crises can be prepared for: There are hurricane barriers in certain major cities, alternative conning positions on major ships, and insurance policies for just about anything. These seek to ameliorate conditions. It's interesting, organizationally, to reflect that we prepare for natural disasters and even hostile acts, but not for the inevitable frailties and peccadilloes of humans, as if we trust people to have learned lessons!

Here are six elements of effective methods to deal with a crisis:

1. *Transparency in communications.*

Tell people what happened. Tell employees, the press, the community, the board, and any other possible stakeholders. In this electronic, social media, snooping media day and age, there are no secrets, and what is surmised will almost always be worse than the actuality. Counsel for candor, and the admission that some facts may simply not be known. It was far worse for BP managers when they vastly underestimated the amount of oil leaking right after the oil-rig explosion. When the truth emerged, they seemed to be either liars or incompetent. If you are clearly being honest, you will get the benefit of the doubt.

2. *The leader exemplifies the behavior.*

Everyone cites the importance of Johnson & Johnson's then-CEO James Burke for personally appearing on all the media during the Tylenol tampering scare, and the difficulty in trying to track down Exxon CEO Lawrence Rawls for a week after the *Exxon Valdez* grounded. Mayor Ray Nagin of New Orleans disappeared into a Four Seasons hotel in Houston while his city was inundated.

When a Merck plant in Puerto Rico blew up, CEO P. Roy Vagelos changed his return plans from California, flew to San Juan, toured the disaster area, and comforted the families of those killed and injured.

3. *Crisis management rests on a foundation of daily beliefs.*

The reason that Vagelos and Burke so quickly acted in the manner they did was that the companies and the leadership embraced such values of honesty, decency, and leadership modeling. You don't create values and behaviors during a crisis; you rely on those that are embedded and practiced. It's tough to suddenly act in a new way; it's far easier to act consistently with normal behavior in abnormal times.

A client might have a disaster preparedness plan that it rips open when certain conditions emerge, but it had better have a continual behavioral set of responsibility and truthfulness if that plan is to be successfully implemented.

4. *Find cause, not blame.*

If you or your client engages in a vendetta, people will keep their heads down and their phones shut off. But if you effectively try to find out the cause and eliminate it, you'll develop far better cooperation early.

Great leaders accept blame and share credit.

5. *Reduce effects first and fast.*

It may be counterintuitive, but before finding cause it may help to assuage pain and remove uncertainties. Provide customers and clients with immediate relief, even before you find how to prevent the situation from recurring.

"Bring back the defective product," "Call this new toll-free number," "Go to this Internet site to secure your refund." Those types of actions will take care of people and give you some time to find out what generated the condition. You take pain reliever before you study the cause of your headache.

Apple responded to the furor about dropped calls on its new iPhone by offering free bumpers for the phone, which could be ordered via an app of course, while also explaining that the condition was not as widespread as was being reported, and the bumpers would take care of the adverse effects that some people were experiencing.

6. *Tell people when it's (really) over.*

Close the loop, whether internally or externally, and let people know that conditions are back to normal (or restored to an even higher standard as a result of the problem being fixed). Allow yourself and your client some good publicity and a sense of closure. Tell the stakeholders what was learned, explain how the operation was improved as a result, and apologize again for the inconveniences or worse.

The Gospel

There are crises and there are crises. Be careful, and urge your client not to overreact. The loss of a client is seldom a crisis. The potential to lose all of one's clients is a genuine crisis.

Figure 12.3 shows what I call the "ambiguous zone." (William Bridges has a similar approach that he calls the "neutral zone.") Most people make themselves comfortable in (or at least tolerate) their existing state.

And, contrary to what we are led to believe, a desired future state is often highly appealing. People are not all that reluctant to change.

However, the *journey* from the current state to the desired state is often threatening. As my son used to inform me when he was very young and I encouraged him to go through a dark, scary ride on the boardwalk at the beach by telling him not to be afraid of the dark: "I'm not afraid of the dark. I'm afraid of what might be *in* the dark."

Normally, engaged in change management, we have the luxury of lighting the way and helping leadership lead the journey. But in crisis that luxury is gone. We have to help more rapidly and confidently through the ambiguous

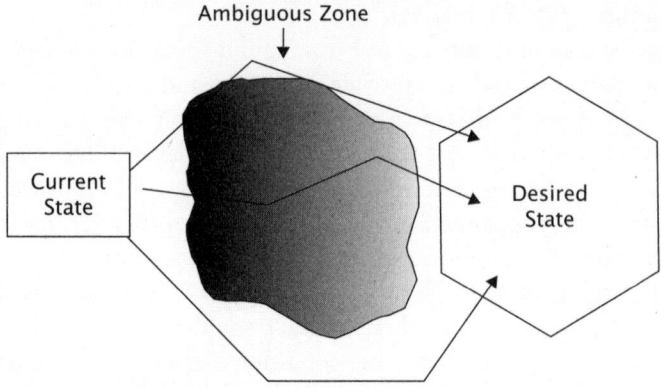

FIGURE 12.3 The Ambiguous Zone

zone. The desired state may resemble an improved current state or a brand-new way of working, but the journey can't wait.

Innovation

The first and foremost thing to remember about innovating is that it is *not* problem solving. Nor is it creativity.

Innovation is *applied* creativity.

By that I mean it's the pragmatic application of new ideas, not merely brainstorming or sterile creation. Problem solving is the restoration of former levels of performance. Innovation is the raising of the bar, proactively, to new levels of performance. (See Figure 12.4.)

Excellent organizations should be constantly engaged in innovation because their competitors probably are not putting pressure on them. So they mainly compete against themselves. For years, giant 3M has had a strategy demanding that 25 percent of new business originate with products that were not in existence five years earlier. (About 75 percent of my business originates in new products and services from the prior three years.)

Your job is to help clients recognize these distinctions, or innovation becomes lost in overall problem solving, quality doctrines, and analytic programs such as lean X, Y, and Z.

In innovative organizations, you should promote this set of 10 beliefs:

1. *Intent, not size, is the key.*

    Any organization can be innovative, even giants like 3M, and small businesses can be bureaucratic and noninnovative, like the

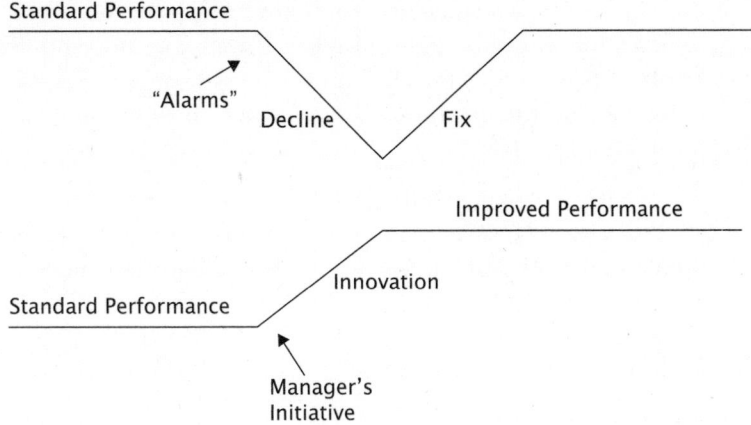

FIGURE 12.4 Problem Solving versus Innovation

corner cleaner who won't return a shirt without the proper ticket, even though you're known there.

2. *Innovation is incremental.*

There is rarely a breakthrough: Ah, we've invented the iPad! Innovation is usually a series of incremental steps or recombinations of existing products and services.

3. *Employees are the main innovators.*

The people dealing with the customers every day are the key sources of innovative ideas and must be included and embraced. This is not about a skunk works or a bunch of dreamers off on a mountaintop. Find out what the customers are demanding or missing.

4. *Innovation must suit the environment.*

You must accommodate the culture (see earlier discussion) or change it. You can't create high-risk innovations in a low-risk environment. Set up paths of least resistance.

5. *Paradigms are made to be broken.*

"But we've never done it that way" is a good reason to do it that way. Plateaus, nests, and comfort zones are not what propel organizations into market leadership. They create complacency and eventual erosion.

6. *Innovation is a learnable skill.*

There are steps to innovation.[4] People can learn it. My doctoral dissertation attempted to prove that behavioral predisposition was the key, and you could hire innovative people if you knew what to look for. Instead, using Merck, Hewlett-Packard, and Marine Midland Bank (now HSBC), I proved just the opposite: Innovation is fostered by the environment, the direct superior, and the skills imparted on the job.

7. *Your environment must encourage innovation, not frustrate it.*

You reward behaviors, not merely victories. You provide the freedom to fail. One year while consulting for Calgon, we implemented a president's award for "the best idea that didn't work," to encourage people to keep coming up with ideas. That was the behavior we were after.

8. *People must be empowered.*

See the empowerment segment (in the "Change Management" section earlier in this chapter). People have to have the decision-making prerogative to influence the outcome of their work. If they do, they can experiment right on the front line. But if they need permissions and approvals, innovation will never work.

9. *Everyone must be educated in the approach.*

You can't have pockets of innovation, because you'll be setting up roadblocks and obstacles—"I don't care what you're trying; I have different objectives." Try to bring entire operating units into the discipline.

10. *The leaders set the vision.*

As in all change, you need a powerful, visible champion who is an avatar of the approaches.

The best sources of innovation for most organizations are:

- *Unexpected success/high growth.* How can you build on the momentum of success beyond plan and expectation, even if it's not yours? The iPhone has generated holders, chargers, apps, and so forth.
- *Unexpected failure of someone else.* Is there a legitimate goal that simply wasn't met by the alternative? British Air pioneered commercial jet travel with the unsuccessful Comet, but Boeing realized the design flaws and dominated commercial jet airframes for decades after.
- *Recombination of technology.* As Steve Jobs of Apple says, "We jump on the next big things." The idea is not to provide a phone or a book reader, but a multipurpose personal aid.

- *Public perception change.* The advertising industry is geared to this. In the United States, billions of dollars have been spent on weight loss in the form of exercise equipment, health club memberships, dietary aids, and surgery. Yet the population is heavier than ever.

- *Demographic shift.* The nature, education, income, age, and residence of customers are constantly changing. Most people tend to think that younger age groups have the most discretionary spending money. That's false: It's actually those over 60, with no more need to save for college tuition, housing, and so on.

Innovation is what helps companies and consultants leap forward and upward. Let's examine in the final part of this book how you deal with the heights.

Notes

1. *Top Management Strategy: What It Is and How It Works*, by Ben Tregoe and John Zimmerman (Simon & Schuster, 1980). Go out of your way to get the original, as the newest version, taken over by Mike Freedman, is a disaster that barely credits the originators at all.

2. You can see my book, *Best Laid Plans* (HarperCollins, 1990; Las Brisas Research Press, 1994), for that!

3. For an excellent discussion of this point, see Margaret Wheatley's *Leadership and the New Science*, 3rd edition (Berrett-Koehler, 2006).

4. See my book with Michel Robert, for example: *The Innovation Formula* (HarperBusiness, 1988).

Proverbs
Consulting Success

How you sow, grow, reap, and create value for yourself and others.
Work is merely fuel for your life.

13

Ethics of the Business
What's Legal Isn't Always Ethical

When Bad Things Happen to Good Consultants

Most ethical transgressions within organizations are the result of the individual doing something *to help the organization* and not for personal gain. Of course, you'll find the latter, but a great many people feel that as long as something is legal, it's proper. That's simply untrue.

They're called courts of *law*, not courts of *proper conduct*.

Case Studies

The president of a $600 million subsidiary called me on a Sunday evening, apologized for the interruption, but told me he needed some urgent counseling. He was having a meeting the next morning with his vice president of sales and his vice president of human resources. The former was requesting a slap on the wrist for a district manager, and the latter wanted him fired.

It seems that a field salesperson purchased an iPad expressly because the clients in her territory frequently had to send her equipment plans to review and needed a quick turnaround. The device allowed her to rapidly respond, keep an archive of past plans, and not have to tote around a laptop.

Her district manager learned of this when she casually mentioned that she had that capability if he needed to contact her in a similar fashion. He told her that she was very innovative and shouldn't have to bear that expense, and to reimburse herself by charging a fictitious client lunch once a week until the iPad was paid off. At a regional meeting, the salesperson mentioned the arrangement to a colleague, who then asked his district manager for the same arrangement, and that manager quite properly blew the whistle.

The president asked me what I would do. Here's what we established:

- There was no personal gain or attempt for personal gain.
- The company had no reimbursement policy for these devices (but perhaps that needed changing).
- The district manager had initiated an unethical procedure.
- The salesperson could have refused but did not.
- A clear message had to be sent since this was now public knowledge.
- The district manager and salesperson had excellent records.

Thus, the sales vice president wanted a slap on the wrist, and the HR vice president wanted a termination. What would you have advised?

What I advised, in view of the bullet points, was to publicly reprimand both people, to deny the district manager participation in the bonus plan that year, and to send a clear policy on such issues to the entire company. The president agreed.

This may not be your response or even the best response, but it worked. It was the right thing to do. Ethics are about "doing well by doing right."

In contrast, a human resources vice president in a major New York bank called me in because he had evidence his staff was cheating on expenses, charging lunches with no clients present, charging supplies that didn't exist, and so on. He asked me to find out why this was rampant and what do to about it.

After a half-day of interviews, I found out that the vice president was entitled to fly first class, but instead cashed in the tickets, flew coach, and pocketed the difference. Everyone knew this because he bragged about his "extra income."

The Gospel

People don't believe what they read or hear. They believe what they see.

A hospital CEO in Rhode Island was showing me around his operation, and pointed to plaques on every wall in every corridor extolling the hospital's "basic values." The fourth one down was "We value our employees." (It's always the fourth one down; these must be preprinted by a Successories subsidiary somewhere in Albania.) Yet right in front of these signs you could see management berating subordinates, doctors ignoring nurses, and unfettered arrogance.

The CEO told me he was perplexed why morale was so poor.

I asked him, "Bill, do you think people believe what they read on the walls or what they see in the halls?"

Consultants can easily become sucked into these whirlpools of erratic ethical behavior. And whether it's for the company, or for the individual, or for the team, or for the cause, it can undermine the best-structured project in the world.

Here's what you should look at: Do the core values of the place match the operating values of the place?

For example, Merck had a very clear core value: "We believe in creating the highest degree of scientific application and directing it against the major areas of human health suffering." No one joined Merck to get rich, as you would a Wall Street trading firm, or to move public opinion, as you would a Madison Avenue advertising firm. They joined because they believed in the core values. At the operating level, they treated each decision the same way: "Does my alternative support the company's core beliefs?"

You'll find organizations where the core beliefs (the plaques on the walls) are from a distant galaxy. The core beliefs (what actually guide people's daily actions) are far different. The company believes in contributions to the environment and world-class building materials, but the people at ground level believe in making their monthly quotas and trying to avoid making too many overnight trips to customers.

Often, it takes a consultant to surface the cognitive dissonance.

Case Study

I was conducting an ethics workshop as part of a project for a large retail finance organization. The president and 20 top officers were in the room. I posed this problem:

Suppose you were interviewing a key manager from the competition for a job at this firm. The candidate pulled out a sheaf of papers with his current employer's letterhead and a large stamp that said "Confidential." He then excused himself to visit the rest room, leaving the document in front of you.

Of 20 people, one said he wouldn't touch it and would terminate the interview, but 12 said they'd read it, and seven said they'd copy it.

The president was outraged. "That's unacceptable!" he shouted. "We don't do things like that here!"

After a brief, uncomfortable silence, one of the vice presidents said, "John, how do you think we put together your Monday morning briefings?"

Financial Follies

The idea in a professional services firm that you run as a solo consultant is to maximize pretax expenditures and minimize after-tax expenditures. However, there is a difference between tax avoidance and tax evasion. The major difference is that the latter can land you in jail.

Work with your attorney and accountant to maximize the deductions that are allowable, and what can be legitimately placed in your firm's bylaws as benefits. You can usually deduct a home office that meets certain criteria, non-reimbursed (by insurance) medical expenses, certain memberships, and other items. But the laws change and even certain states have restrictions.

Assiduously track your expenses, so that you can charge clients for project-related costs (travel, lodging, and so on) and have the company pay for office-related expenses (equipment, supplies) and for professional development (workshops, books).

As for your clients, use the proposal to stipulate payment terms and be inflexible in their payment. If you're not paid as specified, stop working and tell the buyer, "We have a problem." Never argue with accounts payable people or accept "It's just our policy." Your policy is what you agreed to with your buyer.

As far as ethical conduct related to finances is concerned, however, here are seven guidelines:

1. *Never double-dip on expenses.*

   If you're visiting more than one client, expenses should be pro-rated. Never, ever charge twice for the same expense. (On one occasion two clients' accounts payable areas demanded only original receipts to reimburse me for a trip to see both of them. I told them that since there was only one original copy, whoever took it would have to pay all the expenses. They quickly decided to accept copies.)

2. *Charge what the client pays for its own expenses.*

   I travel solely first class, but I charge my clients for coach airfare domestically and business class overseas, because that's what they normally do for their own people. I stay in luxury hotels, but charge the equivalent of a Marriott room in that town. I take limos, but charge for cabs.

   I let the buyer know this and explain it on my invoice. The client isn't obligated to support your lifestyle choices, only for reasonable expenses. If you're successful, you can absorb the difference or conform to the normal procedures.

3. *Don't nickel-and-dime.*

I find it hysterically comical when my attorney bills me $3,042.44. I know the $42 is for copies and the $.44 is for a stamp! Don't charge your client for postage, telephone, fax, courier, or administrative work. Those are simply costs of your doing business.

4. *You can charge differing amounts to different clients for similar work.*

If I'm coaching client A to help a supervisor with a $100,000 budget and 10 people, and coaching client B to help a vice president with a $10 million budget and 400 people, I will charge different amounts even if the methodology is the same and the time frames are identical.

That's because in value-based fees, you charge according to your contribution to the value of the project, which is undoubted higher in terms of the improvement for the vice president. There's nothing wrong with that.

There would be something wrong in charging different fees for two people in the same client company doing identical jobs with identical need and an identical approach from you. (And besides, people talk and compare notes.)

5. *Never cut corners with the client.*

Deliver what you promise. If you promise a customized survey for the fee you've quoted, don't substitute a computerized, generic vehicle. If you promised to visit four offices and six clients, don't settle on three offices and four clients. (This is why it's never a good idea to cite specific deliverables or numbers.)

Think of the fourth sale first. Invest what you have to.

The Gospel

People generally compromise themselves ethically with finances when they are desperate. The best preventive action is to build a thriving practice so that you're never desperate.

6. *Never hide revenue.*

If someone makes out a check to you, personally, and not your company, endorse it over to the company. Don't try to hide the income in your personal account.

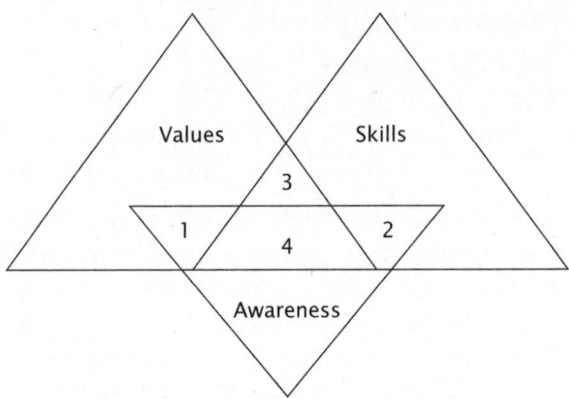

1. "Would act" but can't, because of lack of skills.
2. "Should act" but won't, because of lack of values.
3. "Could act" but doesn't, because of lack of awareness.
4. "Will act" because all elements are present.

FIGURE 13.1　Factors for Ethical Effectiveness

7. *If the client offers nonfinancial benefits, they are usually taxable.*

Airplane tickets, clothing, meals, gifts, tickets to athletic events, theater tickets, and so forth constitute taxable income. You must report them. If you're receiving something of demonstrable value, you must declare it. In most cases, you're better off politely declining such benefits. (And don't think you can run a business on bartering.)

In general, for you and your clients, the chart shown in Figure 13.1 shows the conditions under which you are most like to act ethically:

- You have the values and know what's right and wrong.
- You have the skills to do what is required.
- You have the awareness to understand when something is questionable.

Ethical conduct isn't situational, and financial matters are not an exception to proper behavior. Just because something is legal (e.g., substituting a less expensive product that performs the same way) doesn't mean it's ethical, because that is not what the client has paid for or expects.

You should expect ethical consideration from the client: paying bills on time, recognizing legitimate expenses, and not attempting to build in more services for the same amount of money.

And the client should expect the same from you.

Protection and Plagiarism

There are people among us who spend more time trying to cheat and connive than they would ordinarily have to invest in an honest day's work. One emotionally damaged puppy puts fictitious "biographies" of me on his web site (he claims I was born in Canada), and critiques my work (including things I've never said) so that he can raise his stature on search engines using my name, enabling him to sell suspect services. Several people have told me that they've initiated legal action against him.

But that type of person isn't the problem. He's a marginal character. It's the people who simply take your stuff and claim it as their own who can be more than a mere nuisance.

I found one guy in Australia simply reprinting famous small-business guru David Maister's blog entries as his own! Verbatim! If David reported that he had just come from a book signing event in Amsterdam, that's what appeared on this guy's site, except with *his* name! I wrote to ask how he could have the audacity and absence of brains to do that and, of course, received no reply.

There is an excellent Web resource, Copyscape (www.copyscape.com) that permits you to enter any of your web pages and you will be notified immediately of any other places they appear. Using this, I found two people who had appropriated entire pages of my Mentor Program to use for themselves. When contacted, they immediately collapsed, telling us the pages were just "placeholders" until they developed their own copy (or, more likely, until they were caught).

Google Alerts will pick up whatever keywords you enter and provide a daily summary of where they have been used. You can check your name, your trademarks, your competition, your hot topics, and so on. I often find my work on sleazy free-download sites where people all over the globe are trying to make money by stealing intellectual property (and entire books) and offering them for free while attracting advertisers! There is no bottom to the illegal, unethical well.

We've covered legal protection devices earlier in the book (copyright, trademarks, and so forth). In this section I want to explain redress and escalation.

1. *Subordinate ego.*

    Just because someone uses a phrase (e.g., "exponential learning") that you have used repeatedly doesn't make the individual a criminal. If someone uses your trademarked work (e.g., "The Exponential Learning Workshop"), then you have a case. This is the advantage of registered trademarks: The overwhelming weight of the law is on your side.

2. *Don't fall for scams.*

Every month I get a notice from some obscure company in Asia that my company name and trademarks are going to be used by someone over there unless I file to protect them and, of course, remit a hefty fee. These are scams.

Make sure you have a good trademark attorney to whom you can simply forward these if you're ever worried about them.

3. *Ignore the insects on the windshield.*

Don't spend $5,000 to protect $100. There are some people who will sell your work or rip off your property for very small gain. Not only is trying to stop them expensive, but it actually gives them more publicity than they would ever otherwise merit or receive.

4. *Escalate your responses.*

I recommend you create a very simple sequence:

- Send an e-mail or letter yourself to the offending party. You might find that it's an accident or a misunderstanding, or they may fold their tent right there.

- If that doesn't work, have your attorney fire a shot across the bow. A nice, threatening letter will often take care of things. It should cost you an hour of your attorney's time. (Lawyers, incredibly, mostly bill in six-minute increments!)

- If the shot across the bow doesn't deter them, make an assessment about further legal action. If you take such action, make it clear that you will insist they pay all legal costs as part of your suit. Be sure to do a careful cost analysis as to whether this is worth it.

- If you proceed, leave it to your lawyer and get back to work. Don't stay up nights over this stuff.

I'll remind you that a very strong brand makes the provenance of intellectual property self-evident, and is the best deterrent against people trying to claim your work as their own.

The Gospel

Success, not perfection. Make it clear you'll stop egregious cases of theft, but don't shoot yourself in the foot by obsessing about who is using your stuff.

As the economists say, "on the other hand":

Be rigorous and disciplined about what you appropriate, cite, or claim. This is a chapter on ethics, not merely your own protection. If you use someone else's exact words, intellectual property, model, or illustrations, you must attribute them. While it's true that you cannot copyright or otherwise protect concepts, you can protect the formats and models that support and convey them.

If you are writing an article or a book, or creating a workshop, or delivering a teleconference, and more than about 15 percent is attributable to others, I'd advise that you're relying too much on other sources, *even if you're giving them proper attribution.* I've always been fascinated by authors who continually rely on someone else's work, using their quotes and models. Why should I read their work, if the original source is available to me?

The spoken word is hard to protect (as opposed to a song or a speech, which also appears in writing and can be copyrighted). You may want to publish some version of even informal and extemporaneous speeches you make to protect the content. An introducer once used one of my own stories to introduce me to his conference. He had stolen so much from so many, he didn't realize that the odds had run out and he was using stolen material from that day's presenter!

Remember: You keep what you bring to a client. The client keeps what was the client's before you arrived. What you create at the client is work product belonging to the client and to you unless otherwise negotiated.[1]

Imitation is the sincerest form of flattery, except when it diverts money from your bank account to someone else's. Then it's simply a crime.

When to Refuse Business or Fire Clients

Here is an immutable law: Lousy prospects make horrid clients. They don't magically metamorphose into responsible, respectful, professional partners just because they've begun to pay you.

They become worse.

If a prospect treats you poorly (late for appointments, last-minute cancellations, rude speech and behavior, allowing interruptions from the staff, and so on), as hard as it may seem, I suggest you move on. Just mention that the project doesn't seem right or you don't feel the buyer is sufficiently committed. The money may be attractive, but you'll lose your shirt.

I guarantee many of you will ignore me, and all of you who ignore me will say later, "I should have listened to him." So, in advance, I told you so.

The Gospel

Not all business is good business, just as not all food is good food or all music is good music. Stay away from experiences that you know aren't going to be good for you.

Here are four other reasons to refuse business:

1. *It's not consistent with your values.*

I have never done downsizing work, because I feel it's an unethical response to errors made by senior management. ("We goofed, so let's move the hurt to them.") You may find prospects whose objectives are legal, but not ethical (we've discussed this dichotomy earlier). Hiding information from people whom it affects, tricking customers, and deliberately fooling investors would certainly fall into this category.

I will never touch anything related to multilevel marketing (aka a Ponzi scheme), which I believe provides no value to the environment and enriches people who are first approached at the expense of the people who are attracted later.

2. *The labor is too severe.*

No matter what you do with subcontractors or client people, your personal involvement will require too much time, hazardous travel, poor working conditions, and so on.

Another reason is that you'll be forced to be away during momentous family events.

3. *You don't believe in the product or service of the client.*

I've noted multilevel marketing. But you also may have objections to services that you feel are unfair to the elderly, or discriminate against ethnic groups, or are made with questionable labor practices overseas.

These may be legal, and others may feel they are ethical, but you are never obliged to accept a client whom you find objectionable, as long as you are not discriminating based on factors such as ethnicity, age, gender, disability, race, and so forth.

4. *The work is primarily not your strength.*

It's fine to subcontract work that others do better than you (or you can't do at all), but it should be a minority part of the project, say 25 percent or less. If it's between that and 50 percent, you may want a partner with the missing capabilities. But if it's more than half the work, you're better off referring the business to a consultant who can handle the preponderance and take either a subcontracting role yourself or simply a finder's fee.

There are rare occasions when you already have secured business and are actively engaged but must end it. It happens to all of us.

- *The client stops paying.*

  The greatest leverage (and often *sole* leverage) you have with a client is to cease the work. That's a radical step, but you must do so when the client doesn't meet the payment terms for fees or expense reimbursement within a reasonable time.

  Clients will cite economic downturn, cancellation by one of their big customers, technological failure, and so forth. But the fact is that you are a small business, you can't pay your mortgage with your client's promises, and you're not the client's bank from which the client can borrow money.

  The more leeway you give, the more you'll be taken advantage of. You'll be on the absolute bottom of the accounts payable list.

- *The client attempts to enlarge the project.*

  Sometimes scope creep isn't gradual or modest, but a calculated, overt plan. When the client starts asking to include new areas, more people, additional studies, and so forth—and refuses to consider an amended proposal to accommodate the additional value—it's time to stop. These requests won't go away, and the client has felt that once you've begun you can't afford to stop. (This is why you should always get paid in advance or receive a minimum of 50 percent of the fee in advance.)

- *The buyer does not live up to the stated accountabilities.*

  The joint accountabilities in the proposal are intended to ensure success by allocating what you can best do and the buyer can best do. If the buyer reneges and doesn't provide support, or act as sponsor, or assign key personnel, the project will fail and you'll be blamed. That's why these things are in writing. (This includes the buyer disappearing and not responding to your communications.)

Fortunately, if you have a strong and trusting initial relationship, none of these horrors should happen. But sometimes we're fooled; sometimes buyers change; sometimes conditions radically change. Don't throw good money after bad.

Here are some preventive actions, beyond the solid relationship building:

- Frequently discuss progress with the buyer to ensure you share common perceptions of progress and improvement.

- Use the metrics in the proposal as your template to gauge progress.

- Try not to accede to even modest scope creep. Once that drawbridge is lowered, the moat is no longer relevant.

- Follow up the day after a payment is due and not received. Don't follow with accounts payable, but with your buyer. Be polite but professional and firm.

- Learn language such as this: "I appreciate your financial difficulties, but I'm sure you can also appreciate mine. I'm a small business and can't tolerate unexpected interruptions of cash flow. I'm going to have to insist that I'm paid per our legal contract, and that you seek relief in other areas, not with me."

Don't be afraid to hire legal help if you have uncollected debts. This is a business. I guarantee your bank would hire legal help to come after you.

Doing Well by Doing Right

George Merck's aphorism "Do good and good will follow" appeared in Merck's annual report and in other collateral. For the dozen years I consulted with Merck and could observe firsthand, it appeared to me that people there believed in it and operated on that premise.

The core values and the operating values were completely consistent.

There are two dimensions that affect us as consultants. The first is how we counsel and advise our clients. My position has been consistent in that we must apprise our buyers of any ethical transgressions we find, regardless of whether they are integral to our particular project. We would notify our client of a fire, or of large-scale internal theft, or of some other material threat to the client's well-being.

Case Study

While working for Calgon, I toured a remote warehouse where water purification chemicals were stored. One of the reasons I was doing this was because company management virtually never did and was making assumptions about how orders were received and fulfilled.

In the warehouse I found calendars with pictures of nude women on the wall.

"What is that?!" I asked one of the employees.

"Miss March," he blithely replied.

I went into the supervisor's office and told him that because women worked in and visited the warehouse regularly, this was a violation of rules about preventing a hostile workplace, and the company could be sued.

"It's only Miss March," he said dismissively.

When I debriefed with the president late that day, I mentioned the encounter, and the president was incensed. He told me he'd take care of it immediately. I told him he had three problems:

1. The calendar had to come down.
2. His frontline management needed training in these matters.
3. His human resources people were asleep at the switch (no monitoring).

I told him he could handle this with his own people, but I'd also be happy to help him if he required it. (He did.)

So we help out clients with issues that are of immediate and dangerous impact (or startling opportunity) insofar as at least pointing them out. If we're engaged to work on them, and it's within our competency, then that's fine, too. As long as we are pursuing our client's legitimate self-interests and not merely our own, that's an ethical position.

And that transition brings me to the second major aspect of this segment—how we act.

I've already discussed the obvious, such as not double billing clients for expense reimbursement or traveling at excessive cost. But there are other ethical aspects of a solo or boutique practice.

Five Commandments for Ethical Conduct and Consideration

1. *Are you contributing to the community?*

   Are you playing a role in your surrounding community? You may be part of the chamber of commerce or sponsoring a Little League team to get your company's name in front of people. But I mean are you also playing roles to contribute and not gain? Are you serving on town boards, participating in fund-raising (either giving or soliciting), and helping with local events? Do you visit the senior center, or provide help in cleanup efforts? Do you participate in the food bank or help out at holidays?

2. *Are you contributing to the profession?*

Professions grow as people in them challenge, contribute, debate, and engage. Too many professional groups merely convene so the members can lie to each other about how well they're doing, or express conceptual frameworks that they've painstakingly created and that can't possibly be used in the real world.

Have you taken leadership positions in professional groups? Do you take on free interns who are trying to fulfill college credit obligations? Do you create and share successful models, concepts, and methodology? Do you create and/or engage in mastermind groups? (If the bromide were true that you should never be the smartest person in the mastermind group, then there would never be such a group at all, correct?)

3. *Are you providing pro bono work?*

Aside from any marketing implications, are you using your specialties and talents to help a local school, charity, or arts group? (Some communities have talent banks to which you can offer your skills.) Are you helping people not for money or marketing, but simply for the purpose of helping?

It's amazing how relatively little work can make a huge difference in organizations that don't have a hint of a clue about how to set strategy, or resolve conflict, or create accurate budgets, or implement technology effectively.

4. *Are you coaching and mentoring?*

There are people who are unable to pay for the help they need but are legitimate candidates for coaching (they don't simply want something for nothing). They recognize the need for professional development, which would probably leverage their progress.

In every single workshop I conduct there is at least one scholarship participant. No one knows who they are, and I never provide the benefit to anyone who asks me for it. But it's easy to tell who could use it if you're involved in the aforementioned activities, and my selections are based on potential and enthusiasm. I never ask scholarship participants for any repayment, ever.[2] What you do may take the form of free publications, free workshop seats, accompanying you on a call, free teleconference participation, and so forth.

5. *Are you refusing inappropriate requests?*

With the best of intentions (and sometimes the worst), clients will ask you to assist them by:

- Revealing the specifics of coaching conversations.
- Revealing specific names behind anonymous survey responses.
- Revealing employee conversations and comments that you overheard while engaged in other work.
- Sharing confidences that you have agreed to keep with others.
- Sharing inappropriate information about other clients.
- Providing false or misleading reports to the board or other managers.
- Taking sides in political, internecine conflicts.

If you're going to advise your client on how to act, then you have to know how to act, and walk that talk.

Notes

1. See an attorney if my rule of thumb is insufficient, and you'll get the entire concept in 200 pages instead of my paragraph.
2. Not surprisingly, a few people who have asked to attend something for which they'll pay me later have never paid me back or even raised the issue again. I don't do that anymore.

Chapter 14

Exit Strategies
Nothing Is Forever

Building Equity

At some point you will leave your firm or it will leave you. We know this. So you might as well prepare for it!

In this first segment, we'll discuss building the worth and value of the firm—the equity. If you recall, there are two models that are desirable in this business.

Model #1: The solo practitioner, who has no full-time employees, has relatively few physical assets, may not have an office that is owned outside the home, and takes virtually all profits out of the firm yearly to use personally.

Model #2: The boutique firm, which you own and which has physical assets such as an owned office, employees, and infrastructure, and where the owner invests a proportion of the profits back into the business each year in the form of salaries, benefits, expansion needs, and so forth.

I'll talk about building equity for both models here, and you can apply what is most applicable to the type of practice you have built or are building. Bear in mind *that it's never too early to begin planning for high equity, but it can be too late.* And, as I admonished earlier, confusing these two models will lead to disaster in most cases and seriously undermine equity, since no one wants to buy a flying goat, no matter how nice the wings look that you've strapped onto it. If you try to force it to fly, you will simply wind up with a very unhappy goat.

> ### The Gospel
>
> You can start building practice or firm equity from the first day. The problem is that many consultants don't consider it until the last day.

In order to build the value of your business in others' eyes and for the purposes that will follow in the remainder of this chapter, irrespective of whether you attempt an outright sale or other alternatives, here are seven ways you can create an actual flying machine with proper aeronautics:

1. *Maintain strong lists and databases.*

    Keep track of everybody and everything, which is easier today than ever before thanks to technology. Don't merely track clients; record the people in client companies, their titles, and their contact information. Keep track of prospects, proposals *that were rejected,* leads, and recommendations.

    Inside Tip: Track these people when they move, and purge your lists regularly by sending an e-mail or newsletter or offer—you'll be notified of bounces. The qualitative aspect (up to date) is more important than the quantitative aspect (thousands of inaccurate contacts).

2. *Retain strong, long-term relationships with key vendors.*

    Pay local people first—designers, Web experts, printers, accountants, lawyers, and so forth. Make sure they are contacted regularly even if you don't have business for them directly. Keep them loyal to your practice.

    Inside Tip: Do something annually for key local people, such as an office party or summer picnic. Offer occasional pro bono work. Most important, send them referral business.

3. *Create and protect intellectual property.*

    Turn your intellectual capital into salable intellectual property. I have dozens of plaques on the wall showing trademark registrations in my company's name. (This is also important if you're ever looking for investors.) Make sure all of your work is copyrighted. Keep track of legal actions and their resolutions.

    Inside Tip: Track revenue by products, service, or offerings. Your bookkeeper can do this easily. Show the income generated and the projected growth at a conservative rate.

4. *As you get older, consider increasing your salary and benefits.*

Most of us are convinced that we have to reduce our W-2 (taxable) income and use pretax dollars if possible. However, as we get to a point where our departure from the business becomes more and more a possibility (which may be at a relatively young age for those already highly successful and seeking other adventures), the income we personally receive becomes an asset of the business. It's profit to a buyer.

Inside Tip: You can increase personal income and still take tax deductions by increasing your charitable contributions, for example. Or you can simply enjoy the money or put it away for the next stage of your life.

5. *Gather and constantly refresh testimonials.*

Ironically, highly successful practices often have testimonials that are 10 years old because they never feel the pressure to ask for more or make them more contemporary! You need to demonstrate that the practice is continuing to attract and delight clients.

Inside Tip: Don't be bashful about refreshing old testimonials. Go to supportive people and ask if they'll update testimonials that are several years old. This is also why video testimonials are so powerful—there is seldom a time frame connected with them, as long as no one is wearing bell-bottoms!

6. *Maintain visibility in media.*

Never cease publishing newsletters, blog items, articles in print sources, interviews, and so forth. This should be easier than ever, relying on your prior publishing and contacts. Maintain visibility, even if it's mainly in the narrow fields you may choose to serve.

Inside Tip: Try to secure columns, which are evergreen and seldom sunset unless the publication is sold or your own quality diminishes. I've published with some sources for over a decade.

7. *Update your look.*

Invest in upgrading your web site, logo, blogs, collateral material, and so forth. Your look may not be dated, but even famous brands (e.g., Coke and FedEx) change their look occasionally. With a loyal client base and visibility, you're not going to lose customers just because you change the paint on the place.

Inside Tip: It's easier, less expensive, and far more coordinated to do this when you also change your technology—improve your web site, blog, and/or chat rooms; change computers; upgrade your remote services (teleconferences, webinars); and take advantage of technology advances you can't afford to miss in any case.

Licensing Intellectual Property

Licensing intellectual property (IP) requires that you *have* intellectual property! We've discussed the importance of this earlier in the book.

If you sell your company, the IP becomes a potential asset and part of equity. If you don't sell your company, it remains an asset that may be sold or licensed. (Many years ago, John Humphrey was chairman of a training firm called Forum. He told me that when his bankers were loath to lend money without tangible collateral, he'd take them to the bank vault and show them his original materials, trademarks, and so forth, precomputer. It may be apocryphal, but it's a great visualization.)

Here are some criteria for the desirability and equity potential of IP:

- Is it selling well now, generating income of its own?
- Is it likely to sell well in the future?
- Can it be readily updated and kept relevant?
- Is it amenable to varied media and delivery sources?
- It is cross-cultural, applicable globally?
- Can it be delivered with minimal overhead and costs?
- Can it be sold and delivered completely independent of you?

You may choose to license on a situational basis: Someone may ask to use your IP with one of their projects.

You may choose to license on a time-frame basis: for a year, or five years.

You may choose to license in perpetuity, provided that certain conditions are maintained—in effect, a sale.

You may choose to license to a company for internal use, or to individuals for public use (and with their clients).

The Gospel

If you are a solo practitioner, licensing IP is the exception to not being able to sell your business. You can sell parts of it!

What are most conducive to meeting the aforementioned criteria that you should consider developing with that objective in mind?

- A workshop or seminar that can be delivered by any skilled professional and is not dependent on you, as it would be if people were attending specifically to see you discuss a book you wrote.

- A teleconference series with a significant number of subscribers in which the content hasn't always been yours and the delivery hasn't solely been from you.

- A book that others take to develop multiple media. (These are notoriously lucrative for the writer, but highly dangerous for the people trying to convert the material to profitable delivery mechanisms.)

- A proprietary model (e.g., for strategy formulation or the acceleration of sales closing), which others can implement on their own.

- An Internet-based chat room, answer center, or moderated discussion that others can take over.

- Newsletters, podcast series, and other regular delivery systems to which people subscribe.

- A system that is an approach to a general market and even your name with it. (You can license, e.g., "Alan Weiss's Million Dollar Consulting® System," including workshops, materials, audio, video, and so forth, for exclusive ownership in a variety of countries.)

If you want to orient these and other properties you develop to maximize licensing potential, you should be ruthless in discriminating among those that generate serious revenue, those that merely support other things you do, those that are solely dependent on you, and those that you just keep around for comfort, like pets. There is nothing like a track record of business to convince people to license your property.

Let's use a workshop as an example. If it's two days in length and a client pays $25,000 to place 20 people in it, you should demonstrate that there is a demand for this item at least once a quarter—there's a $100,000 business right there. You should demonstrate that it's been delivered by your own subcontractors and/or by client personnel, showing that you are not required personally for it to be a success. You may be able to show that someone else actually sold a couple, which you then delivered, proving that you're not even necessary for the sale.

You get the idea. If that number is two per quarter, and you've been doing this for five years running, and you deliver only half of them yourself, you then have a potential licensing fee of $200,000 to $1,000,000.

How did I arrive at that? If someone wished to license this for a year, the assumption would have to be that they could triple your sales by focusing on this full-time (or more than you do, since it's a subset of other value you provide). That would be 12 per year at the lower number, or $300,000, generating a $100,000 profit for the licensee. However, if they wanted a five-year agreement, you might lower the fee to $150,000 per year, or $750,000, while the licensee stands to make about $1,500,000 over that period.

If someone wanted to have rights in perpetuity, then these figures might easily generate a million-dollar license arrangement—all based on your delivery of a workshop that is uniquely yours about once a quarter. *When people see a reliable track record, they begin to pay for potential.*

I chose a workshop for simplicity, but this process applies to sophisticated consulting approaches, coaching, and other methodology just as well, and often far more lucratively.

In considering licensing candidates, approach the other party as you would a prospect. Make sure the chemistry is right. Perform due diligence. Do not agree to be paid out of future profits. You're not a bank.

Consider putting these provisions in place:

- The license is for the licensee only, and may not be sold or inherited or otherwise transferred.

- Quality criteria must be met (client feedback, time frames observed, and so on) as a condition of keeping the license.

- If payment is annual, it must be received in full by a certain date.

- You may randomly audit the delivery and results.

- Certain aspects of the work may not be changed or altered.

- Under no circumstances can the licensee compete with you.

To enhance the license, you can offer options, such as continual updates of the IP as you evolve, personal appearances on occasion to help in promotion, ongoing training and refreshers for the licensee and his or her support team, and mention in your promotion and publicity campaigns.

If you develop sufficient IP, you can create a million dollars of non-labor-intensive income during your career. The time to start thinking about it is now, not when you plan to get out of the profession!

Achieving Life Balance

Life balance is a bit of a deceptive phrase, since it implies a fulcrum with a balanced platform hovering above it. But life balance isn't about 50/50 relationships and work and life weighting.[1]

Let's establish a few basic tenets:

- You don't have a "work life" and a "business life." You have *a life.* There is no advantage to compartmentalization, and there are some huge time disadvantages.

- Wealth is discretionary time. You can work so hard and long earning money (which is merely fuel) that you actually erode your wealth.
- When you, as most of us, are a refugee from a large organization and become a solo practitioner to control your fate, you all too often wind up working for a tougher, more unreasonable boss.
- TIAABB: There is always a bigger boat. You can't compare yourself to others, and size doesn't mean a thing. There are plenty of unhappy people on huge yachts.
- No one ever uttered on their death bed, "I wish I had brought on a few more clients and spent less time with the grandchildren."

Life balance is about fulfillment, exercising your talents, attracting and caring for loved ones, and leaving the place a bit better off than when you found it. You don't have to be a megabillionaire to do that.

The true measure of generosity is not how much one gives, but how much, after giving, one has left over.

—Joseph Epstein, from A Line Out for a Walk
(W.W. Norton, 1992)

The Gospel

Life balance is really about life fulfillment, and that will differ from person to person.

I was conducting a session on life balance for entrepreneurs at Boston University on one occasion, and a very successful attorney said, "I love my work, I am fulfilled by helping my clients meet their goals, and I do that 80 hours a week. What's wrong with that?"

"Do you have a family?" I asked.

"Yes, a wife and three boys."

"How do they feel about your 80-hour weeks?"

There was no answer to that. Life balance has to be in harmony with those around you, and particularly your loved ones. The late, great strategist Peter Drucker observed that companies are not like plants or animals, deemed successful by merely perpetuating the species. Organizations are judged by the contributions they make to the surrounding environment.

Why would people be any different? Figure 14.1 shows Abraham Maslow's famous hierarchy of needs. Note that Maslow, a distinguished psychologist, is best known for these building blocks, *but there is no empirical evidence, and there are no longitudinal studies of any kind, that validate their application in the modern workplace.* In fact, Maslow had a far better insight when he admonished that, if the only tool you have is a hammer, you're apt to see every problem as a nail.

The hierarchy presupposes that we progress, sequentially, from the need for basic survival to security and ultimately to what Maslow calls self-actualization, which is the utilization of our talents on a regular basis. I'm going to pose a slightly different view.

I believe we actually move among these levels. We move because of work, life, emotional, psychological, interpersonal, and physical factors that tend to shift, change, and adapt. Traumatically, if we are fired, we fall down these steps to the bottom level; but even if we are just faced with a change at work (new boss, new assignment, cutbacks, new technology, and so forth) we may find

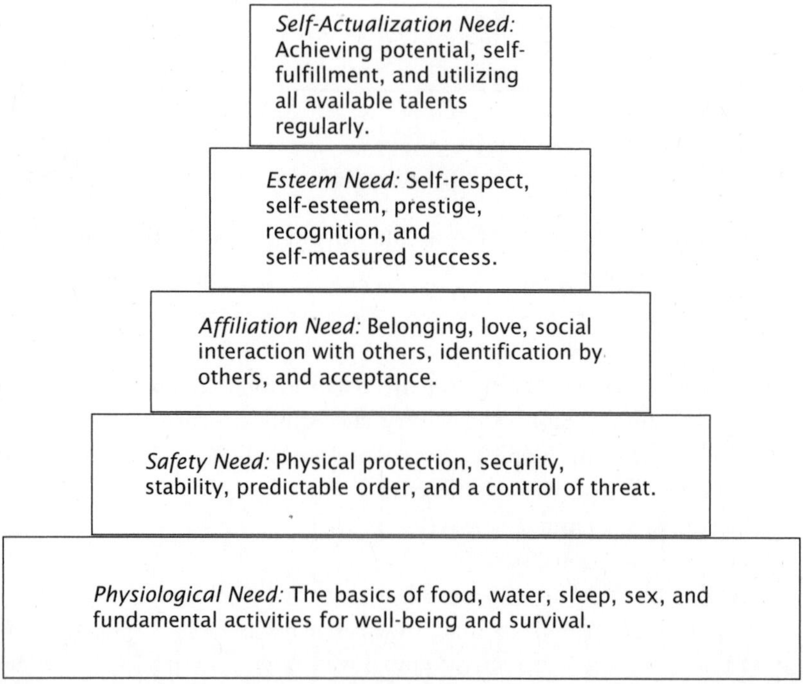

Self-Actualization Need: Achieving potential, self-fulfillment, and utilizing all available talents regularly.

Esteem Need: Self-respect, self-esteem, prestige, recognition, and self-measured success.

Affiliation Need: Belonging, love, social interaction with others, identification by others, and acceptance.

Safety Need: Physical protection, security, stability, predictable order, and a control of threat.

Physiological Need: The basics of food, water, sleep, sex, and fundamental activities for well-being and survival.

FIGURE 14.1 Maslow's Hierarchy of Needs

ourself moving from an upper level down to affiliation since we need commiseration or comfort in the face of change.

My advice to you is this: We all have certain talents, and we all are capable of developing more over the course of our lives. Some are thrust upon us (computer use) and some are voluntarily sought (singing lessons). Here's the key, and where Maslow was right: *The more we are able to utilize the full diversity of our talents every day in our lives, the happier and more productive we will be.*

Note that I didn't say "our work lives." Woody Allen, the famed director and former comic who has released another new movie as I write this, plays jazz clarinet every Saturday with a group in a New York café. That's how he exercises that talent, not otherwise required in his work.

Life balance is about a healthy distribution of talents utilized at work and at play. To me that means not a 50/50 split, but certainly not a 0/100 or 100/0, either. If few of your talents are applied in your profession, then you're going to have long and lonely days, highly stressed, and relatively unproductive. If few of your talents are applicable in your personal life, then you're going to spend too many hours at work and be a rather boring or cantankerous person socially.

You don't need to use talents daily—I wouldn't think that scuba diving or opera singing would fit into most weekly routines—but you can exercise them by creating the opportunities during the year. Talents require differing levels of involvement. I like to write every day, but scuba diving twice a year is fine. (If I needed to scuba dive daily, I'd become an instructor.)

I knew a manager at Merck with a decent but not great operatic voice. He would arrange to get into La Scala and similar venues when they were closed, go out on the main stage, and sing an aria! He had done this in a dozen places and loved telling about it!

You are in this profession as a means to generate fuel (money) to create wealth (discretionary time). In the course of that pursuit, you should be able to exercise existing and new talents on a regular basis. This will maintain your health, happiness, and heart. When you join in these pursuits with loved ones, who support your talents as you support theirs, there is no greater feeling.

That's life balance.

Finding Successors and Buyers

If you do intend to sell your company (or if you are looking for people to purchase your intellectual property or franchises), and assuming you've done a fine job creating and manifesting equity, then you need to find investors.

Here are seven routes to that destination:

1. *An equivalent operation that is seeking to expand.*

There will be myriad firms like yours that are looking for dramatic expansion. Your firm may be in the same type of consulting and would help consolidate their market, or it may be different and synergistic and provide new markets. Over the years, you should be developing professional relationships through trade associations so that you can approach these other principals with such an offer.

It's very important to pursue this principal-to-principal so that secrecy is maintained, because rumors, worries, and resistance from employees can undermine these negotiations before they begin.

2. *Allow an employee buyout.*

If you have long-term employees, you may already have provided them with a small piece of the business. In any case, a core group of employees might decide that the company they know from the inside is a great purchase. You'll need to consider a leveraged buyout, whereby they put down a deposit and pay the balance out of their profits over an agreed-upon time frame.

In this scenario, you are better off with a small number of purchasers and clear decision making, and they need to limit their own salaries and bonuses until you are paid off completely.

The Gospel

Valuation of a company is a job for professionals. Professional services firms are often valued at one to three times sales, or six or more times earnings. Prepare to maximize these a few years before your intended sell date.

3. *Find people in other countries.*

It's common for entrepreneurs in other countries to want to dominate a market by importing methodology with a strong brand and track record of success. Look for opportunities where translation isn't required. South Africa, Singapore, Australia, Canada, New Zealand, Ireland, and the United Kingdom would be of highest potential for materials in English, for example.

This is why there is tremendous benefit in global travel and work during your career, so that these contacts can be built. These investors might want to franchise your work in their country, license certain property, or purchase something outright.

4. *Look for hungry start-up people.*

I met a speaker once who was very good on the stage, but whose material was limited. He opted to purchase the intellectual property of another, retiring speaker in totality, and mesh that into his offerings.

You'll find people with money who are starting second careers and who need the jump start of an existing business, infrastructure, clients, methodology, brands, and so on. You become, in effect, a turnkey operation for them to purchase. You never know. I've had doctors, lawyers, sex therapists, and nuclear submarine captains in my Million Dollar Consulting® College.

5. *Consider your family.*

Do you have children, siblings, cousins, or other family connections who may be interested in owning the firm? It's wise to have such children involved for several years and gradually take over the business, which is not uncommon. You'd be available for backstage guidance and the occasional intervention with a long-term client.

Beware: Family connections can also be the worst connections if people don't act professionally, and it's always problematic to have family members owe you money!

6. *Target a much larger firm.*

Years ago there was a concerted effort by publishers such as the Times/Mirror Group, McGraw-Hill, and Prentice Hall to purchase training companies and boutique consulting firms under the (false) premise that they were all in the information exchange business.

While this turned out to be disastrous for the purchasers, it was a financial boon to the purchased firms. It may be that a huge firm would find that your practice fits nicely into one of its growing businesses, or helps to launch a new one. For the huge firm, money is never a problem. (Never agree to an employee contract during transition, which is typically a couple of years. This is a reason for your company to have a separate brand from your name. The only thing worse than sweating blood for your own business is doing so for someone else's. Don't sell your firm to become someone else's employee.)

7. *Break it up.*

Especially if you're a solo practitioner, but even in a boutique business, consider separating out intellectual property, workshops, speeches, books, Internet presence, consulting models, retainer clients, and so on into distinct, salable entities. Make sure you sever interrelationships, and sell what you can to the most appropriate, relevant, and eager parties.

As long as clients are respected and supported, this fragmentation can work, and you may even choose to retain certain elements that require little labor but provide a great deal of gratification for you.

All organizations come to an end. There is no reason to maintain them merely for the sake of doing so. However, retirement isn't a fixed concept in our profession. So what you choose to perpetuate, terminate, or otherwise change is totally up to you. If you've built a substantial operation that isn't to be left to your family, then you probably need a buyer. If you've generated a lot of money with a solo practice, you don't really need a formal ending point.

Keep these criteria in mind:

- Will I be able to provide for my loved ones in a lifestyle we find attractive?
- Will I be challenged and my talents be used without letup?
- Will my clients be cared for and supported properly?
- Will my intellectual property and other items of worth be appropriately represented and valued?
- Will I be proud of what I've done?

Transitioning

If you agree at all with what's been said thus far in this chapter, you'll probably agree that making a transition can be vastly different for different people. Personally, I never plan to retire in any kind of conventional sense, but I do plan to continue to steadily reinvent myself.

Case Study

"Tom" was a friend of mine for a long time. He had worked in private industry, watched consultants work with his company, and then joined one of those consulting firms. Eventually, he purchased the consulting firm with a colleague when the founder retired to Florida, still a quite vital 70-something.

Over the years they built the firm into a $4 million boutique business with distinguished clients and a staff of six. Tom and his partner ran the place idiosyncratically, often like cowboys, but had a great time and did excellent work. Ultimately, the partner became ill and Tom bought him out. The partner later passed away.

Tom ran the place, living the good life, with a long-term marriage and daughter. In his early 60s, he decided to sell to a huge consulting/accounting firm. However, the buyer demanded that he remain with the company for two years to oversee the transition period. Being an instant partner in the huge parent was appealing to Tom's ego.

However, Tom had to go through basic training, was away for long hours, and was junior to all existing partners. What he called "amusing" and "awkward" I found humiliating and ridiculous. Tom became seriously ill, and was able to leave the new company on disability without violating his contract.

I think that illness saved his life.

Here are my guidelines to you for a successful transition—major reinvention, if you will—in leaving or altering your business, no matter your age or years in operation.

- Start planning at least five years before you anticipate a major shift. Don't start scrambling around with a few months' cushion. Do what makes sense gradually: build equity, create stronger brands, look for potential buyers, explore an employee buyout, see if the family is interested, begin licensing, and so forth. If you end up going beyond five years without major change, there is really no harm done.

- Protect yourself from forced change. Carry the largest disability insurance policies available. Create an executive officer position or find key subcontract people to whom a great deal of work can be delegated. Maximize your remote work, such as retainer business and distance coaching. License approaches to clients.

- Put your own oxygen mask on first. You are not running a corporate welfare system. Consider what is best for your family and you, not your employees, vendors, or even customers. You are under no obligation to provide lifetime employment, nor to share the proceeds from a sale with people who do not have a financial investment in the business. Employees are not partners.

The Gospel

"Transition" denotes time investment, not abrupt and traumatic change. Think "metamorphosis."

- Don't think in terms of all or nothing. You may well retain certain aspects of what you're doing (e.g., speaking and writing), sell others (coaching practice), and terminate the rest (consulting work). You may retain the company name or start a new one. (This is why having multiple brands adds to flexibility. You can retire some and maintain others.)
- Assess your financial position with expert help. Have your financial advisor and attorney consider your passive income, active income, retirement benefits, tax situation, and so forth. This may well influence the type and form of practice you decide to perpetuate or to terminate.
- Consider perquisites and peripheral benefits that may disappear. You may enjoy travel to certain spots, meaning you'd want to retain that client or commitment. You may revel in the gratification of coaching, which would suggest you'd want to continue offering that service in some form. It's never solely about money; it's about gratification and wealth (discretionary time).
- Review long-term commitments. You will want to:
  - Arrange to retain certain clients and commitments.
  - Transfer some obligations to others and forewarn the clients.
  - Gracefully end or not renew certain relationships.
  - Transition some things to lower frequency, shorter duration, or remote rather than on-site work.
  - Cease depending on certain sources of income that will disappear.
  - Resist engaging in certain commitments that will exceed your time frames.

You have options, depending on the extent of your leaving or retaining certain aspects of your practice. To be fair, you need to apprise all interested parties of what the near-term future holds.

- Consider where you intend to be geographically. You may not move an inch. You may move halfway around the world. Technology makes it easier to remain in touch, but not necessarily to travel or to interact in person. What activities and commitments best suit your future locale? Will you have the equivalent technological access, support people, travel ease? These considerations can influence what your future practice looks like.
- What will you use to replace the options you have had to exercise certain talents? Especially if you are largely giving up your practice, or drastically changing it, you have had the ability to stretch your talents at

work. Something will have to replace that or you will become increasingly unfulfilled. It may be pro bono work, or part-time teaching, or mentoring, but you should plan to apply your talents in other ways.

- What will be the extent of your access? Will long-time clients and business acquaintances still have your cell phone number and private e-mail? Will they be encouraged to ask for an occasional piece of advice? Or would you prefer to leave a good deal of this behind and cut the ties? You need to make that clear and to have a personal policy, or you could be drawn back into your old routines but without being paid for doing so!

Transitions can be wonderful if you plan for them, understand your options, and choose carefully what's best for you in your ideal future. In other words, follow the exact same advice you'd give a client.

Note

1. I've got about four pages here, but if you'd like to read about 200 on the subject, see my book *Life Balance: How to Convert Professional Success into Personal Happiness* (Jossey-Bass/Pfeiffer, 2003).

15

Payback and Reinvestment

We Build Our Houses and Then They Build Us

Mentoring Others

Coaching, which I've covered earlier in methodology discussions, is a proactive process used with clients to create behavioral changes and improvement. I've noted that mentoring is far different.

Here, I'm referring to mentoring *not* as a revenue-producing endeavor, but as a contribution to the profession. You may choose to become involved situationally as people approach you, or systemically by providing the options publicly. You may do this as a separate aspect of your business, or you may engage in it despite also offering a formalized, high-fee service elsewhere.

No profession grows unless those who become highly adept and successful within its ranks decide to create and disseminate best practices for others.

Some professional and trade associations perform this function as an aspect of membership—a cosmetic surgery conference organizes a panel discussion among leading surgeons; an architectural group provides sessions as which various design award winners share their creative processes.

But in too many instances, professional associations seem determined to bring every member's level of success down to that of its least successful member!

They eschew excellence because "everyone should have a chance." They don't discriminate between value and contribution because they are envious of success they don't enjoy and, paradoxically, don't want to hear about how it was achieved. (The guys in the back of the hall doing poorly, mumbling to each other that the guest speaker, a spectacular success, is full of hot air, comprise one of the truly ludicrous aspects of many of these gatherings.)

Unfortunately, most local chapters of these organizations constitute a bunch of longtime members trying to justify their own inertia. (An object at rest tends to stay at rest.)

For professions to advance through the success of a maximum number of those who choose to enter the field, those leading the way have to provide the skills, encouragement, examples, thought leadership, and, most of all, the accessibility.

The Gospel

It's one thing to say, "Here's what you do." It's another to offer, "Let's discuss how you do it."

First, here is what's in your self-interest for mentoring others:

- You will learn. I never fail to teach a course, coach someone, or share experiences without learning more myself than anyone else learns. (Why is this more than just a bromide? Because when you have the experience, insights, and perspective, you can appreciate what occurs more than anyone who doesn't.)

- You will keep your finger on the pulse of the profession. It's hard for me to tell you what a new consultant, or a technology consultant, or a consultant in the United Kingdom is going through these days if I'm not consistently interacting with these people. When you're successful, it's too easy to view the world from a jaded and inaccurate perch. (The film critic Pauline Kael, who lived on Manhattan's Upper East Side, became notorious for her line, "How was Richard Nixon ever elected? None of my friends voted for him.")

- You gain perspective about what is a legitimate intervention or approach methodologically, and what simply works because of your own relationships and experiences. I'm constantly and correctly asked, "But that's you, Alan. Can anyone do that?" I have to be certain about what is a validated approach and what is simply a great client relationship or fame from a book. What is really transferable? (This is why so many executive biographies are worthless in terms of others' development—none of it is transferable. How many people have lunch with Henry Ford?)

- Your thought leadership will actually be enhanced. Your processes will be spread, recognition of your contributions will be acknowledged, and your name will continue to be cited as being in the forefront of the profession. (This is of no small advantage when you choose to propose another book to a publisher or to speak at a national event.)

I'm not suggesting that mentoring others is purely mercenary, only that we engage in activities with more passion when benefits also accrue directly to us. That's why we're so good with paying clients!

Some people may come to you seeking advice. In fact, I receive weekly requests to pick my brain or share ideas. I almost always refuse these because they involve far too much of my time ("Can we have lunch?") or they are from people who don't even know what to ask me and have no clue as to what to do with my responses. That's just wasting time, like teaching a seal to whistle or a dog to drive. It's not going to happen, no matter how much time and earnestness are employed.

However, here's what I find useful, pragmatic, effective, and not too labor intensive, which you may find appropriate for your level of success in helping others.

- I always include scholarship people in my programs. I have formalized offerings that consist of workshops, seminars, practicums, and so on. Each has at least one (and usually more) person who I'm convinced can learn and profit but couldn't otherwise afford to be there. I don't ask for financial information, and it has nothing to do with age or years in the profession; I merely extend the offer, no strings attached. (When I've extended the offer at others' requests with the promise to repay me sometime in the future, I've never once been paid back.)

- I will accept people who I believe are truly serious and have learned about the profession, *and have taken the time to learn about me.* For example, when people approach me for help but have not bothered to read *Million Dollar Consulting* (or, now, this book as well), or don't know what I mean by "value-based fees," or don't read my free news-letters, then I'm not convinced they are serious. All of this work is either free or can be borrowed. If you're not interested in my work and approaches, why should I be interested in yours?

- One at a time. I'll mentor someone for a finite period—usually a couple of months—before considering another. I'm there to help them along the way for a while, not to be their career coach ad infinitum.

- I'm reactive, never proactive. Reach out to me when you need something and I'll be responsive and specific. But don't expect me to follow up with you, and don't ask silly questions, such as "What is the full range of things I should know about?" or the insipid "What haven't I asked you that I should have?"

As people come into your life, evaluate whether you have the heart—not merely the intellect—to help them. If you do, accommodate their needs to your own needs. But you have to be committed, and can't accept this responsibility as a time waster or drag on your own life and career.

Not all people are cut out for this career, by the way. You can rarely control others' discipline or talent. When you encounter procrastination, it's virtually always an indicator of fear.

That means that on some occasions, the best possible advice you can give to people is to find other work. The legal profession is not helped by struggling (or dishonest) attorneys; doctors as a group don't profit from huge and justified malpractice claims against some colleagues; teachers are having a hard time getting better pay because it's so hard to get rid of the acknowledged poor teachers, due to ossified union rules.

We can't afford poor consultants in a profession far less regulated than any of those I've cited in the preceding paragraph. We need a profession of high quality and, as mentors, we need to do others the favor—and show them the respect—of directing them elsewhere if they are not going to be able to distinguish themselves (and, therefore, all the rest of us) in this wonderful profession.

Mentoring others is, therefore, one of the most important things we wind up doing if we're qualified by our success, longevity, and temperament. You don't have to do it a lot, but if all of us did it a little, the profession would be far better off and the quality would be evident to all clients and prospects.

Advancing the State of the Art

At the outset of this book, I described a probably not too far-fetched meeting of an early consultant and a client. That transaction—providing an improvement in the buyer's condition in exchange for agreed-upon remuneration—has not essentially changed. (That's because it's the basis for capitalism in general.)

What has changed is the means and devices with which we improve our clients. Frederick Winslow Taylor fostered time-and-motion studies, the height of scientific management, which were later found to be fraudulent and useless. The iconic Hawthorne studies of improving productivity merely by demonstrating that you're paying attention to people later proved to be suspect in their devices and lack of rigor. Even the charming and sexy theories—we discussed Maslow's hierarchy of meeds most recently—are usually not validated in the workplace.

Fads, trends, and mere phrases arrive and depart with the regularity of commuter trains at Grand Central Station on a weekday morning:

- Reengineering
- Lean
- Good to great
- Employee-driven organizations
- Open book management
- Customer-driven organizations
- Post-heroic leadership
- One-minute management
- Quality circles
- Quark leadership

Okay, I made up the last one, but a lot of you didn't immediately notice.

As we climb the mountain of this profession, we have to create trails for others. There may be nothing totally new under the sun—the pharaohs had to employ teams to erect the pyramids, but their motivational devices were different—there are recombinations and additions that maximize effectiveness in changing economies, societies, and technologies.

As an example, Figure 15.1 is a visual I created while writing this chapter to explain a different way of looking at market potential. The traditional bell curve places the great mass of the market in the center. In this depiction, I'm attempting to illustrate a three-dimensional view that is asymmetrical, in that the *value of one's market* depends on its depth.

Hence, as you increase your innovation and interest along the horizontal axis you will encounter apathetic audiences; then pretenders who aren't serious about the profession but are dabblers and dilettantes; then aspirants who have varying degrees of seriousness about growth; then serial developers who tend to consider all growth opportunities, depending on their resources; and finally "hang-tens" (from surfing daredevils) who immerse themselves in the greatest challenges and new techniques.

When one views these in terms of true value of customers and not merely numbers of customers, a very different conclusion can be drawn about where best to invest one's time and money. Although the right edge of the bell curve (a standard deviation away) looks puny, it is, in effect, where the greatest value

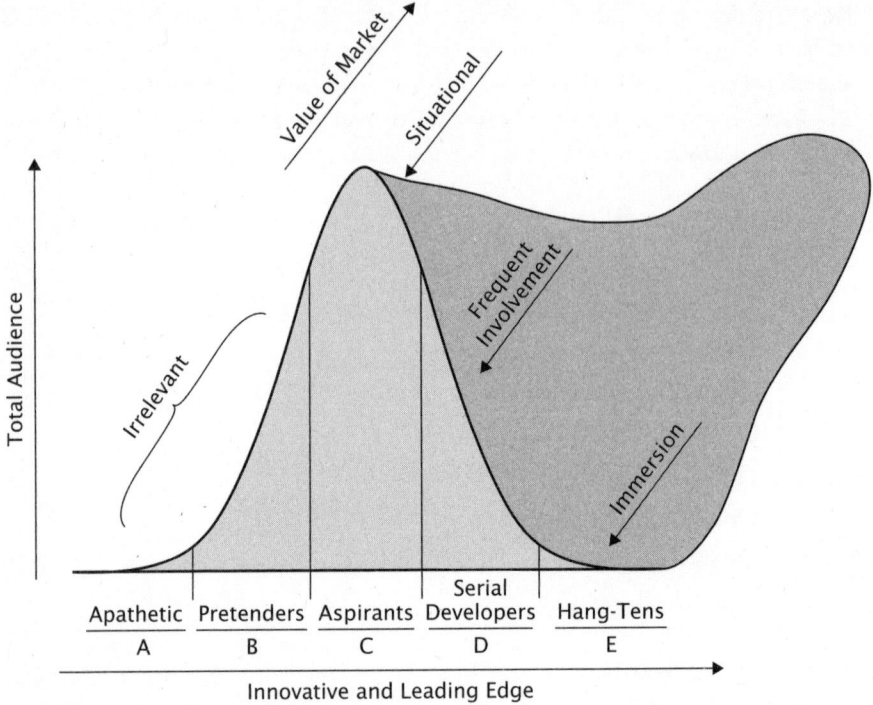

FIGURE 15.1 Market 3-D Bell Curve

market resides for someone who is highly innovative and at the top of his or her profession—someone with a brand and clear intellectual property.

I don't ask that you accept my proposition here, and this is why I didn't present this in the methodology discussions earlier. My point is that this is the kind of state-of-the-art advancement that I'm continually engaged in. You may not buy it, or you may try it and embrace it, but either way you know that I'm a source for this kind of provocative thinking. (And if I created a workshop or teleconference around it, people would attend.)

I think a great many of you are toward the right side of my chart. That's why you're reading this book, and it may well not be the first one of mine you've read. We all have an obligation to create new ways of thinking about and approaching our profession.

For example, there used to be a Big Eight accounting and consulting firm domination, which today is down to about a Big 3.5. Last year, IBM made far more profit from its consulting arm than it did from selling hardware or software. Boutique consulting firms and solo practices are flourishing all over the world, and rapidly growing economies in places such as Brazil, China,

India, and certain Middle East locations will have huge need for bilingual consultants.

Technology is enabling remote, global consulting and producing an exponential growth market. More books are being published than ever before, in hard copy and electronically. Social media platforms are screaming. There is a cacophony of ideas, but most of them are worthless.

Consulting trade and professional organizations are largely nonexistent. The profession is barely regulated anywhere. You can view this as chaos or opportunity, but you must view it as a continuing challenge!

I believe our responsibility in moving the profession forward includes:

- *Sharing our ideas.* We can protect what we need to, but we should be willing to show others and not be afraid.
- *Debunking the charlatans.* The more schlock that we passively allow to exist, the more it degrades the entire profession. (You don't set strategy by remembering the names of your pets when you were young, and you don't accelerate learning by reading things sideways.)
- *Being accessible.* I've discussed mentoring others. We need to be responsive to reasonable inquiries.
- *Being public representatives.* I've written so many letters to the editor and op-ed pieces (including those rejected) that I have separate files for them.
- *Making fun of ourselves, but not the work we do.* I love consultant jokes and can contribute my share. But I'm proud of the contributions I've made to organizations and individuals all over the world, and I'm not about to allow anyone to demean that.
- *Going public.* Don't hide intellectual property. Write books. Speak about it. People will find it in any case, so you might as well make it officially and overtly your own.
- *Paying our dues.* I belong to professional organizations I don't get much from in return, but I should be there ethically and I should be available to them should they need me.

The profession will continue to undergo change as demographics, the economy, technology, attempts at regulation, politics, and other factors dictate. But the core of improving the client's condition will not change.

Fortunately, the state of the art doesn't rely on particle accelerators, billions of dollars in investment, and 14 graduate degrees.

Participation in the Evolution

There is never a need to retire, but there is a need to continue to evolve, to adjust our manner to the times, and to appreciate our successes. After all, we're trying to successfully accommodate environmental change, client change, and our own change.

Our practices should continue to diversify. As our clients become more sophisticated and our own breadth greater, we can see the relationships depicted in Figure 15.2.

When we offer maximum diversity in the eyes of our mature clients—not all things to all people but rather broad-based advisory support—we enter into comprehensive relationships. We can be engaged in a series of projects and in concurrent initiatives, which may also embrace client resources working for the duration, subcontractors, and so on.

If our diversity is high but the client maturity is low, a retainer relationship covering any number of issues may be the best role. You become the trusted

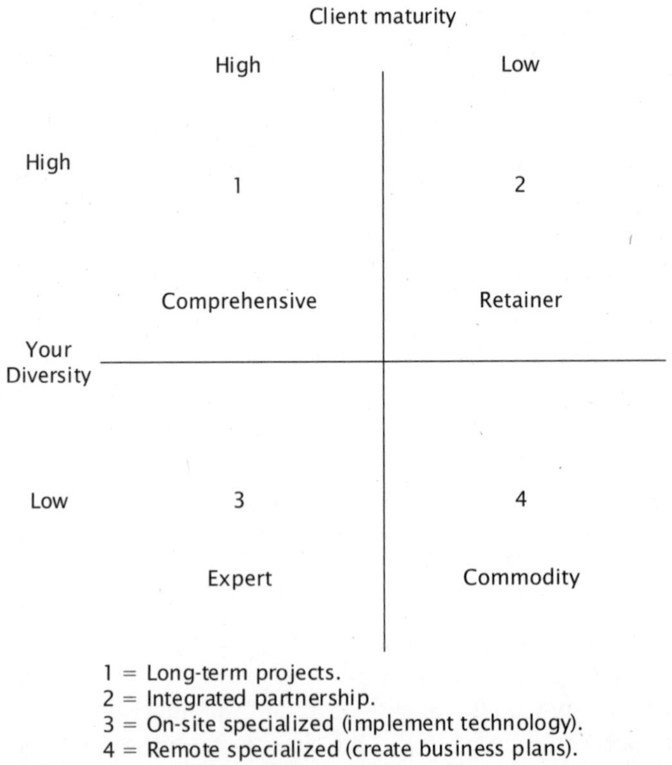

Client maturity

	High		Low
High	1		2
	Comprehensive		Retainer
Your Diversity			
Low	3		4
	Expert		Commodity

1 = Long-term projects.
2 = Integrated partnership.
3 = On-site specialized (implement technology).
4 = Remote specialized (create business plans).

FIGURE 15.2   Diversity and Client Maturity

advisor to a relatively small number of senior people who may contact you relatively infrequently, but you're there when they need you. You may be responding to strategic and tactical issues as that trusted sounding board.

When the client maturity is high but your own expertise remains narrow, you'll tend to be the expert resource. You'll be called in to work on that issue: merger, or compensation, or sales force effectiveness.

Finally, when your diversity is low and the client maturity is low, you'll simply be a commodity, undifferentiated, probably subject to price comparisons.

The first combination will tend to produce long-term, complex projects; the second, an integrated partnership; the third, on-site, specialized help (often seen with technology experts); and the fourth, remote specializations, often in the form of products. You have to make a decision about what you want your evolving practice to look like and how best it will suit your lifestyle.

You may find that you would rather travel less but continue to work with top people, which would point you toward quadrant 2. However, if you prefer to divorce yourself from personal relationships and responsibilities, quadrant 4 would make use of your intellectual property and generate revenue through commodity sales.

Factor into this scenario your own ability to draw people to you. We've discussed the concepts of Market Gravity, becoming an object of interest, and thought leadership. As your practice matures, you should be reaching out less and less and attracting clients more and more (see Figure 15.3).

Most of the best consultants rarely reach out after a certain point. That means you can dictate how you will work with people and under what conditions. You can actually position yourself in the quadrants by filtering and selecting the people who approach you for help.

It's important to lose the mind-set that all business is good business and that it's wrong to turn any business away. Wealth is discretionary time, not piles of money.

The Gospel

Mold your future because I can guarantee you will not like the default position.

You are no longer the person who is concerned about next month's mortgage (or last month's!). Your focus should be on the life you need to create for yourself, your loved ones, and your personal, continuing interest in helping clients and the profession. You own nothing more than that and nothing less.

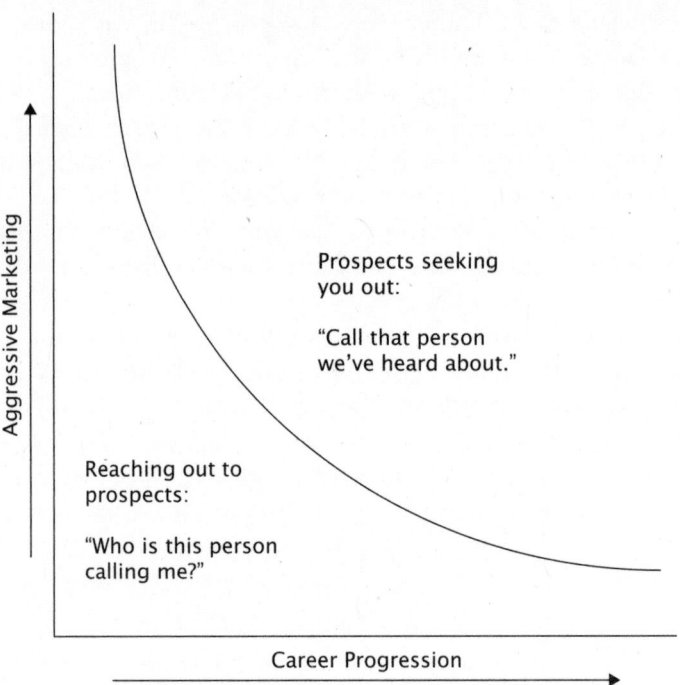

FIGURE 15.3   Reach Out versus Gravity

The Future

One day a woman sat in her work seat suspended a few feet above the floor of her home office, gravity-neutral. An implanted earpiece alerted her to a call from a client working on a moon mining project in an orbiter in geosynchronous orbit. She blinked her eyes in unison and accepted the call.

The client immediately provided a holographic image of his issue, which floated in front of the consultant. As she moved the pieces of the map around with her finger, she showed the client how to change the approach. He thanked her, and mentioned that he hoped to meet her one day, perhaps at the conference in Ulan Bator. The transaction had taken six minutes, part of her yearly retainer to his firm, and she was now due at a virtual conference with her London financial client, so she navigated her chair to her virtual office background area.

She thought she might be working too hard for a modern 2075 consultant.

I started this book talking about our prehistorical consultant, and thought it would be fun to speculate about our consulting descendants in this final segment. For me, the fascinating aspect is that their surroundings will have changed but the profession will not!

I will speculate about a few things that are likely to occur and affect you in the near-term future.

- The number of independent consultants will grow, as people continue to attempt to control their own destinies and they become disenchanted with traditional organizational rigor. (I'm citing true, serious practitioners, not people between jobs or doing subcontracting work.)

- Organizational needs will grow for consultants, since they will be economical alternatives, replacing the resident staffs, which had been underutilized, subject to internal politics, and often without the proper skills.

- Attempts at regulation, certification, and sanction will ebb and flow, but essentially fail, because the transaction is a simple one between those who need help and those who can provide help, and the nature of the help is so diverse and situational that the market is the best vehicle to determine whether the job has been done well. That's not nearly as true in medicine, law, or accounting.

- Technology will enable global reach for everyone, analogous to the small business on Main Street losing its retail customers but more than replacing them on the Internet. Technological prowess in marketing, communications, and delivery will be critical, and consultants will need help in these areas if they cannot do this themselves (and probably are far better off not doing it themselves).

- Informal networks of consultants will form to gather strength from numbers and diverse resources, in competition with formal, large firms but with far less overhead and attached costs. Solo practitioners in Brazil, India, Canada, the United States, and Australia might be bound together by Universal Consulting, Inc., which allows them to land business in Dubai by calling upon their combined international intellectual property, talent, and client lists.[1]

- Hourly and daily billing will be gone except for low-level practitioners, subcontractors, and trainers. The preponderance of important engagements will be billed based on value. (We'll see more and more law firms also shifting to this methodology.)

- The wholesale and retail markets will grow and decline independently based on economic factors, and will increasingly overlap. In other words, consultants will find individual clients in large companies, companies sponsoring individual growth, and individuals coming together in communities to take advantage of group experiences.

- Communities of interaction among peers, in both wholesale and retail venues, will grow and replace traditional trade and professional associations. The communities will be both virtual and real and it will be common to belong to several, all of which create value by dint of membership, affiliation, interaction, and so forth. Consultants will market by creating and fostering these communities in their whole-sale world (e.g., among CFOs or sales professionals) and retail world (e.g., among independent chartered accountants or entrepreneurs).

We're never held accountable for our prognostications, but I would suggest that it's important to contemplate these, add to them, modify them, and otherwise debunk them in terms of your own experience. But whatever the near future you see, you must start preparing for it now.

I've made it a point not to talk about veterans and newcomers in this book. We're all at varied stages of our careers, and many people engaged for a year are doing better than others who are 10 years into their practice. "Ten years of experience" is worthless (and a very peculiar requirement in any search for talent) if it's the same year 10 times over, or even 10 different unexciting and low-growth years. "How long have you been doing this?" is an insignificant question compared to "How well have you been doing this?"

For all of you reading (or listening to) this, tomorrow could be the first day of a new practice, career, or approach. This is a noble profession—which is why the term *bible* is not an inappropriate one from my perspective—in that it is oriented toward improving our client's condition in return for equitable compensation. That improvement and compensation are in the eyes and hands of the two principals: buyer and consultant. They are not subject to governmental regulation, traditional constraints (why do Realtors receive 6 percent?), or arbitrary conclusions. We are in the mainstream of capitalism: payment received in return for value of services rendered.

My concluding advice to you can be distilled into nine points:

1. Evaluate your talents, passion, and market.

2. Orient your time, resources, and energies to aggressively apply yourself to presenting your value to those with the ability to pay for it (Market Gravity).

3. Do great work, and acquire testimonials, endorsements, and references.

4. Minimize your labor intensity while maximizing your value and fees (Accelerant Curve).

5. Focus on the highest-value emerging markets qualitatively, not quantitatively (Market Value Bell Curve).

6. Create and disseminate intellectual property into your market on a consistent and continual basis, protecting all of your work and building strong brands.

7. Create maximum equity in your business and determine how you will capitalize on it.

8. Pay back your general community and specific profession with financial, time, and intellectual contributions.

9. Always remember that true wealth is discretionary time, and that there is *always* a bigger boat!

This has been an incredible journey for me. I'm glad you joined me. I'm honored to be on it with you.

> ### The Gospel
>
> You deserve to be happy and successful. Achieving those goals by helping others to be happy and successful is a great and wonderful privilege.

Note

1. In fact, in consideration of this need, I'm launching the Summit Global Network with two dozen consulting firm members in mid-2011.

Sample Proposal

Situation Appraisal

Since becoming Executive Vice President for XXXXXXXX four months ago, you have discovered numerous strengths in the organization as well as critical barriers to success. These qualities are even more significant given the goal to grow the business at a rate significantly above the historical. While doing so, you are expected to maintain the culture of the organization that is deemed valuable and productive by both your superiors and subordinates.

Your success depends on the creation and successful implementation of a powerful strategy through an organization with the right people in the right roles acting in concert with one another. Past success in building successful relationships with clients and peers will serve you well. However, in this role, you must manage a larger and more diverse organization than before. Further, you have a finite amount of time to demonstrate that you are the right person to lead the organization at this time.

Objectives

1. Provide a professional, external sounding board for you.
2. Develop and implement an integration process to accelerate your success as the Executive Vice President.
3. Provide a professional, expert view of the talent at the top of the organization.
4. Develop a clear, compelling strategy.
5. Develop and use a simple though powerful implementation plan.
6. Increase the cooperation and collaboration among the top leaders to ensure attainment of the goals. Specifically, reduce the friction between two of the Executive Committee members, whose talents are each needed to achieve success.

Measures of Success

1. Agreement between XXXXXXXX and yourself regarding the specific outcomes for which you are accountable.

2. Reduced time to make decisions and increased confidence in those decisions.

3. Increase in revenue while maintaining profit margin.

4. Evidence that the strategy and goals are clear and that behaviors are aligned in support of the plans. Such evidence will include:

   • Spontaneous conversations that indicate such.

   • Increased cooperation.

   • Increase in the number of ideas that come from the lower levels of the organization to the top.

5. Decrease in the number of conversations needed to manage the conflict at the top.

6. Positive feedback from the Chief Operating Officer regarding your performance, both financial and leadership.

Value

• Increase in sales of $1.5 million over the past year will add $300,000 to net profit, taking the total net profit to $1.3 million.

• Decrease in conflict at the top level will reduce time spent in conversation with those involved.

• Decrease in time to market of new ideas or approaches.

• Acceleration of your ability to make a positive impact.

• Create a useful framework for decision making, reducing time to do so.

Methodology and Options

Option 1   For a period of six months, conduct face-to-face meetings with you as needed and provide unlimited telephone consultation.

Meet with each of your direct reports to more fully understand them and the organizational context.

Conduct a meeting of the direct report team to debrief observations and further accelerate your integration.

Meet with the Executive Committee to ensure clarity of purpose and goals and alignment. Create a strategic framework to ensure the attainment of growth and profitability goals.

Meet with you, XXXX, and XXXX to resolve the issues between them and among the three of you.

Meet with you and XXXXXXXX to establish goals and expectations, and to achieve alignment and support for your plans.

Option 2 All the elements of Option 1, plus:

A follow-up meeting of the direct report group at the five-month mark, to identify new opportunities, challenges, and ideas and solidify your leadership.

Option 3 All the elements of Options 1 and 2, plus:

Survey the entire organization to more thoroughly understand the context and any cultural barriers to the effective implementation of your strategy. Analysis and debriefing of results with the direct report team are included.

Timing

The initial interviews and meetings will be completed within eight weeks of the commencement of this project.

The consultation to you and the Executive Committee will continue for a total of six months.

Joint Accountabilities

XXXXXXXX will provide Constance Dierickx, PhD, as the project leader. She will be continually involved in all aspects of the project, and will serve as the primary contact with XXXXXXXX. We will sign nondisclosure agreements as requested, and all work contents remain the property of XXXXXXXX.

XXXXXXXX will provide us with reasonable access to key management people, documentation, and company information, as appropriate, within the time frames outlined. XXXXXXXX will be responsible for scheduling of meetings, and obtaining necessary facilities, equipment, and related support for meetings. XXXXXXXX agrees to the fee structure outlined below and will adhere to the reimbursement of expenses procedures as specified.

Terms and Conditions

Option 1: $60,000
Option 2: $70,000
Option 3: $85,000

Payment terms are one-half fee due upon the signing of this letter of agreement and one-half fee due 45 days hence.

Reasonable travel and living expense are submitted monthly as accrued, at cost, and payment is due upon receipt of the invoice.

This project is noncancelable, and agree-upon payment terms are due as described. You may postpone or delay any part of the work as you deem necessary. The quality of our work is guaranteed. If we do not meet your objectives as stated, we will refund your fee.

Acceptance

XXXXXXXX

Subcontractor Agreements

Solo practitioners often utilize additional help on a situational basis, which is usually called subcontracting. It's important to establish the rules of the road with subcontractors before implementation, so that there are no surprises.

The agreement that follows is meant to constitute the criteria to cover. You may want your attorney to draw up the agreement, though I find that solid relationships are stronger than any legal agreement, and poor relationships will undermine the most airtight legal agreement.

Some hints:

- Utilize people whom you know and trust.
- Even when you don't require help, continue to search for and build relationships for the times you will need help.
- Consider subcontracting when you need help with volume of work, when you need expertise you don't possess, when the work is not of interest or learning to you, or when you are better off with backup.
- Always remember that the client is yours alone.

Sample Subcontractor Agreement

The provisions in this document will govern our relationship while Joan Larson conducts work on behalf of Summit Consulting Group, Inc. at the Acme Company.

1. You will identify yourself as a subcontractor for Summit Consulting Group, Inc. You will not hand out personal business cards or talk about your personal practice at any time.

2. You will do no promotion for your personal business at any time.

3. You will implement according to instructions provided by Summit Consulting Group, Inc., and will not agree to any altered, modified, or new conditions with the client. Any such client requests will be passed on to Alan Weiss for decision.

4. Your expenses will be reimbursed monthly, within 10 days of receipt. You will turn in expenses on the last day of the month. Reimbursement will include airfares at discounted coach rates, taxi fares, meals (not to exceed $75 per day), hotel room at the Marriott Downtown, and tips. All other expenses, including phone, recreation, laundry, and so forth, are not reimbursable.

5. Your payment rate will be $1,500 per day on-site, and $750 per day off-site, as directed and approved by Summit Consulting Group, Inc. You agree that the work assigned to you will be completed within 60 days with a cap of 15 actual days on-site and a cap of 4 days off-site. You will complete the following work, even if it requires additional days, but payment will cap at the levels noted:

   • Conduct 12 focus groups as assigned for 90 minutes each.

   • Analyze and produce reports on each group in progress.

   • Analyze and produce a report for the total group experience.

   • Meet with Alan Weiss at the conclusion to discuss the final report.

   Fees will be paid within 10 days of the submission of your time reports at the conclusion of each month, provided that all individual focus group progress reports have been submitted.

6. All work created and all materials provided you are the sole property of Summit Consulting Group, Inc. You may not cite this organization as your client in conversation or in writing, and all communications with Summit Consulting Group, Inc. and Acme are confidential and subject to the nondisclosure agreement you have signed.

7. You will conduct yourself professionally, observe business ethics and courtesy, and meet the work requirements described. Failure to do so in the opinion of Acme and/or Summit Consulting Group, Inc. will result in termination of this agreement and cessation of payment.

Your notarized signature below indicates full agreement and compliance with these requirements:

_____ Notary, including signature, date, and seal:

Joan Larson

Date: _____

Virtual Appendix

We have created an ongoing Virtual Appendix on my web site with updated references.

Please visit http://summitconsulting.com, click on the bookstore, select this book, and you'll find a link to the Virtual Appendix. No password is required. I hope this will keep this book relevant and personally helpful for many years.

About the Author

Alan Weiss is one of those rare people who can say he is a consultant, speaker, and author and mean it. His consulting firm, Summit Consulting Group, Inc. has attracted clients such as Merck, Hewlett-Packard, GE, Mercedes-Benz, State Street Corporation, Times Mirror Group, The Federal Reserve, The New York Times Corporation, and over 500 other leading organizations. He has served on the boards of directors of the Trinity Repertory Company, a Tony-Award-winning New England regional theater, Festival Ballet, and chaired the Newport International Film Festival.

His speaking typically includes 30 keynotes a year at major conferences, and he has been a visiting faculty member at Case Western Reserve University, Boston College, Tufts, St. John's, the University of Illinois, the Institute of Management Studies, and the University of Georgia Graduate School of Business. He has held an appointment as adjunct professor in the Graduate School of Business at the University of Rhode Island where he taught courses on advanced management and consulting skills. He once held the record for selling out the highest priced workshop (on entrepreneurialism) in the 21-year history of New York City's Learning Annex. His Ph.D. is in psychology and he is a member of the American Psychological Society, the American Counseling Association, Division 13 of the American Psychological Association, and the Society for Personality and Social Psychology. He has served on the Board of Governors of Harvard University's Center for Mental Health and the Media.

He is an inductee into the Professional Speaking Hall of Fame® and the concurrent recipient of the National Speakers Association Council of Peers Award of Excellence, representing the top 1 percent of professional speakers in the world. He has been named a Fellow of the Institute of Management Consultants, one of only two people in history holding both those designations.

His prolific publishing includes over 500 articles and 40 books, including his best-seller, *Million Dollar Consulting*, and *Getting Started in Consulting, Third Edition.* His books have been on the curricula at Villanova, Temple University, and the Wharton School of Business, and have been translated into German, Italian, Arabic, Spanish, Russian, Korean, and Chinese.

He is interviewed and quoted frequently in the media. His career has taken him to 55 countries and 49 states. (He is afraid to go to North Dakota.) *Success Magazine* has cited him in an editorial devoted to his work as "a world-wide expert in executive education." The *New York Post* calls him "one of the most highly regarded independent consultants in America." He is the winner of the prestigious Axiem Award for Excellence in Audio Presentation.

He is the recipient of the Lifetime Achievement Award of the American Press Institute, the first-ever for a non-journalist, and one of only seven awarded in the 60-year history of the association.

He has coached the former and present Miss Rhode Island/Miss America candidates in interviewing skills. He once appeared on the popular American TV game show *Jeopardy*, where he lost badly in the first round to a dancing waiter from Iowa.

Index

A.D. Little, 4
Accelerant curve, 64–67
Administrative support, 24–27
Affiliations, 59–60
Allen, Woody, 237
Alliances
  defined, 83
  guidelines for, 82–83
  revenue sharing in, 82–84
Ambiguous zone, 205
Announcements, use of, 63
Anticipating needs, 7
Attention, loss of, 28
Attorneys, 19–20
Authorship
  art and science of, 100–101
  expression of, 98–100
  marketing tool with, 57
  platforms of, 99
  promotion and, 57

Barr, Chad, 56
Benefits
  nonfinancial, 218
  types of, 39
Blind case studies, 158
Blogs
  global, 92
  investment in, 64
  marketing with, 58
  updating of, 231
Books. *See also* Authorship
  commercially published,
    98–100, 98–101
  promotion of, 57
  self-published, 98
Booz, Edwin G., 4
Booz Allen Hamilton, 4
Bossidy, Larry, 182
Brand pyramid, 78
Brands
  blogs and, 64

creation of, 77–78
defined, 75
expanding via, 78–81
networking with, 77
requirements for, 75–76
solo practitioners and, 76
tenets for, 71
Bridges, William, 205
Buffett, Warren, 109
Bundles, 50
Buyers. *See* Economic buyers

Cameron, James, 96
Career development
  consultants role in, 185–186
  evidence of, 184–185
  implications of, 187
Careers, dueling, 28–30
Case studies
  business ethics, 213–215
  development of, 158
  implementation, 134
  proposals, 132
  transitions, 240–241
  types of, 158
Celebrity
  community interactions with,
    111–112
  success trap in, 107–108
  talent and, 107
  thought leadership and, 95–98
  value-based fees and, 101–104
Chapter C, 20
Checking accounts, 23–24
Choices, limiting of, 50
Clients. *See* Economic buyer
Clinton, Bill, 96
Coaching
  assignments, 164
  distinctions of, 164
  ethical responsibility of, 226
  history of, 163

success criteria for, 165–166
training *versus,* 176–177
Cold calling
  best prospects for, 59
  success from, 61
  trust factors in, 59–61
Collins, Jim, 103
Commercial publishing, 98–99
Committees, 188–189
Communication
  criteria for, 192
  overview of, 190–191
  transparency in, 204
Communities
  celebrity interaction with, 111
  concept of, 18
  ethical responsibility to,
    225–226
  future growth in, 256
  growth cycle of, 112–113
  virtual, 110–111
Conceptual agreements
  for coaching, 165
  defined, 46
  equation for, 38
  metrics of, 121–122
  objectives of, 46–47, 121
  proposals and, 120–123
  success metrics in, 47–48
  trust relationships and,
    120–121
  value-based fees and, 98
  values in, 48–49, 122–123
Conflict resolution, 169–172
Consultants
  alliances among, 81–84
  concluding advice to, 256–257
  forms of, 9–12
  function, 9
  independent, 255
  informal networks of, 255
  IT, 10–12

Consultants (*Continued*)
practice structures for, 30–34
role of, 3–6
types of, 5
Consulting business
compartmentalization
of, 239
expansion of
disengagement and, 152
global, 90–92
overview of, 78–81
referrals and, 84–87
retainers and, 87–90
maturity of, 252–253
refusals, 222–224
selling of, 237–240
transitions in, 240–243
Consulting marketing model, 34
Consulting profession
ethical responsibility to,
225–226
evolution of, 252–254
future of, 254–257
needs, forms of, 9–12
professional responsibility
to, 251
Content, 11
Content experts, 5
Contractors, 10
Copyright
common phrases and, 22
ethical guidelines for, 219–221
registering, 21
trademark *vs.*, 21–22
Creating needs, 7
Credit, purpose of, 24
Crisis management
effective methods for, 204–205
overreaction and, 205–206
preparation and, 203–204
Cultural change, 201–203

Delegation, 26, 41
Delivery model, 40–41
Delivery people, 83
Diagonal approach
content in, 11
process in, 12
trust in, 12
Disability, 22
Disengagements
dynamics of, 146
formal, 145

long-term leverage in,
156–159
reasons for, 222–224
references from, 154–156
referral business from,
148–151
repeat business from, 151–154
successful, steps to, 146–148
testimonials from, 154–156
Drucker, Peter, 109, 235
Dueling careers, 28–30

Economic buyers. *See also*
Nonbuyers
acceleration curve and, 66
accountability role of,
134–135
behavior of, 134–137
claims by, 22
conceptual agreement with,
46–49
defined, 6
finding, 118
firing of, 221–224
identification of, 43–46
jettisoning of, 56
long term leverage from,
157–159
maturity of, 80–81
multinational, 90–92
needs of, 7–9
peer claims with, 119
proposal demands by,
129–132
references from, 154–155
referrals from, 52, 84–85
resources, using, 41
role of, 133–136
saying no to, 137–138
scheduling meetings with,
119–120
shifting work to, 26
testimonials from, 154–155
tracking of, 230
trust relationships with,
118–119
value-based fees and, 37–40,
103–104
80 percent ready move principle,
200
Emotional connections, 61
Emotional resources, 27–30
Emotional support, 27–30

Employees. *See* Staff
Empowerment, 199
Empty rubrics, 51
Equity building
intellectual property and,
232–234
tips for, 229–231
Errors and omissions, 22
Ethical conduct
case studies on, 213–215
commandments for, 225–227
copyright, 219–221
copyright and, 219–221
for financial matters, 216–218
Expenses. *See also* Income
billing of, 126
ethical guidelines for, 216–217
Expertise, 59
Exploration, 153–154

Facilitation
challenges of, 168–169
defined, 166
intellectual capital and,
166–167
steps for, 167–168
Facilitators, 5
Family teams, 188
FedEx, 128
Feedback, unsolicited, 29, 192
Fees. *See also* Value-based fees
determination of, 107
global client, 91–92
hourly/monthly, 255
negotiation of, 131–132
nonpayment of, 223
subcontractor, 105–106
Financial issues. *See also* Income
alliances and, 81–84
commingling of funds, 23–24
ethical guidelines for, 216–218
insurance, 22–23
priorities, setting of, 24
retirement, 23
Firms
career development at,
184–187
change management in,
198–200
committees at, 188–190
communication at, 190–192
crisis management in,
203–206

cultural change in, 198–200
development strategies for,
195–198
feedback at, 190–192
innovation at, 206–209
leadership in, 179–181
loyalty in, 15–16
principals of, 32
succession planning in,
182–184
teams building at, 187–190
Franchising, 106

Generalists, 15
Gitomer, Jeff, 95
Glass-Steagall Act, 5
Global consultations
best practices for, 90–91
blogs, 92
fees for, 90–91
forms of, 90
technology and, 255
Goggle Alerts, 219
Goldsmith, Marshall, 95
Good to Great (Collins), 103

Hawthorne studies, 248–249
Hays, Woody, 128
Hierarchy of needs, 236, 249
Human resources (HR)
departments, 16
Humphrey, John, 232

IBM, 6, 250
Implementation
clients' role in, 133–136
midcourse corrections for,
141–144
scope creep in, 136–141
stakeholder role in, 136–138
subordinates role in,
134–135
Improvements, measures of, 38
Income. *See also* expenses
accelerant curve and, 67
distribution formula, 83–84
ethical guidelines for, 217–218
increasing, 14, 231
increasing, impact of, 123
sources of, 78
tracking of, 230
Incorporation
basic options for, 19

professional advisors for, 19–20
tax benefits of, 20–21
Independent consultants. *See*
Solo practitioner
Individual retirement accounts
(IRAs), 23
Information technology (IT)
consultants
diagonal approach for, 11–12
potentials for, 10–11
Innovation
defined, 206
promotion of, 206–208
sources of, 208–209
Insourcing, 16–17
Insurance, 22–23
Intangible benefits, 39
Intellect, 60
Intellectual capital
conveyors of, 95
facilitation and, 166–167
function of, 97
Intellectual property
building equity with, 230
creation of, 97–98
licensing of, 68, 232–234
maximizing potential of,
233–234
repository of, 63
Interim teams, 188
Interpersonal methodologies
coaching, 163–164
conflict resolution, 169–172
facilitation, 166–169
negotiation, 172–175
skills development, 175–178
iPads, 71, 98–99
IRAs. *See* Individual retirement
accounts (IRAs)

Jack-of-all trades, 50–51
Joint accountability, 125–126,
261

Labor intensity, 40–43
Leadership. *See also* Thought
leadership
consistency in, 180
crisis management by, 204
function of, 95–98
group, 63–64
key issues in, 180–181
messages sent by, 179

social media groups, 63–64
succession planning by,
182–184
Legal issues
copyright protection, 21–22
incorporation, 19–21
liability, 22
Leverage
defined, 50
long-term, 156–159
principles of, 50–52
Liability, 22
Licensing
fees for, 106–107
intellectual property, 68,
232–234
Life balance, 234–237
Limited liability companies
(LLCs), 20
Long-term leverage
case studies and, 158
creation of, 156–157
experimentation and, 159
key contacts and, 157–158
use of clients name in, 157
Loyalty, 15–16

Mager, Bob, 48, 176
Maister, David, 219
Malpractice. *See* Errors and
omissions
Management consulting
history of, 4–6
ongoing needs of, 6–9
Market 3-D bell curve, 250
Market gravity wheel
defined, 55
development of, 56
elements of, 57–58
reach-out *versus,* 43
referrals and, 84
thought leadership and, 97–98
Marketing. *See also* Promotion
accelerant curve for, 64–67
with cold calls, 59
mind-sets for, 68–69
nonbuyers and, 40
priorities quadrants, 79–80
promotion techniques for,
69–70
technology strategies for,
70–73
with social media, 62–64

Markets
plans, evolution of, 13–14
retail, 255
wholesale, 255
Maslow, Abraham, 236, 249
McKinsey, James, 5
McLuhan, Marshall, 96
Media, 231
Meetings
preparation for, 130
scheduling, 119–120
Mentoring
distinctions of, 164
ethical responsibility of, 226
professional value of, 245–246
self-interest aspects of,
246–248
Merck Pharmaceuticals, 204
Merck, George, 224
Methodology
advances in, 250
belief in, 42
determination of, 117
fees and, 217
husbanding of, 139
importing, 238
negotiation of, 174–175
options, 125, 260–261
Metrics
conceptual agreements,
121–122
proposal, 124
success, 47–48
Midcourse corrections
causes of, 141–142
skills building in, 144
thermal layer in, 142
Million Dollar Consulting
(Weiss), 9, 99, 247
Mind-sets, 68–69
Morita, Akio, 7
Mossberg, Walter, 70, 95
Multimedia, 63
Multimedia testimonials, 155

Nance, John, 96
Needs
personal/professional sets
of, 9
types of, 7
underpinnings of, 8
Negotiation
consultants role in, 173

methodology for, 174
musts in, 172–173
parties to, 174–175
wants in, 173
Networking
band, 77
informal, 255
practice of, 58
short-term/long-term, 97
trust and, 59
Neutral zone, 205
Nonabuse guarantees, 155–156
Nonbuyers
dangers of, 44
identification of, 43
recommenders among, 45
references from, 155
testimonials for, 155
Nonprofit organizations, 17

Objectives
conceptual agreements,
46–47, 121
conflicts over, 169–170
proposal, 124, 259
questions related to, 47
Occam's razor, 141
Options
clients', 125
incorporation, 19
proposal, 125, 260–261
Organizations. *See* Firms
Outsourcing, 26, 41
Overdelivery, 140

Parachute business, 66
Payback activities
mentoring, 245–248
professional advances,
248–251
professional evolution,
252–254
Peripheral benefits, 39
Personal needs, 9
Position papers, 58
Preexisting needs, 7
Pro bono work, 58, 226
Process, 12
Products and services, 79
Prohibition, 202–203
Promotion. *See also* Marketing
shameless in, 67–70
techniques for, 69–70

Proposals. *See also*
Implementation
acceptance of, 127
buyers' demands, 129–132
case study for, 134
closing of, 130–132
components of, 123–127
conceptual agreement and,
120–123
delivery of, 128
economic buyer and, 118–120
joint accountability in,
125–126
launching of, 130–132
methodology in, 125
objectives in, 259
options in, 125
phases to avoid in, 128
process of, 117–118
reviewing, 128
sample, 259–262
simplification in, 129
situation appraisal, 259
submission of, 127–129
success metrics for, 260
terms and conditions of,
126–127, 261–262
timing, 261
timing of, 125
values, 260
Protection
financial, 22–24
intellectual property, 21–22,
219–221
plagiarism and, 219–221
Pseudo-isolation, 71
Public speaking, 58

Questions
for economic buyers, 44–45
for metric development,
47–48
for objectives, 47
for values articulation, 49

Reach-out, 43
Real wealth, 14
References, 154–156
Referrals
client, 84–85
criteria for, 149
disengagements and, 148–151
expansion potential in, 86

importance of, 84
indirect, 86–87
nonclient, 85–86
solicitation of, 52
Reinvention
success levels and, 108–109
thought leadership and, 109
timing of, 107–108
triggers for, 109–110
Relationships
conceptual agreements and,
120–121
dueling careers and, 28–30
work demands and, 28
Repeat business
addition mode in, 152–153
defined, 151
expansion mode in, 152
exploration in, 153–154
transference in, 153
Request for proposal (RFP), 7
Resources
administrative, 25–27
emotional, 27–30
Response, speed of, 71
Retainer-type work, 68
Retainers
advantages of, 87
arrangements for, 88–89
disadvantages of, 88
successful, keys to, 89
Retirement, 23, 240
Return on investment (ROI)
formula, 147
Right-on-time learning, 17–18
Risk, fear of, 27–28
Risk/reward ratio, 28
Robbins, Tony, 96
Roth IRAs, 23

S-curve navigation, 109–110
Scope creep
antidote for, 141
avoidance of, 139–141
conditions promoting,
139–141
defined, 88
effects of, 138
responsibility for, 140
solo practitioners and,
136–137
Self-publishing, 98
Service marks, 21

Shared values, 34
Situation appraisal, 123–124,
259
Social media. *See also specific
platforms*
investment in, 64
leveraging of, 63
negative aspects of, 62–63
tenants for, 71
thought leadership and,
97–98
Solo practitioners
branding and, 76
distinctions of, 31–32
-firm principal hybrid, 33
increase in, 255
intellectual property and,
136–137, 232–234
scope creep and, 136–137
SOSO label, 78–79
Speaking. *See* Public speaking
Specialists, 15
Staff
accountability of, 134–135
buyouts, 238
contracts, 239
development of, 181
downsizing of, 27
implementation role of,
134–135
importance of, 25
requirements for, 25
suggestions for, 25–26
virtual, 25
Stranger teams, 188
Strategy
default position of, 195
defined, 196
driving forces of, 197
failure of, 196
responsibility for, 196–197
Subchapter S, 20
Subcontractors
agreement, 262–263
fees for, 105–106
function of, 10, 42–43
IRS rules for, 35
Subordinates. *See* Staff
Success
assuring, 117–120
attributes of, 12–13
coaching criteria, 165–166
demonstrating, 145–148

generic parameters of, 14–15
metrics for, 47–48, 260
trap, 107–108
Succession planning
approaches to, 184
career development and, 185
defined, 182
recruitment and, 182–184
Support
administrative, 25–27
emotional, 27–30
systems for, 30

Talents, distribution of, 237
Tangible benefits, 39
Task forces, 188
Tasks, simplifying, 26
Taxes
for corporations, 19–20
for nonfinancial benefits, 218
for solo practitioner, 31, 216
IRAs and, 23
reduction of, 231
Taylor, Frederick Winslow,
4, 248
Taylorism, 4
Teams
building of, 187
characteristics of, 189–190
defined, 188
manifest of, 189
types of, 188
Technology
effective use of, 70–73
future advances in, 255
philosophy for, 72–73
Terms and conditions, 261–262
Testimonials
consult produced, 156
marketing with, 58
multimedia, 155
nonbuyers, 155
obtaining, 154–156
refreshing of, 231
written, 155–156
Thermal layer, 142–144
Thought leadership
characteristics of, 95–96
defined, 95
intellectual capital and, 97–98
reinvention and, 109
3M, 108
TIAABB, 14

Time
  demands on, 28
  investments, reduction of,
    40–43
  issue of, 181
  utilization of, 200
Timing
  proposals, 125, 261
  reinvention, 107–108
Trademarks, 21
Training. *See also* Career
    development
  coaching *versus*, 176–177
  context of, 175–176
  effective, steps for, 177
  strategic goals and, 178
Transference, 153
Transitions
  case study, 240–241
  guidelines for, 241–242
  near-term appraisals for,
    242–243
Transparency, 204
Trends
  corporate loyalty, 15–16
  in HR departments, 16

insourcing, 16–17
right-on-time learning,
    17–18
volunteerism, 17
True buyers. *See* Economic
    buyers
Trust
  affiliation-based, 59–60
  defined, 12, 118
  economic buyers and,
    118–119
  emotionally-based, 61
  expertise-based, 59
  intellect-based, 60
Trust pyramid, 60
Twitter, 63
Typing, learning to, 26

Unsolicited feedback, 29

Vagelos, P. Roy, 180, 204
Value distance, 7–8
Value-added, 7
Value-added tax (VAT), 35
Value-based fees
  benefits of, 39–40

celebrity and, 101–104
clients condition and, 37–40
criteria for, 105
defined, 102
ethics of, 217
Values
  bases of, 122, 260
  conceptual agreements and,
    48–49
  impact of, 122–123
  proposal, 124
Vendors, 42, 230
Virtual assistance, 25
Visualization, 27
Volunteerism
  impact of, 226
  increasing, 17
  networking by, 58

Waiting period, 22
Web sites
  marketing with, 58
  tenants for, 71
  updating of, 231
Welch, Jack, 182
White papers. *See* Position papers